ELISABETTA PROPERZI NELSEN - CHRISTOPHER CONCOLINO

LITERARY FLORENCE

Walking Tours in Tuscany's Capital

June 2, 2018

*To Phil,
after 40 years of
friendship, my book on
Florence.
Happy Birthday!
elisabetta*

nuova immagine

To our parents

Maps by Stephanie Dal Pra

Photographs by Mike Nelsen Photography

We would like to express particular thanks to our colleague the late Ruggiero Stefanini, professor at UC Berkeley, for his philological expertise and affectionate advice; to Francesco Falasca, whose unexpected and charming assistance (just when we needed it most) proved invaluable in helping us bring our project to completion; and to Fabio Scarpelli, for having verified our remarks about the Church of Santa Croce, Florence's cathedral and Piazza Mentana.

ISBN 88-7145-240-2

© nuova immagine siena, 2006
Via San Quirico, 13 – I-53100 Siena
Tel. 0577- 42.625 – Fax 0577- 44.633
http://www.nuovaimmaginesiena.it
e-mail: nuovaimmagineeditrice@tin.it

Printed by Arti Grafiche Nencini (Poggibonsi, Siena)

Table of contents

Preface
Florence: Jewel on the Arno

*Io dal mio poggio, / quando tacciano i venti fra le torri / della vaga Firenze,
odo un Silvano / ospite ignoto a' taciti eremiti / del vicino oliveto...)*
Ugo Foscolo, *Le Grazie*

*I from my hilltop / When the winds hush among the towers / Of fairest Florence, hear
a wood-god / Unknown guest of the silent hermits / Of the nearby Olivet...*
Ugo Foscolo, *The Graces*

Just as Foscolo in the first years of the nineteenth century was moved to recall
Florence's mythological and literary past in *Le Grazie*, many others before
and after him were also inspired to write in this city, Tuscany's capital. Most, if
not all, of the places where these writers lived have hardly changed, and so it's
possible to uncover traces of their lives in Florence's palaces, streets and city
squares. This book identifies these places and arranges them in eleven itineraries. The sites offer a feast for the eyes that is singularly and justifiably famous
– but immeasurably enhanced by the appreciation of each location's historical
and literary importance.

But Florence has attained the status of a literary homeland for other reasons.
For Dante in exile, it represented the city loved, hated and lost forever – yet
retrieved allegorically both in Heaven and in Hell. Florence therefore becomes at
once the locus of historical and personal memory par excellence as well as the
center of his poetic imagination. This same metaphorical connotation has also
appealed to non-Florentines. For a writer of tragedies from Piedmont such as
Vittorio Alfieri or for the Milanese novelist Alessandro Manzoni, Florence was
the place to absorb Italy's literary tongue in person and "rinse [one's] clothes in
the Arno," to use Manzoni's words. For the romantic Ugo Foscolo, it was the cus-
todian of Italy's poetic and artistic greatness, which he identified particularly with
the tombs in the church of Santa Croce, a virtual pantheon of creative personalities. One of Foscolo's contemporaries, Elizabeth Barrett Browning, found her second homeland in Florence and fervently supported the *Risorgimento*, Italy's nineteenth-century movement in favor of unification and liberation from under the
yoke of Hapsburg and Bourbon domination. In stark contrast to this, Dante's
home town was a city of exile for Dostoevsky, who completed *The Idiot* across the
street from the Pitti Palace. Other foreigners such as E.M. Forster and D.H.
Lawrence saw the city's refined Renaissance beauty balanced by the spontaneity

and naturalness of its inhabitants, while John Ruskin interpreted Florence as a "jewel box" in which he could rediscover Gothic art in the nineteenth century.

These literary walks aim to retrieve an urban past that offers the reader places rich in history, curiosities and poetic memory. Nonetheless, Florence has changed over the centuries and must now deal with contemporary problems facing any city – even though it still proffers a Medieval and Renaissance environment and, as such, the quintessential tourist destination. Automobile and motorbike traffic unfortunately contribute to a certain level of noise pollution, but the itineraries included herein help the reader's imagination return to a *silent* dimension in the literary past. In walking through Florence's streets, all visitors – be they tourists, scholars or the merely curious – will enjoy reading aloud the engraved words on the plaques marking each literary site, which still function as a source of inspiration for writers today.

Introduction
Florence and Italian Literary Tradition

F or centuries Florence has been fertile ground for men and women of letters. From the Middle Ages on several literary trends were either born or substantially shaped by writers of Florentine origin. During the second half of the thirteenth century, the *Dolce Stil Novo* represented a fusion of the rift between physical and spiritual love in the creation of the angelic woman as love-object. In this way love for a woman became the means to reach spiritual perfection, which Dante's *Divine Comedy* articulated in a poetic voyage through the three realms of the afterworld: Hell, Purgatory and Heaven. As both author and character, Dante finds redemption through Beatrice. Her presence is salutary in a spiritual sense, and as a poetic figure she is an allegory of both the Church and Christ.

In the fourteenth century Petrarch tore open that fusion of ideas in a revolutionary way by desiring the object of his love, Laura, and emphasizing how deep personal feelings conflicted with his religious beliefs. The originality of his love poems were such that they were widely imitated throughout Europe during the Renaissance and continued to resonate with poets up through the twentieth century. Indeed, thanks to Petrarch, Italian letters were identified for centuries with poetry rather than prose.

The folktale is something of an exception. This genre had existed since the Middle Ages as a written form of oral story telling and is generally an expression of popular rather than aristocratic language and culture. Some collections, such as the thirteenth-century *Novellino* (the work of an anonymous Florentine writer) and Franco Sacchetti's late fourteenth-century *Trecentonovelle* (Three Hundred Folktales) include moral messages attached to the end of each tale. Others, mostly comical, continued to be written in the Renaissance – while also trying to duplicate the success of Boccaccio's *Decameron*, which is recognized as the highest achievement in late Medieval prose. The *Decameron* perfectly balances oral traditions with an elaborate narrative style based on Cicero's Latin.

Fourteenth century Florence also saw the birth of Italian historical writing in Dino Compagni's *Cronica delle cose occorrenti ne' tempi suoi* (Chronicle of the Things Happening in His Time, 1310-1312) and in Giovanni Villani's *Cronica fiorentina* (Florentine Chronicle, 1320). Both historians rely on a medieval vision of history as the result of sin and divine justice, but Compagni's patriotism and sense of personal outrage over the political events of his time are expressed vividly in the pages of his *Cronica*. Villani's text is rich with detail about Florentine daily life in the fourteenth century.

The late fifteenth-century Florentine court of Lorenzo de' Medici, known as "The Magnificent," was a kind of literary laboratory where all sorts of genres were tested and tried out. Lorenzo himself was the epitome of the refined amateur or dilettante: he toyed with writing carnival songs, formal love poetry and even pretended to write as a peasant praising the rustic charms of a farmyard lass. As a patron of the arts he fostered works by others, notably Luigi Pulci and Angelo Poliziano. Pulci was one of the first Italians to give literary form to the medieval Roland story, which had circulated for centuries throughout the peninsula in oral ballads, sung or narrated by itinerant troubadours. Pulci's comical *Morgante* (1478) adds a twist to this genre – the chivalric epic – and precedes significant contributions made to it later. Poliziano is remembered for the elegant simplicity of his narrative poem in honor of a joust won by Giuliano de' Medici, Lorenzo's brother. A wholly different genre is represented by the *sacra rappresentazione* or mystery play – a popular form of religious theatre, often with musical components. It began in the fourteenth century and reached a particularly high level of development and standardization during the fifteenth century before its decline in the High Renaissance. All of these works must be seen, however, as complementary to the fifteenth-century outpouring of writing in Latin, the language of Italy's classical forebears and therefore of everything most worthwhile emulating, at least from Florentine humanists' perspective. Their studies were strongly philological because the analysis of classical texts required an accurate knowledge of Latin and Greek. This lead in turn to the discovery and translation of ancient texts, and on occasion their findings even had political implications. Lorenzo Valla was able to show that the belief in Constantine's gift of temporal power to the Church was based on a false Latin text, since close study showed that it was rife with grammatical and lexical contradictions as well as anachronisms. Scholars such as Coluccio Salutati, Giannozzo Manetti, Giovanni Pico della Mirandola, Poggio Bracciolini and Marsilio Ficino (Neoplatonism's principal theorists) expressed their thoughts in treatises, letters and orations.

Sixteenth-century Florence is characterized by its production of works in many genres, though none predominated. Treatise writing was one of these, which reflected the birth of the social sciences (separating rational analysis from moral considerations for the first time) and the centrality of the human subject (ever more independent from Christian dogma). *The Prince* (1532) by Machiavelli is the most salient example because it presents the first view of politics as a science unconditioned by religious issues. Much earlier, the humanist Leon Battista Alberti had published *Della famiglia* (*On the Family*, 1432), a collection of dialogues on the institution of the family seen as a utopian ideal of social relations and economic prosperity. These ideas anticipated descriptions of the ideal courtier's life in the sixteenth century, though they were greatly transformed by Baldesar Castiglione in his *Il cortegiano* (*The Book of the Courtier*, 1528), who accounted for many changes that had come about as part of the general shift from seigniory (non-hereditary rule by an aristocrat) to principality. More than just a manual on courtly manners, Castiglione's book sets forth an actual philosophy of ideal professional and social behavior. At the same time, courtly taste in reading tended more and more towards the chivalric epic, represented by Matteo Maria Boiardo's *Orlando innamorato* (1506) and Ludovico Ariosto's *Orlando Furioso* (1532). The latter, especially, mixes the Roland story with Arthurian legend in a successful blend of fantasy and history that Ariosto expresses in typical ironic style. Its popularity all over Europe was so great that it even inspired Cervantes' *Don Quixote*.

Imitating Petrarch's poems, much lyric poetry continued to be written in the sixteenth century as well, including works by women such as Vittoria Colonna, Veronica Gambara, Tullia d'Aragona, Gaspara Stampa, Veronica Franco, Isabella di Morra and Laura Battiferri (wife of the Florentine architect and sculptor Bartolomeo Ammannati). The latter half of the century came under the increasing sway of the Italian Counter Reformation, whose reactionary conservatism colored most aspects of cultural life, though it also produced Benvenuto Cellini's *Vita* (1562), or autobiography, which exults in the creative power of individual genius – a point of view more typical of an earlier Renaissance perspective.

Indeed, just as Mannerism gave way to the Baroque in painting and the figurative arts, Michelangelo's *Rime* (rhymes) and Torquato Tasso's melancholic *Gerusalemme liberata* (*Jerusalem Delivered*, 1581) preceded the seventeenth century's preoccupation with a poetry of rhetorical preciousness and the idea that the writer's principal duty was to instill "meraviglia" or amazement in his audience. Gian Battista Marino and his followers were most representative of this tendency, but later in the century scientific writers in Florence such as Francesco Redi and Lorenzo Magalotti countered it in sober prose that was heir to the emphasis Galileo placed on clarity and rational language when describing physical reality (especially his *Dialogue Concerning the Two Major World Systems, the Ptolemaic and the Copernican*, 1632). The *Seicento* (or seventeenth century) also saw the flowering of Italian Opera, which was born in Florence in the wake of Count Giovanni de' Bardi's interest in creating a modern equivalent of ancient Greek theater and music. The earliest surviving fruit of this initiative is the mythological-pastoral drama *Euridice* by Ottavio Rinuccini, set to music by Jacopo Peri and Giulio Caccini in 1600. The non-musical improvisational theater known as the *Commedia dell'arte* had already been well established by then and continued to be popular for the next 150 years.

In the mid-eighteenth century Carlo Goldoni reformed the *Commedia dell'Arte* by eliminating improvisation and masked stock characters and increasing character development. It also became a theater based on Florentine speech rather than Venetian (the language of Goldoni's native Venice). In somewhat different fashion Pietro Metastasio undertook a reform of Baroque opera's complexities. Beginning with *Didone abbandonata* (*Dido Abandonded*, 1724) he intended to return its libretto to classical ideals of clarity and stylistic dignity. These goals were also espoused by the Arcadian Academy in Rome (and its outlying poetic "colonies"), which encouraged its members to find inspiration in the pastoral-utopian myths surrounding ancient Greek Arcadia. More or less at the same time Italy began to respond to the cultural stimuli of the Enlightenment, which came to it largely from England and France. Notions of social justice, equality, reform and progress found their way to Italy as did a certain emphasis on rational thought and empirical observation. Milan was the northern pole of this culture, disseminated in part by Pietro Verri's newspaper *Il Caffè*, and was also home to Cesare Beccaria and Giuseppe Parini. The latter wrote a hugely entertaining satire of contemporary aristocratic mores (*The Day*, 1763-1801) and the former an argument for the abolition of torture (*Essay on Crimes and Punishments*, 1764). The southern pole was Naples, where social theorist Gaetano Filangieri envisioned a radical reworking of social structures, as he explained in his *Scienza della legislazione*, (Science of Legislation, 1780). Earlier in the century Giambattista Vico, another Neapolitan, produced pioneering work in historiography. Altogether distinct from Enlightenment thought, his monumental *New Science* is partly anthropological and partly linguistic in approach and describes a cyclical theory of history that is nonetheless ever-changing due to unique differences that condition all historical circumstances. During the century's second half Vittorio Alfieri settled in Florence and wrote tragedies recalling biblical and ancient heroes. In this respect they are neoclassical even as their heroes' struggles against tyranny have more than a little in common with Enlightenment notions of social justice. Alfieri's protagonists are intensely individualistic and in this they prefigure the personality of the Romantic hero.

Following suit, the nineteenth-century Italian hero yearns not only for self-realization through love but for the peninsula's political unification and emancipation. Ugo Foscolo's epistolary novel *The Last Letters of Jacopo Ortis* (1802) makes this plainly clear as does his poem *I sepolcri*, which takes Florence's church of Santa Croce as its point of departure. In fact, Italian Romanticism tended to express itself in patriotic terms, and nowhere is this clearer than in the historical novel, which rose to prominence after the great success Walter Scott's novels enjoyed in England. Set in the remote past, the Italian historical novel is a tale of resistance against oppression, with the result that it was interpreted as an allegory of Italian opposition to Austrian and Bourbon domination (*i.e.* the *Risorgimento* mentioned in the Preface). Because it was written in contemporary spoken Florentine, Alessandro Manzoni's *The Betrothed* (1827) is the most important, but there were numerous others, such as Francesco Domenico Guerrazzi's *La battaglia di Benevento* (The Battle of Benevento, 1827) and Massimo d'Azeglio's *Ettore Fieramosca* (1833). These same goals were pursued in lyric poetry by Aleardo Aleardi and Giovanni Prati. As was true throughout Europe, Romantic lyric poetry in Italy (including Foscolo's) privileged descriptions of nature as a mirror of individual introspection. This technique was originally a Petrarchan invention, but Giacomo Leopardi's *Canti* (1831) modernized it in a new interpretation of traditional poetic forms and language in order to convey his own kind of existential pessimism. Nature imagery continued to hold a place of prominence through the end of the century, especially in Giovanni Pascoli's and Gabriele D'Annunzio's poems and in Antonio Fogazzaro's novels: all works in which a generation's values seem to falter. In recognition of this fact their authors have often been remembered as "Decadents." After Italian unification in 1861, however, Italians had difficulty coming to terms with its results: debt, economic depression and the apparent betrayal of egalitarian ideals. Some, known as the *Scapigliati* (the Dishevelled), rejected the consequences of industrial capitalism and took refuge in dark kinds of personal and literary irrationality such as the supernatural. For others, the historical novel's patriotism gave way instead to the influence of French Naturalism (known as "verismo" in Italy), which was more useful in pointing out the deleterious effects of heredity and environment on individuals and families. Giovanni Verga, its best known voice, wrote fiction that focused mostly on the disenfranchised in rural Sicily (especially in *The House by the Medlar Tree*, 1890). Others turned their attention toward the aristocracy, such as Federico De Roberto (in *I Vicerè*, 1894) and Luigi Capuana (in *Il marchese di Roccaverdina*, 1901) or, like Emilio De Marchi, toward the urban working class (as in his *Demetrio Pianelli*, 1890).

In the years preceding W.W. I the crises of nineteenth-century values were exacerbated further. Darwin, Freud and Nietzsche had posited revolutionary shifts in accepted notions of geologic time, the psyche and spirituality, but the changes in paradigm they foresaw arose as cultural manifestations only later. Italo Svevo and Luigi Pirandello articulated these feelings of unease in systematic ways and are therefore recognized as Italy's prose Modernists. Svevo's novel *The Confessions of Zeno* (1923) takes the existence of the unconscious for granted, while Pirandello's novels and many plays (especially *Six Characters in Search of an Author*, 1921) argue in favor of a fractionalized concept of reality whose meaning can only be determined in relation to points of reference constantly in flux. As industrialization increased, the urban working class organized itself in unions while cities continued to grow larger. In reaction to this and the spread of technological culture in general (*i.e.* positivism) some young bourgeois intellectuals in Florence published literary journals in the first two decades of the twentieth century. *Il Leonardo* and *Hermes* sympathized with D'Annunzio's conception of art as an elitist aesthetic experience, while the more important *La Voce* (1908-1916) was a forum for cultural self-examination and debate. Another Florentine magazine, *Lacerba*, had Futurist adherents on its editorial staff (Aldo Palazzeschi and Carlo Carrà), and Filippo Tommaso Marinetti, the movement's founder, had published work in *Lacerba*. In Marinetti's *Technical Manifesto of Futurist Literature* (1912) Italy was introduced to the poetic concept of "words in liberty," which abolished traditional syntax, punctuation and grammar in order to express the immediacy and frenzy of modern life. Futurists, who considered technology and war harbingers of necessary social innovation also supported Italian colonialism and the invasion of Lybia in 1911. A certain return to the classics, however, ran counter to all the Futurists' energy. It was most typically represented by *La Ronda*, an important literary journal published in the early twenties, whose contributors tended to be interested in questions of literary form and writing not compromised by ties to contemporary social realities. Giuseppe Ungaretti, Salvatore Quasimodo and Eugenio Montale, the Hermetic poets of the twenties issue in part from this same environment. Many members of the cultural avant-garde often met in Florentine cafès, such as *Giubbe Rosse*, *Paszkoswki* and *Gilli*, as they did in all the largest Italian cities during the century's first half. The advent of Fascism in 1922 certainly narrowed Italian cultural horizons, but it was also a period when new trends continued to take shape. Alberto Moravia's *The Time of Indifference* (1929) was an existential novel, while Elio Vittorini's *Conversation in Sicily* (1939) broke with Italian narrative traditions and adapted clearly foreign influences in creating a new lyrical realism. At the same time, Dino Buzzati explored the fantastic in fiction having surrealist overtones, as in his novel *The Tartar Steppe*, 1940. Many of these writers published in the Florentine magazine *Solaria* (1926-1936), which was open to intellectual contacts with writers all over Europe. Some writers were officially protected by the regime, such as D'Annunzio and Pirandello, while others were exiled because their works were in opposition to it. After W.W. II a number of novelists discussed the war's devastating effects on the everyday lives of working class people and farmers – as well as the problems inherent in the process of reconstruction. Referred to as Neorealists they used terse modern sentences in describing local and regional issues, often including reflections on the experiences of partisans who had fought in the Resistance (1943-45). Among their most important works are Cesare Pavese's *The Moon and the Bonfires* (1950), Carlo Levi's *Christ Stopped At Eboli* (1945), Primo Levi's *If This is a Man* (1947) and Vasco Pratolini's *Family Chronicle* (1947). The 1950's saw the development of still different narrative modes. Giuseppe Tomasi di Lampedusa's *The Leopard* (1958) is a nostalgic return to the historical novel, while Giorgio Bassani's *The Garden of the Finzi-Contini* makes use of memory in much the same way that Proust did. Newer developments in verse included works by poets known as *novissimi*. Andrea Zanzotto is their best known representative, whose poems mix dialectal forms with traditional language. At about this same time Italo Calvino emerged as one of the most prominent writers in Italy, largely because of his efforts to find continually new directions for fiction. From his own kind of neorealism he moved on to experiment with mixed genres of his own invention combining fable (as in *Our Ancestors*, 1960) comedy, fantasy, science fiction (as in his *Cosmicomics*, 1965) and allegory. Just as the controversial filmmaker and writer Pier Paolo Pasolini had done, Calvino also participated in national and international debates on issues of cultural importance. During the second half of the century there was also a virtual explosion of writing by women as a result of successful political campaigns for civil rights. Natalia Ginzburg's *Family Sayings* (1963) and Elsa Morante's *History* (1974) quietly deal with issues central to women's lives and familial situations while Dacia Maraini presented a more open and systematic criticism of patriarchal society in such works as *The Age of Malaise* (1963) and *The Silent Duchess* (1990). In the early 1980's Umberto Eco produced the much-imitated *The Name of the Rose*, a novel mixing semiotics and detective fiction. Since then Italian literature has moved in many different directions, though it seems certain that prose attracted more writers than poetry in the twentieth century. Social problems and changes in contemporary culture are themes that have appeared in their fiction to a greater or lesser degree. Among them: the advent of the computer age, pollution, inner-city problems, the culture of drug users, homosexuality and the arrival of new immigrants.

Map of Walking Tours 1-10

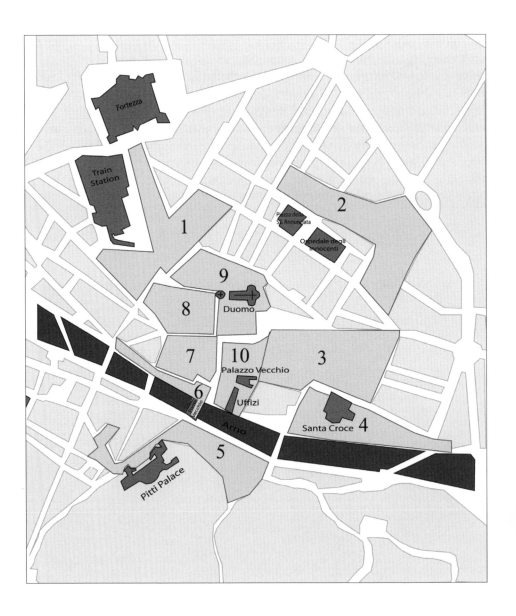

Walking Tour 1

Henry James - Henry Wadsworth Longfellow - Giovanni Boccaccio - Giuseppe Garibaldi - John Milton - Bernardo Cennini - Percy Bysshe Shelley - Alphonse de Lamartine - Carlo Collodi

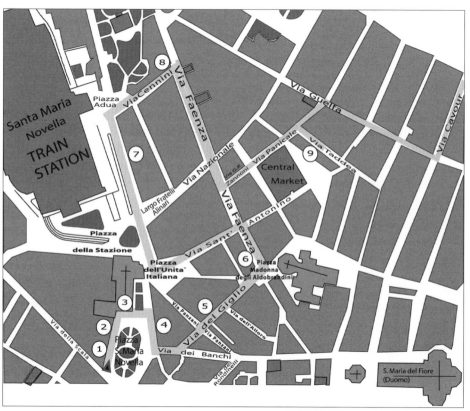

Piazza Santa Maria Novella - Via del Giglio - Via Faenza - Piazza della Stazione - Via Taddea

1) HENRY JAMES (1843-1916)

Piazza Santa Maria Novella 12-16 (red)

As you stand in Piazza Santa Maria Novella with the large black and white façade of the church in front of you, turn around and walk toward the opposite end of the square keeping to your right. The Square's lawn will be on your left. Continue along the length of the piazza towards the arched arcade (Loggia di San Paolo) at the opposite end. At different times James stayed in an apartment in this square on the corner of Via della Scala. It may have been at Number 10, now located in the Loggia di San Paolo, which formerly housed a convent school known as the Convent of the "Leopoldine." It is also possible that his apartment was near Numbers 12-16 (red), as indicated by the address above.

Henry James lived in an apartment here in 1874 that had a sitting room, two bedrooms, a pantry and a balcony – for which he paid $25 a month. Nearby, James often ate at Victor's, a restaurant in Via de' Rondinelli. This is a short street connecting Via dei Cerretani to Piazza Antinori, and it can be reached from Piazza Santa Maria Novella by walking down Via dei Banchi to Via dei Cerretani.

The New-York-born James had traveled with his family to England, France, Germany and Switzerland from 1855 to 1860. As a result he was aware of his father's serious interest in contemporary cultural developments while still a boy. This early exposure to continental cultural life led him to acquire what he called the "European virus." Indeed, many of his works deal with Americans living in Europe, and he himself never returned to the United States after 1911, becoming a British citizen in 1915.

James first arrived in Florence in 1869 when he was twenty-six. At that time he stayed at the Hotel de l'Europe in Piazza Santa Trinita and was amazed by the city's beauty, especially the Uffizi and the Pitti Palace – although he suffered from serious constipation, which he complained about in letters to his family, describing it as "perfect torpor and inaction of the bowels" that made him "as yellow as an orange." His older brother William (the philosopher later known for *The Varieties of Religious Experience*, 1902) jokingly referred to this as Henry's "moving internal drama." James returned to Florence in 1872 and again in the following year, when he was joined by William. In fact, the novel *Confidence* (1879) reflects many of the two brothers' experiences together that year. But after seeing Rome, James' opinion of Florence began to tarnish, for whom the city where the Renaissance was born then seemed just "a vulgar little village" with a cold climate. All the same, towards the end of 1874 he started work on his *Florentine Notes*, which are essays containing his observations on Florentine art, architecture and social customs (now included in his *Italian Hours*, 1909), which also contains the chapter "Autumn in Florence." During the same year he began the novel *Roderick Hudson* (1876), which presents a recurrent theme: the cultural conflict between Americans and Europeans. Often the American is characterized as simple and innocent in contrast to the refined but corrupt European. This theme is not explored fully in *Roderick Hudson*, but it is reworked with great subtlety and complexity in subsequent novels such as *The American* (1877) and *The Europeans* (1878). These, which do not privilege one culture over the other, have American protagonists that almost suggest a fusion between opposite ethical traditions. Later, however, novels such as *Daisy Miller* (1879) and *Portrait of a Lady* (1881) raise this dialectic with even more disquieting ambiguity, so that Europe tends to be identified with death and America with vitality. *Portrait of a Lady* also includes many Florentine settings. *The Princess Casamassima* (1886), whose heroine Christina Light was first introduced in *Roderick Hudson*, is a continuation of that earlier novel and includes its Italian setting.

James' address changed repeatedly in Florence. While working on *Portrait of a Lady* he stayed at the Hotel de l'Arno near the Ponte Vecchio, from where we know he wrote ironic words of congratulations to George Eliot's second husband, John Cross, who would later attempt to drown himself in a Venetian canal while on his honeymoon. In 1886 and 1887 he also stayed frequently with wealthy friends, and briefly rented an apartment in the Villa Brichieri in Bellosguardo, which is in the hills above the Oltrarno side of the city. James had always wanted to live in Bellosguardo, and so he fulfilled a dream going there. From his room he could look over the city's domes and towers as well as view Fiesole and the Apennines beyond. Here he wrote *The Aspern Papers* (1888). This novel is based on an anecdote told to him by the stepbrother of the writer Violet Paget, who published under the name Vernon Lee and was living in Florence while James was. It's narrated in the first person by Jeffrey Aspern, who recounts his attempts to lay hands on letters written by Shelley and Byron but owned by an old woman and her daughter. James' comments on Violet Paget, who was his friend, are nonetheless curious and funny. For example, he flatly described her as ugly, quarrelsome and perverse – though he also considered her the only one in Florence with a mind. Perhaps this fact should be seen in relation to the size of James' social circle, since it appears that his friends were almost exclusively American and British expatriates. These were often women of means who opened their salons to select members of the expatriate community. Among them were Teresa Guiccioli, a niece of Byron, and the Baroness Zunch.

At the same time, James continued to travel but was certainly in Florence in 1887 when there were celebrations marking the completion of the cathedral's façade. In his *Florentine Notes* James wrote that its red, white and green exterior "may be the image of some mighty hillside enamelled with blooming flowers" making it "one of the loveliest works of man's hands." He attended a ball given for the occasion at the Palazzo Vecchio by King Umberto I and Queen Margherita and went dressed in red and black Renaissance costume.

2) HENRY WADSWORTH LONGFELLOW (1807-1882) — Piazza Santa Maria Novella 6-15

From James' address walk toward the large church of Santa Maria Novella keeping the square on your right. You will see the following plaque on your left opposite the part of the square in which the lawn ends and the paved area in front of the church begins.

Henry Wadsworth Longfellow (1807-1882)   Henry Wadsworth Longfellow (1807-1882)
poeta americano nelle lingue neolatine   American poet, master of romance
maestro traduttore della Divina Commedia   languages and translator of the Divine
tra le fiorentine dimore ebbe questa nelle   Comedy, among his Florentine homes
Piazza che fu detta "La Mecca degli stranieri"   had one here in the square called "the
                                            foreigners' Mecca"

The most widely-read American poet of the nineteenth century, Longfellow was a professor of modern languages first at Bowdoin College in Maine, where he studied alongside Nathaniel Hawthorne, and then Harvard, where he was professor of Modern and European literature before he decided to dedicate all of his energy to creative writing. In 1839, when he was thirty-two years old, he published the volume of poetry *Voices of the Night*, which gained him wide popular success that grew even further after *Ballads and Other Poems* came out three years later. His best-known works include the narrative poems *Evangeline* (1847), *The Song of Hiawatha* (1855) and *The Courtship of Miles Standish* (1858). Based on North-American history, *Evangeline* is a tragic love story of two young Acadians (i.e from Nova Scotia) who were forceably separated on their wedding day in 1775 and only reunited in old age. *Evangeline* sold 37,000 copies in ten years, an enormous success for that time. *The Song of Hiawatha*, which is perhaps Longfellow's best work, is a re-elaboration of North-American Indian myths about the miraculous birth of an indigenous hero and bringer of peace: Hiawatha. As in James Fenimore Cooper's novels (see Walking Tour 9, Site 54), native-American culture became the object of a search for authentic origins – as well as the invention of an idealized past seen more through the eyes of poetic imagination than through those of a real anthropologist, as in Washington Irving's work. Hawthorne's passion for Dante led him in 1881 to organize the Dante Society at Harvard, the first one in the United States. Previously, from 1867 to 1870, he had completed an English translation of the *Divine Comedy* which he undertook as a distraction from his second wife's tragic death. While she was melting sealing wax to amuse her children, her gauze clothing caught fire and she was burned alive. The main strength of Longfellow's translation is that it aimed to be faithful to the original. It is clear, easy to understand and also maintains the rhythm of Dante's eleven-syllable verse, although the lines don't rhyme the way Dante's do, which make use of his distinctive "terza rima" or three-lines of interlocking verse. His is a fine translation that can still be recommended.

During his first voyage to Europe he arrived in Florence on New Year's Day 1828 and probably stayed there throughout the winter before heading south to Rome. The *Letters of Henry Wadsworth Longfellow* relate his experiences in Italy at that time, and a few of them were written in his passable, though flawed, Italian. He particularly enjoyed going to the theater in Florence, where he rubbed elbows with the cream of international high society. We also know from his correspondence that it was easy for him to read and understand spoken Italian, but unfortunately he had the tendency to use Spanish words in place of Italian ones when talking. In his opinion, the language spoken in Florence was also more grammatically correct than elsewhere, though Longfellow found the Florentine accent "harsh." In fact, his attitude toward Italy in general was less than enthusiastic. Writing that he felt no excitement over it (as he admits in one letter), he travelled through Italy with "just enough curiosity to[stay] awake." Despite this, Longfellow gave us a panorama of his impressions in "Italian scenery," which evokes the beauty of the landscape surrounding the Benedictine abbey of Vallombrosa outside Florence: – Night rests in beauty on Mont Alto. / Beneath its shade the beauteous Arno sleeps / In Vallombrosa's bosom, and dark trees / Bend with a calm and quiet shadow down / Upon the beauty of that silent river.

3) Giovanni Boccaccio   Church of Santa Maria Novella and
(1313-1375)   Piazza Santa Maria Novella

Turning to your right, you will again see the large façade of the gothic church of Santa Maria Novella. The façade was designed by Leon Battista Alberti after Boccaccio's death (see also Walking Tour 4, Sites 19 and 22).

> *[N]ella venerabile chiesa di Santa Maria Novella, un martedì mattina, non essendovi quasi alcuna altra persona... si ritrovarono sette giovani donne tutte l'una all'altra o per amistà o per vicinanza o per parentado congiunte, delle quali niuna il venti e ottesimo anno passato avea né era minor di diciotto, savia ciascuna e di sangue nobile e bella di forma e ornata di costumi e di leggiadra onestà...*
> *Mentre tra le donne erano cosí fatti ragionamenti, e ecco entrar nella chiesa tre giovani, non per ciò tanto che meno di venticinque anni fosse l'età di colui che piú giovane era di loro.*

[O]ne Tuesday morning in the venerable church of Santa Maria Novella there was hardly any congregation there... except for seven young women, each of whom was a friend, neighbor, or relative of the other, and none of whom had passed her twenty-eighth year, nor was any of them younger than eighteen; all were educated and of noble birth and beautiful to look at, well-mannered and gracefully modest... While the ladies were discussing this, three young men came into the church, none of whom was less than twenty-five years of age.

The words above are taken from Boccaccio's best-known work the *Decameron*. Its title, derived from Greek, refers to ten days that the author imagines ten young people spent together during the epidemic of bubonic plague that struck Florence in 1348. Although it's really a book of short stories, the *Decameron* includes an introduction that is a fascinating account of the Black Death. Boccaccio describes the suffering, corruption and cruelty of the Florentines towards each other during a time so horrifying that civilization itself seems to have been destroyed. To escape these inhuman conditions, the ten elegant aristocrats flee to the hills above Florence (just below Fiesole) where they pass the time by telling tales: ten stories a day for ten days. Before they leave the city, however, all of them happen to find themselves in this church, where Boccaccio has them meet and decide to go away.

The invention of this refined party is the method Boccaccio uses to organize his hundred tales, which is referred to as the work's "frame story." On each day the stories follow a different theme, except for those told on the first and the ninth days, when the narrators pick a theme of their own choice. On the other eight days, the themes are chosen by an appointed "queen" or "king" of the day.

We still read Boccaccio today because the *Decameron* offers a wide view of medieval society in realistic situations that are comic, adventurous, witty, sexually colorful, tragic and even otherworldly. Its characters are merchants, priests, laborers, mothers superior, con men, women tragically in love, princesses, vengeful brothers, servants, poets, artists, village idiots, unfaithful wives, kings and prostitutes. Boccaccio wrote these tales when the Florentine mercantile class was just beginning to gain strength and free itself from its feudal, agrarian origins. It was a wealthy city-state, and Boccaccio's work attests to the rise of this new social class that developed along with the beginning of capitalism, born in Florence. Nonetheless, Boccaccio's plots were not entirely original since he also relied on widely-known oral and written sources. The *Decameron* was much imitated during the Renaissance, especially after Pietro Bembo's treatise on linguistics *Le prose della volgar lingua* (The Style of Written Italian, 1525) declared it to be the ideal model for all writers of prose. While its tone is sometimes conversational, its syntax and grammar are often very elaborate because Boccaccio consciously derived them from Cicero's Latin prose. Formal written Italian is still affected by it.

Many of the Florentine places where Boccaccio's tales take place can still be identified today – especially when the tales are comical. For example, Peretola, the location of Florence's airport, is the site of two of the *Decameron*'s most famous tales: the fourth tale of the sixth day (whose protagonist is Chichibio) and the ninth tale on the fifth day (whose main character is Federigo degli Alberighi). Guido Cavalcanti, Dante's friend, was one of the principal poets of the "Dolce Stil Novo" (Sweet New Style), the Florentine poetic school of the late 13th century. He is the main character of the ninth tale of the sixth day, where he walks down Via Calzaiuoli (then Corso Adimari) from Orsanmichele to the Baptistry. At that time, the site of Florence's cathedral, Santa Maria del Fiore, was occupied by a cemetery, where Guido was teased (in this tale) by a group of rowdy citizens. Via Calzaiuoli also appears in the eighth tale of the ninth day, whose main characters are Filippo Argenti and Biondello. Argenti, famous for his temper, had a house here. Calandrino, Boccaccio's best-known comic simpleton, together with his companions Bruno and Buffalmacco appear in several tales at different locations. In the eighth day's third tale these two fellows convince Calandrino that he is invisible, and they chase him along a portion of the Mugnone (now an urban stream) up to the San Gallo Gate (the present-day Piazza della Libertà). This stream is still largely visible, since it flows behind the Fortezza da Basso and Le Cascine (Florence's large public park) before it enters the Arno. Two other streams, the Africo and the Mensola, appear in one of the best of Bocaccio's minor works, the *Ninfale fiesolano* (The Nymphs of Fiesole) a narrative pastoral love poem. Africo is a shepherd in love with Mensola, a nymph – both of whom are changed into streams after their deaths. The Africo can be seen where it runs into the Arno at the foot of Via Piagentina between the Lungarno del Tempio and the Lungarno Cristoforo Colombo. Moreover, if you follow Via Piagentina northeast away from the Arno, you will find that it becomes Via Lungo l'Affrico after Piazza Leon Battista Alberti. The Mensola flows into the Arno three miles east of Florence where Via Gabriele D'Annunzio reaches the village of Ponte a Mensola (reachable by taking city bus number ten). Santa Maria Novella, besides its place of prominence in the *Decameron*'s Introduction, also provides the setting for a number of tales. In the eighth day's ninth tale Buffalmacco tells Mastro Simone to meet him here in order to play a practical joke on him. At the end of the tenth day of storytelling, the three young noblemen say goodbye to the seven young ladies and accompany them back to this church: "e i tre giovani, lasciate le sette donne in Santa Maria Novella, donde con loro partiti s'erano, da esse accommiatatosi, a' loro altri piaceri attesero, e esse, quando tempo lor parve, se ne tornarono alle lor case" (and the three young men, after having left the seven women at Santa Maria Novella, whence they had set forth, said goodbye to them and set out to find diversions elsewhere. When they decided that the appropriate time had arrived, the women repaired to their homes).

Boccaccio may have been born in Florence or Certaldo, a small town thirty miles southwest of Florence near San Gimignano. (Certaldo has a museum dedicated to Boccaccio and he is also buried there in the church of San Jacopo). His father was a wealthy merchant and moneychanger, although very little is known about his mother, probably of very humble origins. In fact, Boccaccio's father recognized him legally only in 1320. When the boy was thirteen, he was sent to Naples to work as an apprentice in a branch of the bank owned by the Florentine Bardi family. At that time, Naples' Angevin court under King Robert I was home to a stimulating intellectual environment that welcomed the traditions of chivalry and poetic courtly love that had first arrived in Italy from France and Provence about a hundred years earlier. This milieu was also enriched by the numerous foreign visitors that arrived at the city's port, spurring the growth of Naples' economy. Indeed, Boccaccio moved easily between members of refined aristocratic society, the ascending affluent merchant class and the colorful and imaginative Neapolitan populace. Accordingly, these eclectic influences led him to abandon his studies in canon law and to take up primarily literary interests. So when Cino da Pistoia (one of the poets in Dante's poetic circle) came to teach at Naples' university, Boccaccio was able to gain first-hand knowledge of the "Dolce stil novo." Boccaccio's years in Naples (from around 1326 to 1340) were the happiest time of his life, and one of his first loves is probably reflected in the novel *Elegia di Madonna Fiammetta* (Elegy of Milady Fiammetta, 1343-1344). Fiammetta, or "little flame" is both a metaphor for love and an alias for Maria d'Aquino, an illegitimate daughter of King Robert. Unfortunately, when the Bardi bank had serious financial problems Boccaccio had to return to Florence where he remained for the rest of his life till his retirement in 1375 to Certaldo. Florence was where he met and befriended Francesco Petrarca (Petrarch), with whom he corresponded for years, and it was also where Boccaccio witnessed the plague of 1348, which killed his father and his second stepmother. During his last years, Boccaccio was charged with giving the first public readings and commentary on Dante's *Comedy*, which Boccaccio defined "divine" in his *Trattatello in laude di Dante* (Short Treatise in Praise of Dante), thereby giving the work its present title. The readings took place in the church of Santo Stefano, parts of which are now incorporated into the Pandolfini chapel in the church of the Badia Fiorentina, in via del Proconsolo at via Dante, opposite the museum of the Bargello. As you enter from via del Proconsolo, the Pandolfini chapel is the first one on your right.

Besides the *Decameron*, Boccaccio also wrote the poems *Caccia di Diana* (Diana's Hunt, 1334), *Filostrato* (Defeated By Love, 1335, 1339 or 1340) and *Teseida delle nozze d'Emilia* (Emilia's Nuptials and Theseus' War Against Thebes, 1339-41). The latter two works are written in stanzas of eight lines whose final syllables rhyme according to the pattern: ABABABCC. This rhyme scheme in combination with the eight-line stanza was later imitated in Renaissance epic-chivalric poetry by Luigi Pulci, Matteo Maria Boiardo, Ludovico Ariosto, and Torquato Tasso. In addition, Boccaccio produced the novels *Filocolo* (Labor of Love, 1336-38) and the *Ninfale d'Ameto* (Ameto's Nymphs, 1341-42), which is interspersed with poetry in Dantesque tercets. The *Corbaccio* (1365-66, perhaps from "corbacho" or "whip" in Spanish, or else from the Italian pejorative for "ugly crow") is a misogynous work in prose that may perhaps be evidence of Boccaccio's amorous frustration in middle age. Other works include his love poetry published under the title *Rime* (Rhymes), and a series of Latin works: *De montibus, silvis, fontibus, lacubus, fluminibus, stagnis seu paludis, et de nominibus maris liber* (Book on the names of mountains, forests, springs, lakes, rivers, ponds or swamps and seas, circa 1360); *De casibus virorum illustrium* (The Fates of Illustrious Men, 1373); *De mulieribus claris* (Famous Women, 1361-62), and the twenty-four *Epistole* (Letters).

4) GIUSEPPE GARIBALDI   Piazza Santa Maria Novella 21
(1807-1882)

With the church of Santa Maria Novella behind you, walk along the square's left side with its green lawn on your right. On your immediate left you will see the following plaque on the second-story wall to the left of the large entrance at this address:

"Da questa casa Giuseppe Garibaldi	From this house Giuseppe Garibaldi
soldato costante dell'Italia e dell'umanità	constant soldier of Italy and humanity
il 22 ottobre 1867	on October 22, 1867
al popolo plaudente	in front of cheering crowds
indirizzava le memorabili parole	spoke the memorable words
o Roma o morte	"Rome or death!"
preludiando la spedizione di Mentana	anticipating his arrival in Mentana
che restituiva	where he gave back
all'Italia	to Italy
la sua capitale	its capital and
all'umanità	to humanity
il libero esame.	free choice.
Questa lapide	This plaque
a eterna memoria	in eternal memory
posero i garibaldini toscani	Garibaldi's Tuscan troops dedicated
oggi 2 luglio 1882."	Today: July 2, 1882

Garibaldi is remembered today principally as a general and the military strategist of Italy's three wars of independence (1848, 1859 and 1860). He was called "l'eroe dei due mondi," or "the hero of the two worlds" because he fought as a volunteer in several South-American wars of independence, including Uruguay's, from 1834 to 1848. Garibaldi's greatness is attributed especially to the forces he led in 1860 from Quarto (near Genoa) to Marsala (in the Province of Trapani) on Sicily's extreme western tip. His landing at Marsala is known as "la spedizione dei Mille," or "the expedition of the Thousand." This military strike spearheaded the liberation – first of Sicily – and then of all of southern Italy from under the yoke of Spanish Bourbon domination. A great military success, his expedition in 1860 is still renowned for its speed of action and for the grass-roots support given him by people throughout Italy. He embodied the very idea of the people's hero. The plaque at this site refers to Garibaldi's plans to conquer Rome in 1867 – after most of Italy had already been unified in 1861 under Victor Emmanuel II, formerly the king of Piedmont and Sardinia. Garibaldi lost this battle for Rome (the last remnant of the Papal State), but he opened the way for the Eternal City to become the capital of unified Italy.

In addition to these accomplishments, he also left a number of writings which are still not well known. For example, his war reports, daily military orders, proclamations and public speeches were only published from 1934 to 1937. These appeared in three volumes as *Discorsi politici e militari* (Military and Political Works). He also wrote his memoirs, the *Memorie autobiografiche*, which are available in English both as *The Memoirs of Garibaldi* and *The Autobiography of Garibaldi*. This work recounts his time in Uruguay, his return to Italy and "the expedition of the Thousand," which Garibaldi considered the most glorious moments of his career. The book begins with a declaration of patriotism and affirms the author's belief in the need to create a republic, but it also recognizes the monarchy's important role in leading the peninsula to independence.

His many letters were also published under the title *Epistolario* (Correspondence) in 1885, while the volume *Lettere ad Anita e ad altre donne* (Letters to Anita and Other Women, 1926) includes letters to his wife Anita, a Brasilian creole woman who died in his arms while crossing the swamps outside Ravenna.

However, Garibaldi was also the author of a few historical novels. This genre was particularly popular during the first half of the nineteenth century when Italy was ruled by a variety of foreign powers. The historical novel allowed writers to emphasize national political ideals and romantic sentiment. It was also a means by which contemporary yearning for freedom, independence and unification could be represented within the context of earlier historical settings. Alessandro Manzoni was the founder of this genre in Italy, although Walter Scott's novels were already well known precedents at the time.

Garibaldi wrote four of them between 1870 and 1874: *Cantoni il volontario* (Cantoni The Volunteer, 1870); *Clelia* (The Rule of the Monk, 1870); *Manlio* (Manlius, 1870) and *I Mille* (The Thousand, 1874). All of these works are somewhat anticlerical in nature because they tend to depict the most powerful members of the clergy as corrupt and lascivious, while the novels' sympathetic characters are always revolutionary patriots. An unusual aspect of *I Mille* (considering it's a nineteenth-century novel) is the female character Marzia, who is both an ethnic minority and a militant revolutionary. She is a beautiful young Jewish woman who is subjected to the sexual advances of a high Church dignitary. To escape, she disguises herself as a man and sets sail with Garibaldi's expedition of the Thousand. Among the novel's other vicissitudes, Garibaldi describes the conditions of revolutionary women who were sent to Palermo as messengers for the general's troops. These pages, which reflect actual historical events, testify to women's participation in the struggle for Italian independence, which has often been neglected by traditional historians. The novels do suffer from a certain lack of stylistic refinement, but they are also invaluable as historical documents since they provide a depth of detail and description about Italy's wars of independence. Moreover, given Garibaldi's obvious sympathy for his co-combatants, these works show his gratitude for their sacrifices.

At the same time, the "hero of the two worlds" also wrote poetry. His poems are characterized by a wild beauty, as one can see in the long autobiographical poem *Carme alla morte*, or Ode to Death (1911).

5) JOHN MILTON   Via del Giglio 29 (red)
   (1608-1674)

From number 21 Piazza Santa Maria Novella, proceed to Via dei Banchi, the first cross-street on your left. At the next corner turn left again in Via del Giglio and cross the very busy Via Panzani. Look for a plaque on the second story of the building on your left just before you reach Via dell'Alloro, the next cross-street on your right:

Qui nel palazzo dei Gaddi è tradizione che soggiornasse negli anni 1638 e 1639 John Milton trovando a Firenze l'Italia dei classici

According to tradition, John Milton stayed here in 1638 and 1639 in the home of the Gaddi family, finding Italy of the classics here in Florence.

Known for his seventeenth-century Christian epic poems *Paradise Lost* (1667) and *Paradise Regained* (1671), Milton came to Florence in his early thirties to complete and refine his already vast erudition. For him Italy was "the home of humane studies and of all civilized teachings," and Florence was the city where he could discover the roots of his humanistic education and put it to the test. He arrived in Florence on his way south from France after passing through Genoa, Leghorn and Pisa. Milton stayed here on two different occasions: the first time, probably, from late July through September 1638, and later, in March 1639 for two months after having spent several months in Rome. Even as a young man Milton had shown an enormous talent for languages, and it's probable that he read nearly everything available in his time in Latin, Greek, English and Italian. Furthermore, his admiration of Dante and Petrarch made him eager to improve his command of spoken Florentine. Indeed, before coming to Florence, Milton wrote the companion poems *Il Penseroso* (The Meditative One) and *L'Allegro* (The Cheerful One) in 1630 or 1631. These titles (the first one in imperfect Italian) testify to his love for the Italian language. They are meditations, respectively, on Night and Day, and seem to allude to Michelangelo's statues of identical inspiration in the Medici Chapels that Milton would later admire in person. While *L'Allegro* evokes bucolic nature and classical themes dear to writers of Italian Renaissance and Baroque poetry, *Il Penseroso* conjures up moon-lit nights and melancholic thoughts that were precursors of early romantic literature of the late eighteenth- and early nineteenth centuries.

In 1638 Florence was still home to about forty literary and intellectual societies called Academies, which carried on many of the learned traditions begun during the Renaissance. Milton's education and interests naturally led him to gravitate toward them, and soon he was well acquainted with prominent men of letters associated with the Accademia degli Apatisti (Academy of the Apathetic – or the Indifferent) and the Accademia degli Svogliati (Academy of the Listless). In fact, the owner of this house in Via del Giglio was Jacopo Gaddi – the founder of the Accademia degli Svogliati.

During one of his sojourns here Milton undertook a kind of intellectual pilgrimage by going to see Galileo, whom he said had "grown old, a prisoner of the Inquisition for thinking in astronomy otherwise than the Franciscan and Dominican licensers thought." Galileo lived a short ways outside Florence in Arcetri, and was seventy-five years old at the time. Though no longer imprisoned by the Inquisition, (which had left him almost completely blind) he was still under constant surveillance. Seeing him like this, Milton realized that England offered him more intellectual freedom and tolerance (For the entry on Galileo see Walking Tour 4, Site 19). As a consequence Milton came to appreciate this aspect of his native land and rediscovered his own patriotism. Indeed, he thereafter signed his name in Latin "Joannes Miltonius, Anglus" and decided that he would write to celebrate the greatness of England. As William Riley Parker has remarked in his authoritative biography, Milton's stay in Italy marked a turning point in his career. The end of his stay in Florence signaled the close of his youthful period and coincided with the beginning of his mature style. Henceforth his works even echoed the style and vocabulary of sixteenth-century Italian literature. From this point on he tended to write in verse rather than prose. More important, *Paradise Lost's* glorification of mankind resounds with the Italian Renaissance tradition that Milton had studied and absorbed, while his profound interest in the human moral condition can even be considered a remembrance of Dante's *Comedy*.

6) BERNARDO CENNINI   Via Faenza 7
(1415-1498)

From Milton's lodgings continue forward on Via del Giglio toward the large dome of the Medici Chapels in front of you. Before you reach it you will arrive at Piazza Madonna degli Aldobrandini where you should turn left into Via Faenza. Follow Via Faenza to number 7 on your left:

A perpetua onoranza di Bernardo Cennini	In perpetual memory of Bernardo Cennini,
orefice nostro del secolo XV	goldsmith of our fifteenth century,
che per sentore di libri	who, having heard about books
non scritti a penna	not written by hand
ma con segreto inaccessibile	yet by some unattainable secret
impressi a Magonza	printed in Mainz,
immaginò e fuse caratteri	created and smelted type
e in questa città stampò per il primo	and first printed in this city
latine opere ed italiane	Latin and Italian books
squisitamente corrette eleganti	exquisite, precise and elegant,
e così della tipografica arte	and hence of the art of typography
fu comprimario inventore.	was co-inventor.
Qui ov ebbe i natali ai II di gennaio	Here, where he was born on January 2, 1415,
MCCCCXV e visse e tenne officina	living and working in his shop,
i Fiorentini lavoranti di stampa	Florentine typographers and printers
nel MDCCCLXIII	in 1863 longingly
questo marmo desiatissimo posero	placed this plaque with deepest affection.

As stated on the plaque, Bernardo Cennini introduced Florence to the art of printing with moveable type in 1471. His workshop was one of the city's first. He was also known as a gifted goldsmith and collaborated with Lorenzo Ghiberti in the creation of the "Doors of Paradise" (in the words of Michelangelo) for the Baptistry of Florence's cathedral. From 1453 to 1459 he was an engraver for the Florentine Mint and was a maker of punches, dies and presses. Today the only book printed by him is *Il Virgilio* (Virgil), kept in the National Library in Florence.

7) PERCY BYSSHE SHELLEY   Piazza della Stazione 2
(1792-1822)

Follow Via Faenza to Via Sant'Antonino. Turn left into Via Sant'Antonino and continue on into Piazza dell'Unità d'Italia, recognizable by the obelisk at its center. Turn right at the first corner and you will see the Piazza della Stazione ahead of you. Stay to the right, crossing Largo Fratelli Alinari. Ahead of you on your right you will see a large brown stone building that houses a McDonald's restaurant. Walk past it to the building's main entrance at the address above, set farther back from the street. There you'll find a plaque that reads:

> *Tra il 1819 e il 1820 in questi luoghi già di Via Valfonda Percy Bysshe Shelley lavorò al 'Prometeo liberato' compose 'L'Ode al vento occidentale'*

> On this site, formerly part of Via Valfonda, Percy Bysshe Shelley worked on "Prometheus Unbound" and "Ode to the West Wind" from 1819 to 1820

Shelley, along with Byron, Coleridge, Wordsworth and Keats, is one of England's most important Romantic poets and may arguably be considered the epitome of them all. This plaque marks the spot where Madame Merveilleux du Plantis ran a boarding house in the Palazzo Marini. Shelley arrived here when he was 27 years old along with his second wife Mary Wollstonecraft Godwin (author of *Frankenstein* and daughter of Mary Wollstonecraft, who had written the seminal feminist work *A Vindication of the Rights of Woman* in 1792).

Shelley was born to inherit a baronetcy and all the advantages that came with it, but his passionate and rebellious nature led him to reject it. While still a student at Oxford he wrote "The Necessity of Atheism" and was expelled because of it. This abruptly ended his university career, and it also caused a permanent rift between him and his father. In fact, after 1811 – when Shelley married 16-year-old Harriet Westbrook (a tavern keeper's daughter) – the two men never saw or spoke to each other again. Instead, Shelley tried to make a life for himself in London, where he became a devoted follower of William Godwin's radical anarchic and utopian philosophy, which held, for example, that social and legal institutions block full development of human potential. Shortly afterwards, Shelley also fell in love with Godwin's daughter Mary, and in 1814 he took her with him to live in France. Yet despite his free-thinking ways, Shelley didn't want to abandon his wife Harriet. Realizing that it wasn't ethical for him to share the bed of a woman he didn't love any longer, he asked Harriet to join him and Mary and live with them as a sister.

This caused him to be denounced as immoral not only by his family and friends but also by the general public, and Harriet became so desperate that she drowned herself in 1816. The English courts took away the two children he and Harriet had had together and so Shelley married Mary Godwin in 1818 and moved to Italy with her in the same year, never to return to England again. Restlessly moving from place to place, they finally settled in Pisa in 1820 where they formed part of an English expatriate group known as the "Pisan Circle." But while Shelley was sailing with a friend on a short trip from Tuscany to Liguria a sudden squall came up and both men – unable to control their boat – drowned. Neither was seen again till their bodies washed ashore days later. Shelley was cremated and his ashes were taken to the Protestant Cemetery in Rome. Curiously, he had even foretold this fatal accident in the last stanza of "Adonais," his elegy on John Keats' death. There he describes himself as a ship carried out into the darkness where his spirit will join Keats'.

Florence is one of the places where Shelley was able to find refuge from those he felt persecuted him even though he was mostly in poor health and often depressed here. The city's cold winters bothered him too, as we know from a letter dated January 17, 1820 in which he wrote that "Tuscany is delightful eight months of the year. But nothing reconciles me to... such infernal cold as my nerves have been racked upon for the last ten days."

All the same, Florence is where he also wrote some of his most important works – and he even gave the city's name itself to his fifth child: Percy Florence Shelley. In 1819 alone he finished his masterpiece "Prometheus Unbound" and wrote *The Cenci* (a tragedy), *The Mask of Irony* and *Peter Bell* (two satires), *A Philosophical View of Reform* (a political essay), and much lyric poetry. The "Ode to the West Wind" was inspired by the time he spent along the Arno in the Cascine park (on the north side of the Arno along Viale Giorgio Washington, Viale dei Lecci and Viale Abramo Lincoln). In his own words: "This poem was conceived and chiefly written in a wood that skirts the Arno, near Florence, and on a day when that tempestuous wind, whose temperature is at once mild and animating, was collecting the vapors which pour down the autumnal rains." In fact, Florence's influence on Shelley even extends to this poem's rhyme scheme, which is an imitation of the interlaced tercets (or "terza rima") first used by Dante in the *Divine Comedy*. What's more, Dante's experiences as an exiled poet must have touched Shelley and seemed similar to his own, although we can also see his use of this Dantean element as part of the nineteenth century's general rediscovery of medieval culture.

8) ALPHONSE DE LAMARTINE   via Faenza 93
   (1790-1869)

From the site of Shelley's boarding house on Piazza della Stazione, proceed in the same direction to the office of the Lazzi Bus Company at the next corner on your right. As you walk, Shelley's building will be on your right and the train station on your left. Turn right at the corner into Piazza Adua and walk past Via Fiume on your right into Via Bernardo Cennini. Turn left at the first cross street: Via Faenza. Just around the corner you will see this plaque on your left.

Questa casa e il giardino adiacente tra il 1827 e il 1829 appartennero al poeta Alfonso Lamartine

This house and the adjacent garden belonged to the poet Alphonse Lamartine from 1827 to 1829

The 19th century French poet Alphonse de Lamartine was born in Mâcon (Burgundy) to a noble family and raised in a country home fourteen kilometers away in Milly, where he spent a happy and tranquil childhood surrounded by his five sisters. These circumstances probably contributed to his profound affection for the beauty of the natural world and his literary interest in affairs of the heart.

As a boy Lamartine was sent to Jesuit boarding school where he befriended some fellow students from prominent Piedmontese families in northern Italy. He also developed an interest in Italian literature while a student, and so it was certainly no accident that he became especially enthusiastic about the tragedies and autobiography by the Piedmontese writer Vittorio Alfieri, which he read in French translation. Alfieri's works embody pre-romantic ideals, which Lamartine admired to the point of exclaiming (in a letter to a friend): "I love him to the point of madness... There is not room enough for all the points of admiration!" At about the same time Lamartine also read Madame de Staël's *Corinne ou l'Italie* (1807), which he called "mon premier roman" or "my first novel." Indeed, one critic has noted that de Staël's novel led him to see Italy as "the land of his dreams," or in Lamartine's own words: "Cette seconde patrie de mes yeux et de mon coeur" (My eyes' and heart's second homeland). But Lamartine's attitude toward the Italian peninsula was not unique. His mindset was characteristic of other French romantics as well, such as Stendhal (1783-1842), who saw Italy from an idealized point of view. Still, if *Corinne* was his first novel, then Torquato Tasso, author of *Gerusalemme liberata* (Jerusalem Delivered, 1575) was his "first poet" or, as he said, "mon premier poète."

Nonetheless, he first went to Italy in 1811 with one of his mother's cousins and her husband because his parents wanted to separate him from the young woman with whom he had fallen in love. It was at this time that he got his first glimpse of Florence, where he arrived with a letter of introduction to the Countess of Albany, who had been Alfieri's companion and paramour for many years. Lamartine paid homage to Alfieri's tomb in the church of Santa Croce and reverently visited the room where the Piedmontese writer had lived with the Countess, kept by her as a shrine to him (see Walking Tour 4, Site 19 and Walking Tour 6, Site 35). While there, Lamartine fetishistically plucked a piece from Alfieri's quill pen and kept it as a relic. After returning to France in 1812 Lamartine even completed his own version of Alfieri's tragedy *Saul*, but it was never performed, probably because Lamartine's real talent lay in lyric poetry. Indeed, his hero has none of the tragic individuality so unique to Alfieri's work.

Italy was also where Lamartine had several love affairs, such as the one with "Graziella," the woman he recalls in his *Confidences* (1843) and in other poetry, where she may be the same woman transfigured as "Elvire." Nonetheless, prior infatuations with French women such as "Henriette P." (recalled as "Lucy") and Julie Charles – together with his passion for Italian writers – continued to offer him inspiration once back in his native land. Petrarch's poetry, with its pronounced introspection, became a point of reference for him in particular. Indeed, his *Méditations poétiques* (1820) are known for their intimate self-analysis of love and memory.

In 1820 he married the English Elizabeth Birch. Right after the wedding the young couple left for Italy because Lamartine had been appointed Secretary at the French Embassy in Naples, where they lived in a villa on the island of Ischia. His "Chant d'amour" (Love Song) and his "Ode to the Duke of Bordeaux" date from this period, which sum up, respectively, his love for his wife and his political view of the Neapolitan revolutionary movements preceding Italy's three wars of independence. In fact, due to Lamartine's concern over the safety of living in Naples, he and his wife moved to Rome in the following year, where his son Alphonse was born in 1821. There he also met the wealthy and cultured Duchess of Devonshire, who opened her salon to artistic and literary personalities during this transitional neoclassical phase of early Romanticism. Among her most frequent visitors were people such as Alexander von Humboldt and Antonio Canova. Lamartine's sensitivity to Rome's beauty and to the wealth of art and antiquity to be enjoyed there also impressed him immensely, and he dedicated his hymn to liberty "La liberté, ou une nuit à Rome" (Liberty, or a Night in Rome, 1822) to the Countess.

He was forced to return to France in the Spring of the same year when the Bourbon King Ferdinand I expelled the French diplomatic corps from Naples. On his way back to France he stopped in Florence, where he met Carlo Alberto of Savoy, who was living in a wing of Palazzo Pitti. Carlo Alberto later became king of Piedmont and Sardinia, and was the first monarch to favor Italian movements for national independence and unity. In spite of this, Lamartine criticized Carlo Alberto's inconsistent and cautious approach – although his friend Alessandro Manzoni (author of the great historical novel *I promessi sposi*, 1827 – The Betrothed) wrote to him explaining the need to support Italian patriots. (See Walking Tour 6, Site 34).

Lamartine was able to return to Italy only in 1825 when he was again appointed Second Secretary at the French Embassy in Florence. In the meanwhile, his son Alphonse had unfortunately died, but in May 1822 his wife gave birth to a daughter, Julia, named after his early love for Julie des Hérettes. Still, Lamartine loved being back in Florence, which he called "l'Athènes du moyen âge" (the

Athens of the Middle Ages) – while Tuscany was "the garden of Italy," in his words. The city's high society opened its doors to him as did the expatriot French residents. These were years when many of the most important men of letters spent time in Florence; men such as Giacomo Leopardi, Giambattista Niccolini, Giuliano Frullani, Niccolò Tommaseo, Alessandro Manzoni, and Vincenzo Monti (see Walking Tour 3, Site 15; Walking Tour 4, Sites 19 and 23). Even the Florentine sky and the city's climate appealed to him and reinforced his appreciation of the city's past:

Ah! Qui m'importera sur les tièdes rivages
Où l'Arne couronné de ses pâles ombrages
Aux murs des Médicis en sa course arrêté,
Réfléchit le palais par la Muse habités
Et semble au bruit flatteur de son onde plus lente
Murmurer les grands noms de Pétrarque et de Dante.

Ah! Who will take me along the warm banks
Where the Arno crowned by its pale shadows
Lingers in its way past the walls of the Medici,
Where it reflects the buildings the Muse dwelled in
And seems to whisper the great names of Petrarch and
Dante with the flattering sound of even its most sluggish wave.

Lamartine came to know Florence's environs as well, such as the Benedictine abbey at Vallombrosa, about fifty kilometers north of the city. He visited it with his friend Antoir and was so touched by its atmosphere that he described his impressions of it in the twelfth of his *Harmonies poétiques et religieuses* (Religious and Poetic Harmonies, 1830) entitled "L'Abbaye de Vallombrose," (The Abbey of Vallombrosa). Lamartine's praise of the monks' life of prayer typified a shift in the writer's work, evidencing a new interest in spiritual and religious themes.

An odd aspect of Lamartine's fascination with Italy, which might be seen as contradictory, was his strongly critical vein. Hence, after the publication of the Fifth Canto of Byron's *Childe Harold*, Lamartine penned a literary imitation of Byron's verses which was an explicit criticism of the Italians. This alienated him from many people, who openly criticized him in return. As a result, the Neapolitan revolutionary Gabriele Pepe challenged him to a duel for offending Italy, which they fought with short swords. When Lamartine was wounded on his right arm Pepe announced that he was sufficiently satisfied and even dressed Lamartine's wound himself. Indeed, the two men became friends afterward. But Lamartine's closest Italian friend was the writer, historian and patriot Gino Capponi (see Walking Tour 4, Site 19).

In August 1828 Lamartine left Italy and never returned. Although he continued to write in France – where he had a brilliant political career, including being elected to parliament and serving as Minister of Foreign Affairs in 1848 – the restoration of imperial power under Napoleon III meant the end of public life for him. From that point on he lived only from the proceeds of his writing. He died in Paris on February 28, 1869.

9) CARLO COLLODI   Via Taddea 21
(1826-1890)

Return to the corner behind you and proceed along Via Faenza passing Via Cennini on your right. Cross Via Nazionale and turn left into Via Giovan Battista Zannoni. After one cross street Via G. B. Zannoni becomes Via Panicale. Follow it to Via Taddea, which will enter it on your right. In the middle of the block on your right you will see a plaque reading:

> *In questa casa nacque nel 1826 Carlo Lorenzini detto il Collodi padre di Pinocchio 29 ottobre XX*

> Carlo Lorenzini, known as Collodi, the father of Pinocchio, was born in this house in 1826. October 29, 1920.

If there is such a thing as a "global character," Pinocchio is it. Walt Disney certainly contributed to his fame, but he was invented by Carlo Lorenzini and went on to star in the eponymous tale loved by children the world over. Pinocchio was a wooden puppet made by the old carpenter Geppetto who had always wanted a child. The story follows Pinocchio's adventures as a puppet as well as his desire to someday become a flesh-and-blood boy, a desire he eventually realizes. At first glance the tale seems to belong solely to the genre of children's literature, but it also offers psychological observations, provides moral precepts and maintains a solid narrative structure. In other words, the puppet-boy soon learns that he cannot merely live as a wooden puppet because the nature of human life requires him to act according to a specific set of morals and rational forms of behavior. It is interesting too that the tale's moral teachings are never overpowering. They result directly from Pinocchio's adventures and misadventrues (on which he is led to reflect) and can be considered another form of the picaresque (as in Cervantes or the English eighteenth-century novel), a rather marginal genre in Italian literature. Collodi's psychological analysis reflects several different sides of a child's growth: fear of death, relationship to a father figure, desire for a mother, a child's rapport to authority and social constraints (*i.e.* school) as well as the problem of balancing duty with pleasure. The combination of these aspects makes *Pinocchio* a very amusing and comical read for both adults and the young. Some characters have become so imbedded in readers' minds that they are almost part of our collective memory: Geppetto, the Talking Cricket, Fire Eater, the Fox and the Cat, the Fairy with Azure Hair and Lamp-Wick. Many of these characters exist in statue form at the park and sculpture garden *Il Paese dei Balocchi* (Toyland) dedicated to him in the town of Collodi, between Lucca and Pistoia. Indirectly, *Pinocchio* also mirrors the harsh socio-economic conditions around Lucca and Pistoia at the end of the nineteenth century following the unification of Italy. It is no accident then that Geppetto is a poor carpenter and Pinocchio suffers from almost constant hunger. On the other hand, the Toyland that Pinocchio escapes to is not a Land of Milk and Honey – just where he goes to play – but it can be seen as an escape from the severe working conditions that were imposed on any laborer or artisan such as Geppetto. Stylistically, Collodi's prose clearly reflects the tradition of oral story-telling, and its characteristically Tuscan forms of speech prevail over what was considered standard Italian even in the nineteenth century.

Le avventure di Pinocchio: Storia di un burattino (*The Adventures of Pinocchio: The Tale of a Puppet*) was first serialized in 1881 in the *Giornale dei bambini* (Children's Magazine) and then published in a single volume in 1883 when Carlo Lorenzini was middle aged. Earlier he had also written other works for children, such as *Il viaggio per l'Italia di Giannettino* (Giannettino's Voyage Throughout Italy, 1876), *Minuzzolo* (1877), *Occhi e nasi* (Eyes and Noses, 1881) and *Storie allegre* (Happy Stories, 1887). His translation of Charles Perrault's *Contes de ma mère l'Oye* (Tales of Mother Goose) is additional proof of his interest in children's literature, although Collodi entitled it *I racconti delle fate* (The Tales of the Fairies).

In his youth Lorenzini had fought for national liberation during Italy's wars of independence in 1848 and 1859. He had had a career in journalism writing theatrical reviews for the newspaper *Scaramuccia* (Skirmish) and the political journal *Il lampione* (The Street Lamp), which he founded in order to "bring light to those who were groping in the dark." It was in his journalistic writing that he began to use the pseudonym Collodi, the name of the town where his mother was born. She, a seamstress, and his father, a cook, nonetheless saw to it that young Carlo was educated in a seminary. Since both his parents were household retainers at the Palazzo Ginori Lisci in Via de' Ginori, the family chose to live in nearby Via Taddea: a neighborhood of stables and workshops inhabited by coachmen and servants. Among his very first published works is *Un romanzo in vapore: Da Firenze a Livorno* (*A Novel in Steam: From Florence to Leghorn*, 1856), a humorous illustrated guide in praise of travel by steam locomotive. Ten years prior the popular railroad connecting Florence to Leghorn had opened and Collodi wanted to write a travel book that was part guidebook and part novel.

He is buried near the church of San Miniato in the Cimitero Monumentale, also known as the Cimitero delle Porte Sante (see Walking Tour 8, Site 49 to find the house in Via Rondinelli where Collodi lived as an adult).

Walking Tour 2

Giovanni Pico della Mirandola - Girolamo Benivieni - Angelo Poliziano -Benvenuto Cellini - Bartolomeo Scala - Elizabeth Barrett Browning - Arthur Hugh Clough - Walter Savage Landor - Frances Trollope-Milton - Giampietro Viesseux - Pellegrino Artusi

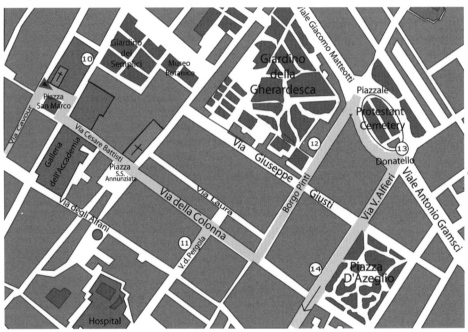

Piazza San Marco - Via della Pergola - Borgo Pinti - Piazzale Donatello -Piazza d'Azeglio

10) Giovanni Pico della Mirandola   **Church of San Marco**
  Girolamo Benivieni   **Piazza San Marco**
  Angelo Poliziano

From Via Taddea, retrace your steps to Via Panicale and turn right. At the next corner turn right again into Via Guelfa and walk three blocks to Via Cavour. Turn left, and after one long block you will find yourself in Piazza San Marco where you will see the Church of San Marco on the opposite side of the four-cornered square. After entering it keep to the left side of the nave and look for a bronze statue between the second and third altars on your left. You will see two large plaques behind the statue of Savonarola sitting (see Walking Tour 10, Site 60). The upper one mentions both Pico della Mirandola and Girolamo Benivieni while the lower one indicates Poliziano's tomb:

Joannes Iacet Hic Mirandula Cetera Norunt — Here lies Giovanni Pico della Mirandola about
Et Tagus Et Ganges Forsan Et Antipodes — whom the Tagus, the Ganges and even the Antipodes

Obiit Anno Sal. MCCCCLXXXXIV — know everything. He died in the year of our Savior 1494

Vixit Ann. XXXII — He lived thirty-two years
Hieronimus Benivenius — Girolamo Benivieni saw to it that these remains
Ne Disiunctus Post Mortem — were buried in this ground so that after death a
Locus Ossa Teneret Quor Animos — divided grave would not separate the bones of those

In Vita Coniunxit Amor; — whose souls were united by love during life.
Hac Humo Supposita Poni Curavit. — He died in the year 1542
Ob anno MDXLII Vix An. LXXXIX — and lived 89 years.

Son qui le ritrovate ossa di — Here are the rediscovered bones of
Agnolo Ambrogini detto il Poliziano — Agnolo Ambrogini, called "Poliziano"
MCCCCLIV-MCCCCLXXXXIV — 1454-1494
che nei più divini linguaggi d'Europa — who was a poet and master of the most
fu maestro e poeta e volle risorta — divine languages in Europe and hoped
l'Atene di Pericle nella Firenze — to restore Pericles' Athens in Florence
del suo Magnifico — under the Magnificent

GIOVANNI PICO DELLA MIRANDOLA
(1463-1494)

Beyond being one of the principal humanists of the fifteenth century, we continue to remember Pico della Mirandola today because of his precocious talent, personal charm, wealth, nobility, tragic life and early death. In the 1450's he was considered the most handsome young man in Florence. His nephew Gianfrancesco wrote that he was "gracious", "tall", "blond" and had a "noble and distinctive gait", "a delicate and rosy complection, light-blue vivid eyes, an attractive face" and "white and regular teeth." His memory was also legendary, and according to one anecdote he was able to recite entire books backwards according to a special method in use during the Renaissance.

He was born in Mirandola, near Modena, in 1463 and studied Latin and Greek early on in preparation for a career in the Church. His father was Gian Francesco Pico, Count of Mirandola and Concordia and his mother, Giulia Boiardo, an aunt of the poet Matteo Maria Boiardo (see Introduction). After studying canon law in Bologna and Arabic and Hebrew at the universities of Padua and Ferrara, he settled in Florence in 1484 where he became familiar with Marsilio Ficino's

Neoplatonism (see Walking Tour 9, Site 55). The result of his interest in it led him to attempt a theoretical mediation between Christianity, other religions and a number of classical philosophical traditions. To this end he planned to organize a meeting of scholars in Rome and published 900 brief statements that were supposed to serve as stimulus for debate: *Conclusionae nongentae in omni genere scientiarum* (Nine Hundred Theses Concerning All Sciences). Some of the statements anticipated ideas that were later developed during the Reformation, and the vast array of medieval and international thinkers he mentions are impressive because they indicate a surprising mental openness at a time when Western scholars were expected to refer only to Christian authors in support of their arguments. In other words, alongside Thomas Aquinas, Aristotle and Plato, Pico also discussed Pythagoras, Jewish Cabalists, Arab commentaries on Aristotle, Zoroaster as well as mystical Hellenistic traditions. Unfortunately, a special committee set up by Innocent VIII condemned all of his *Conclusionae*, which he tried to defend in an *Apologia* to no avail. He fled to Paris where the Pope had him imprisoned anyway. Later King Charles VIII of France released him due to the efforts of several Italian princes, and he returned to Florence where he spent the rest of his short life on a kind of parole looked over by Lorenzo de' Medici. Pope Alexander VI finally cleared him of all charges in 1493, the year before his death.

Pico's many other works include Italian love poetry, Latin poems, religious essays, an argument against astrology, a commentary on the Psalms, another on the first 27 verses of Genesis (*Heptaplus*), and *De ente et uno* (On Being and the One), in which he tries to reconcile Plato and Aristotle. The many letters he left are evidence of the contact he had with humanists from other parts of Italy and of his tolerance in philosophical debates.

He wrote his famous oration "On the dignity of Man" as an introductory speech for the *Conclusionae*. It includes a praise of free will that places humankind on a level that is almost divine in that Mirandola sees the potential in all people to rise either to God-like perfection or lower themselves to the level of animals. In opposition to Christian thought of the Middle Ages which relegated human beings to an inferior and sinful position with respect to God's superiority, Mirandola's concept of free will elevates the human condition to a centrality that revolutionized Western thought. Written as a dialogue, the oration is an obvious expression of the Neoplatonism then in sway with Marsilio Ficino and Cristoforo Landino, the principal exponents of the intelligentsia at the Medici court. As Mirandola has God say to Man: "I put you at the center of the world.... I made you neither heavenly nor earthly, neither mortal nor immortal, so that you would mold yourself in the form that you want as if you were the free and sovereign creator of your destiny." Such an idea conferred great importance and artistic dignity on any human pursuit.

The *Conclusionae* show that Pico was largely in agreement with Marsilio Ficino's effort to point out the basic harmony between Platonism and Christianity. Pico's tireless attempts to find similarities between disparate intellectual traditions led other humanists, his friends, to call him the "Prince of Harmony". Florence was Pico's ideal city and the place that nourished his friendship with Lorenzo de' Medici, Girolamo Benivieni, Angelo Poliziano and the main humanists of the Florentine Academy. Poliziano called him "omnium doctrinarum lux" or "light of all knowledge." Savonarola described him as "a miracle of insight and intelligence" while for Machiavelli he was "a man almost divine." Pico's early death has left an indelible and beautiful impression: the quintessence of youth that rose to its full intellectual potential as part of a Romantic interpretation of the Renaissance. Horace's motto "carpe diem" was a leitmotif of Pico's time; and so it is not a coincidence that one of his sonnets, curiously premonitory, restates this idea in saying: "It is a happy thing when Heaven is friendly to us, to die young; to complete one day then, is better than to wait till evening".

GIROLAMO BENIVIENI
(1453-1542)

You might well ask yourself why this Florentine humanist is buried with Pico della Mirandola. In point of fact, it was Benivieni himself who arranged Pico's burial here: he was so grief-stricken by his younger friend's death that he almost committed suicide. The epitaph above plainly spells out the affectionate relationship between the two men. Benivieni was a poet and part of Pico's and Ficino's Neoplatonist humanist circle. He is known for his "Poem on Heavenly and Divine Love," which was an attempt to summarize Marsilio Ficino's commentary on Plato's *Symposium*. This poem was written in 1486 with an introduction by Pico della Mirandola and further attests to the intense intellectual exchange between the two humanists. Suffering from what we now call depression (once described as "melancholic humour"), Benivieni found it hard to take the initiative in life and preferred to seek protection as court poet to princes such as Giulio Cesare da Varano, lord of Camerino, and eventually Lorenzo de' Medici. Girolamo Benivieni and Giovanni Pico della Mirandola were certainly very fond of each other, and judging from the inscription on their single tomb it would seem that Benivieni wanted to immortalize his love for Pico.

ANGELO POLIZIANO
(1454-1494)

Born Agnolo Ambrogini in the Tuscan town of Montepulciano, this poet and humanist came to be known simply as Poliziano, after the Latin name for his birthplace (*Mons Politianus*). After his father's murder he was welcomed into the court of Lorenzo the Magnificent and while still an adolescent translated three books of the *Iliad* into Latin. His precocious creative vein assured him a promising future: Lorenzo appointed him the tutor of his three-year-old son, Piero, and gave him free access to the Medici library where he composed epigrams, elegies and odes in Greek and Latin. Among his other works are the *Detti piacevoli* (Pleasant Sayings) and the long poem *Sylva in scabiem* (Trees with Mildew), one of his more whimsical compositions, which describes all the various symptoms of scabies.

Poliziano's masterpiece is *Stanzas Begun for the Tournament of the Magnificent Giuliano de' Medici*, a narrative poem that was supposed to celebrate the jousting victory of Lorenzo de' Medici's brother in a competition in Piazza Santa Croce. Instead it's the tale of a young hunter's love for a nymph: a story that is really a pastoral transfiguration of Giuliano's affection for Simonetta Cattaneo, then considered the most beautiful woman in Florence. It is one of the most important works of the Renaissance because its simple but extremely elegant style constituted a single-handed renewal of literature in Italian at a time when most intellectuals preferred to write in Latin. At the same time it returns to classical and mythological imagery that was so typical of the Renaissance in Italy. The *Stanzas* were begun in 1475 but were never completed because Giuliano was murdered during a mass in Florence's cathedral in 1478 when the Pazzi family conspired to eliminate the Medici (see Walking Tour 9, Site 50 for directions to Giuliano's tomb).

Poliziano was much more than a tutor in the Medici household: he was a close friend and advisor to the entire family. Unfortunately, disagreement with Lorenzo's wife Clarice Orisini led him to seek employment for a short time in Mantua at the court of Cardinal Federico Gonzaga. It was here in 1480 that he wrote *The Legend of Orpheus*, a dramatic work based on the Florentine mystery play, but Poliziano was deeply nostalgic for Florence and was able to return there at the end of the same year. He was welcomed back into the Medici household where, at the age of 26, he was awarded a post as professor and scholar famous for his subtle commentaries on Greek and Latin classics. His philological expertise, renowned during his lifetime, is attested to by his writings collected in his *Miscellanea*. After Lorenzo's death Poliziano sought the protection of Lorenzo's successor, his son Piero, through whom he hoped to be appointed cardinal, but this hope was never realized: a source of great disappointment to him.

All the same, Poliziano was an integral part of the Medici court, and his importance to it can be measured by the prestigious portraits of him that the Medici have left us. One is in a fresco by Domenico Ghirlandaio in the church of Santa Trinita, where Poliziano appears in profile. It is in the Sassetti Chapel in the right arm of the transept, where there is a lunette at the top of the center wall. Entitled "St. Francis receives the rule of order from Pope Honorius," this fresco depicts the Loggia dei Lanzi and Palazzo Vecchio in the background. Poliziano is in the foreground leading Lorenzo de' Medici's children up a submerged staircase. Another is in a different fresco by the same artist in the church of Santa Maria Novella. It appears on the right wall of the apse in the cycle narrating events in the life of Saint Zachary. In the bottom-most scene on the right, which depicts the angel as it appears to Saint Zachary, Poliziano is the third figure from the left at the very bottom of the painting. The first figure on the left is Marsilio Ficino (see Walking Tour 9, Site 55).

11) BENVENUTO CELLINI   Via della Pergola 59
(1500-1570)

After exiting the church of San Marco turn left and cross the square into Via Cesare Battisti, following it through Piazza Santissima Annunziata to Via della Colonna. After one block turn right into Via della Pergola, where you will see a plaque on the right-hand side of the street to the left of the entrance at number 59:

> *Casa di Benvenuto Cellini nella quale formò e gettò il Perseo e poi vi morì il 14 febbraio 1570.*

> *Benvenuto Cellini's house, where he sculpted and cast Perseus. He died here later on February 14, 1570.*

Poor and alone, Benvenuto Cellini wrote his unfinished autobiography in Florence from 1558 to 1566, when it must have offered him solace from his enemies and legal problems. A sculptor, goldsmith and medalist, he published treatises on sculpture and on the goldsmith's craft, but now owes his reputation as a writer to the *Vita* (*The Autobiography of Benvenuto Cellini*), in which his experiences unfold as a series of daring feats in a hero's life of adventure. In this sense the *Vita* recounts a succession of events as a work of art – those embodied in a picaresque character – and in doing so becomes one of the first autobiographical novels. For this reason, Cellini's Renaissance titanism is also quite different from Giorgio Vasari's *Lives of the Most Eminent Italian Architects, Painters and Sculptors from Cimabue to the Present Day* (1550-1568), which represents an early attempt to write art history (see Walking Tour 10, Site 61).

The *Vita* touches on childhood memories such as the music lessons his father made him take and his decision to devote himself completely to the figurative arts. As Cellini said, "In Florence I sought constantly to learn from Michelangelo's fine manner, from which I never strayed." During the sack of Rome and the siege of Castel Sant'Angelo in 1527 he helped defend the city from Spanish imperial troops and personally led a band of fifty men to victory. Later he was imprisoned in the same building, and the *Vita* narrates his daring escape from it too. Among other things, Cellini shares his thoughts on his rapport with several popes and his many adversaries. Passionate and instinctual by nature, he was easily aroused to anger, vengeance and even murder – while at other moments his fervid character expressed itself in a positive way, such as in his anecdote about smelting his statue of Perseus (restored in 2000), now in the Loggia dei Lanzi in the Piazza della Signoria. He uses a spoken, spontaneous antiliterary style in describing it and compares his skills in metallurgy to the risks against successful completion of the project (II, 73-8). In this, Cellini's technical skill exemplifies Machiavelli's concept of "virtù," or bravura, and its constant battle with adversity, or "fortuna" (fortune).

From 1540 to 1545 Cellini produced works of art for Francis I of France, such as a salt cellar and the door to Fontainebleau palace, though he spent his final years in Florence. The *Vita* wasn't printed until 1728, existing only in manuscript form up to then.

12) BARTOLOMEO SCALA   **Borgo Pinti 97**
(1430-1497)

From Cellini's house retrace your steps back to Via della Colonna and turn right. After one block turn left into Borgo Pinti and continue past Via Laura and Via Giuseppe Giusti. After the long walled garden on your left you will see the following plaque between numbers 97 and 99:

> *Bartolomeo Scala cancelliere della repubblica illustre storico letterato visse e morì in questo palazzo da lui costruito e dai suoi posteri venduto nel MDLXXXV ad Alessandro de' Medici cardinale che fu Leone XI da cui lo ebbe Costanza sua sorella moglie di Ugo conte della Gherardesca nel MDCV*

Chancellor of the republic and illustrious historical writer, Bartolomeo Scala lived and died in this building built by him and sold by his heirs in 1585 to cardinal Alessandro de' Medici (later Leo XI), whose sister Costanza, wife to Count Ugo della Gherardesca, inherited it in 1605.

Bartolomeo Scala was an important political and literary figure who moved in the same cultural milieu shared by Pico della Mirandola and Angelo Poliziano. His literary reputation didn't shine as brightly as theirs, but his political career certainly did, since he was Chancellor of Florence from 1465 to 1497. As such, his duties included overseeing internal Florentine affairs as well as formal relations with foreign Italian states, among which Milan, Venice and the Papal States were the most important. Born to a very humble family, he nonetheless rose to a position of wealth and great responsibility, and for this reason embodied the self-made Renaissance man. His father was a tenant miller in Colle Val d'Elsa in the province of Siena, a provincial town known as a center of learning, where he was born on May 17, 1430. When he was about twenty years old he moved to Florence in order to study poetry, oratory and law, though he left for Milan in 1454 to work under the humanist Francesco Filelfo. Scala frequented the court of Duke Francesco Sforza, ruler of Milan, whom he knew personally, and the influence that the Duke's secretary had on him came to be of primary importance since he later modeled reforms in Florentine governance on those he had seen in Milan. After returning to Florence, he was made secretary to Pier Francesco de' Medici, a nephew of Cosimo il Vecchio – the latter being the patriarch of the Medici dynasty and a man whom Scala admired greatly. His career grew slowly but steadily, and the period of Scala's greatest influence in Florentine governance lasted from 1469 to 1478, when he worked closely with Lorenzo de' Medici as Chancellor of the Florentine republic. In this capacity he collaborated in maintaining the delicate balance of power that Lorenzo established between Florence, Milan, Venice and the Papal States. After becoming Chancellor, Scala bought the house you see in front of you, designed by Giuliano da San Gallo, where he lived until the end of his life. Its imposing stateliness attests to the power and wealth achieved by its owner.

Bartolomeo Scala's works include 225 letters of official communication between the Florentine republic and heads of state, speeches, essays, and apologues. His poetry includes Latin elegies and eclogues as well as sonnets and other poems in Italian. All of his writing reveals his Latin and Greek education and his profound respect for humanistic studies, although he modestly recognized his own limitations writing to Angelo Poliziano: "if you want to know me – I am just one of the people, a supporter of Latin eloquence, an enthusiastic admirer of the liberal arts, but a man of little learning and barely mediocre abilities." There is even a description of Scala in George Eliot's 1863 historical novel *Romola*, set in Fifteenth-century Florence. It appears on the first page of chapter seven.

13) ARTHUR HUGH CLOUGH	**Piazzale Donatello 38**
GIAMPIETRO VIEUSSEUX	**Protestant Cemetery**
WALTER SAVAGE LANDOR	**(Cimitero degli Inglesi)**
FRANCES TROLLOPE-MILTON	
ELIZABETH BARRETT BROWNING	

From Bartolomeo Scala's house in Borgo Pinti proceed in the same direction to the next corner where you will see the Protestant Cemetery (also known as "il cimitero degli inglesi") on a small hill in the middle of Piazzale Donatello surrounded by a traffic circle. Turn right into the square with the cemetery to your left until you reach its opposite edge. There, after crossing the very busy street toward the cemetery, you will find its entrance.

The two large avenues connected to Piazzale Donatello – Viale Giacomo Matteotti and Viale Antonio Gramsci – were built after 1864 when the city walls were demolished to make way for them as part of Giuseppe Poggi's plan for modernizing the newly-established capital city. This hill lay just beyond the city walls and used to be a favorite place from which to watch soccer matches on the surrounding fields. In 1827 the Grand Duchy of Tuscany sold this land to the Reformed Evangelical Church for use as a cemetery, which was closed to new burials in 1878. This denomination was created through a joint effort of French Huguenots, Italian Waldensians and Swiss Calvinists. The cemetery still belongs to the Swiss Evangelical Reformed Church and is officially called the Protestant Cemetery, although it is generally known as the English Cemetery because of the many English buried here. There are a total of 1409 graves here, including British, Swiss, North Americans, Italians and Russians. The Swiss began to arrive at the end of the eighteenth century and easily integrated themselves into the Florentine community largely because their modest social origins obliged them to work for a living. Many opened cafes, shops and grocery stores that flourished into the nineteenth century. As the Protestant community grew, its members could be buried in the Protestant cemetery in Leghorn, but none existed in Florence. The English, who visited the city for short periods of time and came from largely wealthy or aristocratic families, had no need to become a part of Florentine social fabric. These ethnic groups made up Florence's few religious minorities. The Italian Waldensians had arrived from Piedmont in 1859, and among them was the Robiglio family, whose pastry shop in Via de' Servi 112 (red) is still renowned. (These writers particularly recommend the "budino di riso," a Florentine specialty made from rice).

The cypresses here recall the ones traditionally planted in cemeteries all over Italy, although those found throughout Tuscany belong to the region's natural landscape. A popular saying has it that God made this region so beautiful that he even blessed it with exclamation points.

Arthur Hugh Clough (pronounced "Cluff") (1819-1861)

Walk slightly less than one-half way along the central path that leads up the hill from the gatehouse. At the first break in the hedge on your right is Clough's tombstone, framed by a small laurel hedge.

A close friend of the critic Mathew Arnold, Clough was an English intellectual whose termperament was pulled in many directions at once – just like the religious controversies that rocked Victorian England. Like many English writers of his time, he felt caught between the conservative Tractarians and the Evangelical movement and eventually abandoned the religion of his youth. After very promising studies begun at Rugby under Mathew Arnold, he studied at Balliol College Oxford and went on to become tutor and fellow of Oriel College there until 1848, when he resigned. In the years immediately following he travelled across Europe and first arrived in Italy in 1843 on a relgious tour of the Benedictine monasteries in Tuscany at Vallombrosa, Camaldoli and La Verna. A supporter of independence movements, Clough went to France during the 1848 Revolution and was in Rome from

April through July the following year during Giuseppe Mazzini's brief creation of the Roman Republic. Clough found himself temporarily blocked there when the French laid seige to the city to disarm Mazzini's threat to the Papal States. Clough described the experience in his *Amours de Voyage* (1849), a collection of letters in his favorite meter: the hexameter. In 1853 he travelled to Boston to lecture and see Ralph Waldo Emerson, whom he had met earlier on his European tour. After returning to London later the same year, he found employment for the rest of his brief life in the Education Office as a civil servant. Soon afterwards Clough married Blanche Smith, a cousin of Florence Nightingale. He dedicated a considerable amount of time helping the famous nurse in her efforts to reform military hospitals, and it's even likely he nurtured an unrequited love for her. Ironically, Clough died in Florence from typhus when he was only 42 during a trip undertaken to improve his health. In a letter written on November 29, 1861 to their friend C. E. Norton, Blanche noted that: "[h]e is buried in the little Protestant cemetery here – a very nice little place – where the tall cypresses stand against that beautiful blue sky and the hills look down on it. I love this place now – it is so beautiful. And sad as it is to have him away from home it is not an unfit resting place for him." This thought corresponds to some of Clough's own words as well, for in spite of all his travel he always longed for England: "There is a city, upbuilt on the quays of the turbulent Arno, / Under Fiesole's heights, – thither are we to return? /.../ Sicily, Greece will invite, and the Orient; – or are we to turn to / England, which may after all be for its children the best?" (*Amours de Voyage*, Canto V).

His writing is noteworthy because its language and subject matter enlarged the range of literary expression during his time. His first work was *The Bothie of Tober-na-Vuolich* (1848), a narrative poem whose Gaelic title refers to a forester's hut on the shore of Loch Ericht. In 1849, the following year, he published the collection *Ambarvalia*. During the 1850's he worked on a translation of Plutarch's *Lives* and the long poem *Mari Magno*, organized like the *Canterbury Tales*.

GIAMPIETRO VIEUSSEUX
(1779-1863)

This tomb is to the left of Clough's and is set back from it one row. On top of a raised plinth is a marble casket decorated with oak and acanthus leaves in relief. In the center of one side is an oval portrait of Vieusseux in profile.

Born in Oneglia, Liguria, to a Protestant family originally from Geneva, Vieusseux was principally a merchant until 1819, when he moved permanently to Florence. The "Gabinetto Vieusseux" was his private study, but it became a meeting place three times a week for literary and politically progressive people living or visiting

Florence. At the time, Florence was capital of the Grand Duchy of Tuscany, so Vieusseux's initiative not only worked to make it a more cosmopolitan city but sustained patriots planning Italy's eventual unification and independence. Activists and political theorists from all over the Italian peninsula were able to exchange ideas here, and many such as Niccolò Tommaseo and Gino Capponi also contributed to various journals the Gabinetto published: *L'Antologia* (The Anthology), the *Giornale agrario* (Agrarian Journal), the *Guida dell'educatore* (Educator's Guide) and *La Fenice* (The Phoenix). The *Archivio storico italiano* (Italian Historical Archive), which began publication in 1842, was particularly important for Italians struggling for independence because it published valuable and often rare information that gave them a better sense of their own historical traditions. The Gabinetto's importance is attested to by the caliber of the intellectuals who shared in its cultural life. Giacomo Leopardi, Alessandro Manzoni, Stendhal, Schopenhauer, Thackeray, Dostoevsky, James Fenimore Cooper, Mark Twain and Emile Zola were among those contributing to the Gabinetto's cultural mix during the nineteenth century – followed in the twentieth by Kipling, André Gide, Aldous Huxley and D.H. Lawrence. From its original site in Palazzo Buondelmonti in Piazza Santa Trinita it has moved five times and has resided in Palazzo Strozzi since 1940. It now exists as a major research center, library and historical archive whose *Centro romantico* promotes the study of nineteenth-century European civilization. Eugenio Montale was director of the Gabinetto from 1929 to 1938, Alessandro Bonsanti from 1941 to 1980 and Enzo Siciliano from 1995 to 2000.

WALTER SAVAGE LANDOR
(1775-1864)

From Clough's and Vieusseux's graves continue up the central path until you reach a break in the hedge on your left. Follow the path there toward the cypress tree at the path's end. Before you reach it you will find Landor's simple low tomb abutting a small laurel hedge on your left.

Born in Warwick, Staffordshire, in 1775, Landor excelled in Latin from the time he was an adolescent, when he began to write Latin verses. After arriving in London in 1794 he began to study French and Italian and, because of this, expressed the desire to go one day to live in Italy. Landor became acquainted with Vittorio Alfieri's tragedies and was very proud to have met him once in a bookshop. *The Poems of Walter Savage Landor* (1795) was his first publication. A Latin scholar, Landor translated Oriental texts into epic verses with the title *Gebir*, a reference to Gibraltar. In 1815 he first arrived in Como, Italy with his wife Julia and stayed until 1818. There he responded to Vincenzo Monti's negative remarks about England with insulting Latin verses of his own, and the authorities asked him to leave town because of it. For this reason he went to Pisa until 1821 when he left for Florence to stay for 5 years with a family in the Medici Palace. From 1829 to 1837 the Landors had a villa in Fiesole, where they were happiest. There they could work in their garden and keep a dog too. This was the setting in which Landor composed his most important work, the *Imaginary Conversations* (1824-1829), which are a five-volume collection of invented discussions between great figures of the past. Among these are George Washington and Benjamin Franklin, Pericles and Sophocles, Henry VIII and Anne Boleyn, Milton and Andrew Marvel. There are Italian interlocutors too, such as Dante and Beatrice, and the conversation between Machiavelli and Michelangelo is an interesting condemnation of democracy. These show his admiration of turning points in Italian and world history and his view that Italy's nineteenth-century struggle for unification destined it for greater things. Many conversations are dramatized sketches while others are learned dialogues. Unfortunately, Landor's "combative and explosive" personality meant that he alienated many in Florence just as he had in Como. One of his Italian neighbors is reported to have said that: "all the English are crazy, but this one ... oh boy!" Indeed, after much quarrelling Landor left his wife to return to England. Twenty years later, accused of libel and hounded by creditors, he resurfaced in Fiesole and was soon embroiled in disputes once again. Since he had already left most of his wealth to his children, he suddenly found himself nearly destitute. Robert Browning found him lodging in Siena and then in Florence. He stayed here until his death surrounded by a circle of friends and those who admired him despite his sometimes difficult nature. Younger Florentines referred to him as "the old man with that beautiful little dog."

FRANCES TROLLOPE (1780-1863)

Trollope's grave lies two rows up the hill from Landor's, on your right. It is one of two identical vertical plinths and is the one on your left. The corroded Latin inscription was written by Thomas Adolphus Trollope.

The "indomitable Mrs. Trollope" is now remembered as the author of *Domestic Manners of the Americans* (1832) and mother of the Victorian novelist Anthony Trollope but was a prolific writer in her own right: the author of 35 novels and several travel books. Born in Heckfield, England, in 1779 to a protestant minister, she married at age 30 and gave birth to 7 children, only two of whom outlived her. *Domestic Manners of the Americans* is the fruit of her family's sojourn in the U.S. from 1827 to 1831, which was partly an effort to escape some of the Trollopes' severe financial problems at the time. Leaving her husband behind, Mrs. Trollope and several of her young children sought out a utopian community at Nashoba, Tennessee, where the colonists hoped to prove the equality of blacks and whites and eventually eliminate slavery through education. The primitive conditions and poor sanitation there shocked Mrs. Trollope and induced her to leave Nashoba after only ten days, so the family set out for Cincinnati, known as an Athens of the West. This city sits at the core of her book, a scathing indictment of American behavior – which Trollope found crude, selfish and "money-grubbing." Her account is part adventure story and part reported speech from Americans whom the author lets speak for themselves (a revolutionary technique for its time). It was her first book and caused a sensation in both England and America – which led Trollope to undertake a series of travels and then write about them. Even though she was then already over fifty, she went on to write *Belgium and Western Germany* (1833), *Paris and the Parisians* (1835), *Vienna and the Austrians* (1838) and *A Visit to Italy* (1842). During this same period she also wrote thirteen novels one after another, some of which openly meant to reform social problems such as slavery (*Jonathan Jefferson Whitlaw*, 1836), corrupt evangelists (*The Vicar of Wrexhill*, 1837), child labor abuse (*The Life and Adventures of Michael Armstrong, the Factory Boy*, 1840) and welfare payment to the poor (*Jesse Phillips, A Tale of the Present Day*, 1843). Trollope's travels had given her the opportunity to observe women's lives in a variety of cultures and integrate her reflections on them in writing. She expanded this vein in subsequent novels in which strong female characters were fiercely independent, became fortune hunters in marriage or figured in "conventional" romance novels in order to represent the unconventional woman. From about 1838 on Mrs. Trollope lived primarily in Florence, intersperced with occasional visits abroad and trips to England. Indeed, her home in Piazza Indipendenza became known as a center of social life for the English expatriate community. Among those who attended her Friday receptions there were Charles Dickens, Harriet Beecher Stowe, James Russell Lowell, Nathaniel Hawthorne and George Eliot. While "Fanny" Trollope adored Florence and made sure she was seen amid the swirl of high society in regular attendance at the Cascine Park, she was also familiar with the city's art treasures. Always critical, she had little patience with guidebooks that contradicted each other and reasoned that any visitor would have appreciated the Uffizi gallery much more if it had contained benches for visitors to rest on. Perhaps this suggestion is still pertinent.

ELIZABETH BARRETT BROWNING
(1809-1861)

From Frances Trollope's grave return to the central path that leads to the crest of the cemetery's hill. Turn to your left and continue up that path until you see a stone casket on your left atop six short pillars. It was designed by Lord Leighton (for the principal entry on Elizabeth Barrett Browning see Walking Tour 5, Site 30).

14) PELLEGRINO ARTUSI **Piazza d'Azeglio 35**
   (1820-1911)

Exit the Protestant Cemetery and turn right into Via Vittorio Alfieri. After the first cross street, Via Giuseppe Giusti, you will find yourself in Piazza Massimo d'Azeglio. Keeping the piazza on your left, you will come to number 35 just past the midpoint of the block on your right, where a plaque declares:

> *I cittadini di Firenze e della nativa Forlimpopoli si riuniscono nel ricordare Pellegrino Artusi che qui lungamente operò e morì il 30 marzo 1911. Letterato gastronomo benefattore in questa sua città di adozione dette unità italiana alla varietà linguistica regionale nel suo celebre libro 'La scienza in cucina e l'arte di mangiar bene.' Firenze, 29 maggio 1994. Il Comune di Firenze. Il Comune di Forlimpopoli. L'Accademia Artusiana in Forlimpopoli.*

The citizens of Florence and of his native Forlimpopoli gather together to remember Pellegrino Artusi who worked and died here after many years on March 30, 1911. A writer, gourmet and benefactor in this his adopted city, he gave Italian unity to regional linguistic varieties in his celebrated book "Science in the Kitchen and the Art of Eating Well." Florence, May 29, 1994. The City of Florence. The City of Forlimpopoli. The Artusian Academy in Forlimpopoli.

"Just because I've written about cooking I wouldn't want people to think I was a glutton or a huge eater. I rebel against this less-than-flattering reputation because I'm neither one nor the other. I love beauty and goodness wherever they are found, and I'm repulsed when I see the Grace-of-God wasted." These are the words Artusi uses at the end of the Preface to his famous cookbook published here at this address in 1891, up through the 14th edition. It became a best-seller, was reprinted thirty-five times, and people all over Italy wrote to Artusi at his home here for copies of it until he died in 1911. Piero Camporesi has said that "in a discreet impalpable underground way" Artusi "accomplished the very civilized task of uniting and amalgamating the heterogenous masses of people that only formally were able to call themselves Italian," which he achieved "first in the kitchen and then in the folds of the entire collective unconscious." Primo Levi praised Artusi's affectionate simplicity of language. Written for the burgeoning upper-middle class at the end of the nineteenth century, this work represents a change in cookbook writing. Till then most cookbooks had used many French terms not understood by the general reading public. Not only did Artusi avoid these, but his simple, discursive and often humorous language made it easy for the reader to recreate all sorts of dishes from appetizers to soups, broth, side-dishes, vegetables, noodle dishes, fried dishes, seafood, roasts, stews, boiled meats, sauces, syrups, pastries, preserves, liquors, and ice cream. He even included a category called "tramessi" (or "entremets") that were side dishes served between main courses. In the Appendix there is a category called "Cooking for Weak Stomachs" as well as a variety of sample meal plans for every month of the year.

His advice is to chew one's food well and not eat between meals, which one should consume at regular intervals.

Artusi's family came to Florence after his entire hometown in Romagna had been sacked in 1851 by a group of men headed by the famous bandit Stefano Pelloni, known as "il Passatore." His sister Gertrude had been so traumatized that she went mad and had to be confined to an asylum in Pesaro. Pellegrino was sent to Leghorn to learn the family mercantile business and later established the "Banco di Sconto" (Discount Counter) in Florence. His nose for business was so acute that he retired at age 50 and was able to write. Besides *La scienza in cucina*, he completed two other works. One is the *Vita di Ugo Foscolo* (Life of Ugo Foscolo, 1878) with notes to Foscolo's *Sepolcri* (Sepulchres) and a reprinting of his *Viaggio sentimentale di Yorick* (Yorick's Sentimental Journey). The other is his *Osservazioni in appendice a trenta lettere di Giuseppe Giusti* (Observations in Appendix to Thirty Letters by Giuseppe Giusti, 1881). These two works of literary criticism, it is interesting to note, make use of culinary metaphors and terminology as well.

Walking Tour 3

Giacomo Leopardi - Giovanni Villani - Michelangelo Buonarroti

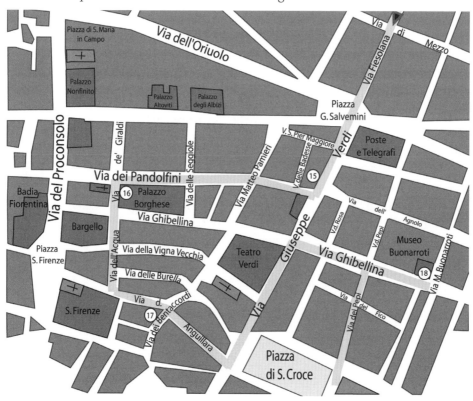

Via Verdi - Via de' Giraldi - Via dei Bentaccordi - Via Ghibellina

15) GIACOMO LEOPARDI   Via Verdi 11
   (1798-1837)

From Pellegrino Artusi's house continue walking in the same direction, keeping the gardens of Piazza D'Azeglio on your left. Cross Via della Colonna into Via Farini and then turn right into Via de' Pilastri, walking past Via dei Pepi on your left. Turn left at the next corner into Via Fiesolana and continue past Via di Mezzo and Piazza Gaetano Salvemini into Via Giuseppe Verdi. After you pass Via San Pier Maggiore on your right you will see a plaque on the second story of the building on your right at the intersection of Via Verdi and Via dell'Agnolo. It reads:

MDCCCCI Per decreto del comune	1901-By municipal decree.
In questa casa dimorò più volte fra	Giacomo Leopardi lived in this house
il 1828 e il 1833 Giacomo Leopardi	several times from 1828 to 1833
e qui agli amici suoi di Toscana	and dedicated here to his Tuscan friends
dedicava i canti nelle cui austere	the poems in whose austere
armonie non vinta dalla sconfitta	harmony the destined note of
delle cose umane persisteva fatidica	Italian hope resounded most generously
la magnanima nota delle italiane	unvanquished by the defeat of
speranze.	human affairs

The "Canti" or "Songs" mentioned on the plaque refer to the poems first published under this title in 1831 and now recognized to be not only Leopardi's best work but also the most significant Italian Romantic lyric poetry (along with Ugo Foscolo's). This site is one of many addresses where Leopardi lived in Florence. Born in the town of Recanati near the Adriatic Sea (in the then-Papal Region of the Marches), the highly educated though largely self-taught Count Leopardi grew up feeling hemmed-in by the narrow cultural horizons of his hometown and by the fact that his impoverished family could not afford to support him away from home (in a period when aristocrats did not work for a living). His first contact with big-city life came when he went to Rome in 1822 in search of literary contacts, but was deeply disappointed, probably because he was unfamiliar with accepted norms of social interaction among the urban intellectual elite. The high point of his stay there was his visit to Torquato Tasso's tomb (the great but desperate Counter-Reformation poet of the sixteenth century who wrote the epic narrative *Jerusalem Delivered* and became the epitome of the misunderstood poet). Nonetheless, Leopardi's own writing did enable him to continue to travel – to Milan in 1825 (where he was put in charge of new Latin and Italian editions of Cicero's complete works) – then to Bologna in 1825 and 1826; Florence (in 1827, 1828, 1830 and 1832-33) and finally Naples (from 1833 to 1837), where he died and was buried not far from Virgil's tomb.

Leopardi first came to Florence to participate in its cultural ferment and was able to meet Giovanni Battista Niccolini (a writer of tragedies), Giampietro Vieusseux, Pietro Colletta (a historian and ex-general), Alessandro Manzoni (poet and novelist), Gino Capponi (historian, economist and writer on educational theory), Pietro Giordani (writer and free-thinker) and Niccolò Tommaseo (novelist and political theorist). (See Walking Tours 2, Site 13; 4, Site 19; and 6, Site 34). These men were all members of the city's liberal intelligentsia that longed for Italy's unification and independence (according to the ideals of Italian Romanticism). Their activities gave birth to the *Antologia* (Anthology), a progressive periodical that promulgated radical changes in Italian political and social structures – and in fact the Grand Duchy of Tuscany (under the Austrian house of Lorraine) outlawed it after twelve years in 1833. Giordani suggested that Leopardi be the *Antologia's* correspondent from the Papal States, but he declined twice because of his lack of experience and interest in politics. Colletta and other intellectuals even funded a stipend for Leopardi, who was chronically unable to support himself.

On top of this, Leopardi wasn't able to enjoy himself in Florence because of a malady that caused his eyes to water and swell. He couldn't write because of it and only went out at night. As if that weren't enough, frequent toothaches forced him to have teeth extracted too. In a letter of June 23, 1827 he wrote that he would consequently be kept from participating in the celebrations the following day in honor of Florence's patron, Saint John the Baptist. He found Florence expensive but wrote, not surprisingly, that he was "tired of life" – though he did mention how kind to him everyone had been in Florence's literary circles. In the same year Leopardi also met Alessandro Manzoni and published his *Operette morali* (Short Moral Treatises). It was very hot during his second trip to Florence, and he complained that the Florentines were more interested in politics than in art and literature. They, for their part, referred to him as the "hunchback," a nickname he had had to endure since childhood. After that summer he returned to Florence a third time in 1830, when he renewed his friendship with Antonio Ranieri and met Mrs. Fanny Targioni Tozzetti, with whom he fell in love – writing four poems in the *Canti* about her. For Leopardi Fanny embodied the well-read woman and combined an ideal of classical beauty with motherly and wifely attributes. She is but one example of many unrequited passions experienced only in Leopardi's poetic imagination. Antonio Ranieri, a political refugee from the Kingdom of Naples, eventually became his lifelong friend. His last stay in Florence was the result of two factors. On the one hand Leopardi wanted to avoid returning to Recanati, and on the other he thought that Florence would be an affordable place to live (in spite of his previous experience). He was also planning to launch a new magazine to be entitled *The Florentine Spectator*, which was to be much less radical than the *Antologia* because its primary purpose was to appeal to a larger and more moderate readership and thereby earn him income from its sale. This project never came to fruition because it was banned by the Austrian authorities, and Leopardi found himself more isolated than ever at a time when several of his friends and patrons associated with the Gabinetto Vieusseux had died or gone into exile for political reasons. He was therefore obliged to rely on Ranieri's help, who had been forced to move back to Naples in the meantime, but promised to support and care for the increasingly frail and destitute poet. In fact, they moved to Naples together in October 1833.

Leopardi's temperament was characterized by an inability to adapt to the social realities of his time and by a continual and painful search for existential meaning beyond that offered by Catholicism. Poetry was the vehicle he chose to express his pessimistic cosmic pain, his deep sense of loss over the passing of time and, especially, his disappointment over unfulfilled youthful expectations. He was educated at home first by his father, who was a minor writer himself with a very good library

of his own. Giacomo had complete access to it, where he studied the most impor-
tant Greek and Latin classics as well as Hebrew, French, English and (probably)
Spanish. He was also influenced by the Enlightenment and soon started writing lit-
erary and cultural essays (i.e., "Saggio sopra gli errori popolari degli antichi," On the
Popular Errors of the Ancients, 1815), translations of Homer, Moscus, Hesiod and
poetry. Among the *Canti* the most beautiful poems are "To Sylvia," "Saturday in the
Village," "Holiday Eve," "Night Song of a Wandering Shepherd in Asia,"
"Recollections," "The Infinite," "Quiet After a Storm," and "The Lonely Sparrow."
Their beauty is also reflected in the *Operette morali*, a collection of imaginary dia-
logues about humanity's difficult and unhappy relation to the natural world and to
life itself. Among the most important are the "Dialogue between Nature and an
Icelander" and "Dialogue between Federico Ruysch and Some of his Mummies."
Leopardi also kept a notebook of personal and literary musings, published as the
Zibaldone (Working Notebook), which is essential in coming to a complete under-
standing of his work.

16) GIOVANNI VILLANI   **Via de' Giraldi 2**
    (1280 ca.-1348)

From Leopardi's lodgings turn right into Via de' Pandolfini and follow it past Via
delle Badesse, Via Matteo Palmieri, Via del Crocifisso and Via delle Seggiole. Turn
left into Via de' Giraldi, where you will see the following plaque on your left shortly after turning the corner:

Giovanni, Matteo e Filippo Villani qui	Giovanni, Matteo and Filippo Villani had their
ebbero le loro case e vi dettarono	houses here, where they recounted their
le cronache fiorentine	Florentine Chronicles to their scribes.

The brothers Giovanni and Matteo Villani were both merchants and chroniclers
of Florentine history. Giovanni held the highest public office in city government
three times under the city's late-medieval government: an oligarchy of the aristocracy and the wealthiest bourgeoisie organized in guilds. As was common at the
time, he was imprisoned for two years for political reasons and died in the great
epidemic of bubonic plague that swept through Florence in 1348. In accordance
with medieval concepts of history his *Cronica fiorentina* (Florentine Chronicle,
1320) begins with an overview of Western history according to Biblical sources but
is recognized as important due to its detailed information about Florentine events
up to 1382. The *Cronica* was published in ten books only in 1537, and then again in
1554 in twelve books. The last six books are the most interesting because they discuss the economic and political events during Giovanni's lifetime and also contain
the first biography of Dante Alighieri. The author's style is dry and unadorned, and
events are narrated year by year according to a strict chronological order that aims
at being dispassionate and objective. Foreshadowing the Renaissance, Villani con-

sidered Florence the heir of ancient Rome's greatness. As he states: "I, John, citizen of Florence, considering the present greatness and nobility of our city, think it's necessary to remember and recount such a famous city's origin and birth, fortunes and misfortunes, as well as the events of its past."

His brother Matteo continued his work up to 1363 but with heavily moralistic overtones. In the same way Matteo's son Filippo took over from his father and brought the *Cronica*'s events up to 1364. From 1381 to 1388 Filippo also wrote the "Book on the Origin of the City of Florence and its Illustrious Citizens."

17) MICHELANGELO BUONARROTI (1475-1564)   Via dei Bentaccordi 15 (red)

Continue in the same direction from the Villanis' address in Via de' Giraldi. Cross Via Ghibellina, where Via de' Giraldi becomes Via dell'Acqua, and follow it till it ends. At Via dell'Anguillara turn left, proceed past Via Filippina and then turn right into Via dei Bentaccordi. Shortly afterward you will see a plaque on your right.

Casa dove Michelangelo Buonarroti	The house where Michelangelo Buonarroti,
nato a Caprese nel Casentino	born in Caprese in the Casentino, [an area in
visse gli anni della sua giovinezza	Tuscany] lived the years of his youth.

The artist known principally for his frescoes in the Sistine Chapel in Rome, the "Pietà" in Saint Peter's Basilica and the gigantic statue of David in Florence, was also a poet. His poetry was published only after his death by his grandnephew in 1623, who printed only 137 out of the 302 poems now known to exist. Many of them were left incomplete and only jotted down in the margins of letters and sketches so that there is no coherent thematic development from one poem to the next nor from the beginning to the end of any compilation of his poems. Enzo N. Girardi has divided them into three periods: Apprenticeship (1503-1532); the period from 1532 to 1547 (which includes the poems dedicated to his friend, poet Vittoria Colonna); and Maturity (from 1547 to 1560).

Many of his poems echo the opposition between physical and spiritual love that Neoplatonists felt to be so important – as well as the idea that artistic perfection is not the result of individual creativity. Instead, the Neoplatonists believed that the artist merely eliminated what was unnecessary from raw materials in order to unveil pre-existing artistic form: "The best of artists never has a concept / A single marble block does not contain / Inside its husk, but to it may attain / Only if hand follows the intellect" (Sonnet 149). Michelangelo's poems are not particularly easy to understand, although they do repeat common Petrarchan themes: old age, solitude, fragility of the human body, and religious suffering. In Michelangelo's words: "My course of life already has attained, / Through stormy seas, and in a flimsy vessel, /... What will become, now, of my amorous thoughts, / Once gay and vain... / There's no painting or sculpture now that quiets / the soul that's pointed toward that holy Love / That on the cross opened Its arms to take us."

Michelangelo came to live in this house with his father during his first year of life and lost his mother when he was six years old. He started school when he was ten, but we know that he preferred drawing early on and would run off to watch artists working. His father wanted him to pursue literary studies, but he preferred to train as an apprentice painter in Domenico Ghirlandaio's workshop (where he was paid instead of having to pay, as was then normal). Two years later he was already one of several young artists protected by the Medici court, so that he was able to study sculpture with Bertoldo di Giovanni, who was in charge of Lorenzo de' Medici's collection of ancient statues in the gardens adjoining the church of San Marco. Michelangelo would also go to the church of the Carmine to study Masaccio's frescoes but loved to tease his classmates. According to Benvenuto Cellini's *Autobiography*, he provoked one of them, Pietro Torrigiano, to the point that he punched Michelangelo in the nose, giving it the characteristic shape still visible in the bust in Casa Buonarroti. Under the Medici he was given a room in the Palazzo Medici-Riccardi (at the intersection of Via Cavour and Via Martelli) and knew court luminaries such as Angelo Poliziano. His early years in Florence were therefore crucial in shaping his personality as one of the greatest and most widely known artists of the Renaissance. He later left for Bologna and then Rome (in 1494), but lived again in Florence from 1501 to 1502 (when he created the statue of David) and from 1515 to 1532. Although he lived the latter part of his life in Rome where his sculpture, painting and architecture earned him fame and wealth, he left proof of his love for Florence in an interesting madrigal. He addresses his city lamenting its present-day moral decadence in a way that recalls Dante's own concerns: "For many, Lady, no, for a thousand lovers, / You were created, in an angel's shape; / Now Heaven seems asleep ... / Return to us, your mourners, / The sun of your eyes." Among Michelangelo's other writing, his *Letters*, first published in 1875, are extremely important because they give an unguarded and personal account of the artist's daily life.

18) MICHELANGELO BUONARROTI   Via Ghibellina 70
(1475-1574)

From Michelangelo's childhood home retrace your steps to Via dell'Anguillara and turn right. At Piazza Santa Croce turn left into Via Giuseppe Verdi and follow it to Via Ghibellina, into which you should turn right. Pass Via della Rosa and Via de' Pepi on your left and you will see the Museum of Casa Buonarroti on your left at the intersection of Via Ghibellina and Via Michelangelo Buonarroti. Inside the entrance, over the doorway in the far wall of the second vestibule is this plaque:

Questa casa comperata a' suoi dal divino Michelangelo fatta ornare di pitture e arricchita de' modelli de' disegni degli scritti del grande zio da Michelangelo pronipote il cavalier Cosimo Buonarroti lasciò per testamento alla città con tutto il suo mobile prezioso l'anno MDCCCLVIII.

This house, which the divine Michelangelo bought for his relatives, was enriched by his second nephew Michelangelo [the younger] with paintings, models, drawings and writing by his illustrious uncle. Mr. Cosimo Buonarroti left it to the city in his will along with all of its furniture. 1858.

This museum contains some of Michelangelo's very first works. He bought it for his nephew Leonardo di Buonarroto, whose son Michelangelo the Younger later filled with his great uncle's works. The family died out in the nineteenth century with Cosimo Buonarroti.

Walking Tour 4

Dante Alighieri - Michelangelo Buonarroti - Vittorio Alfieri - Niccolò Machiavelli - Leonardo Bruni - Ugo Foscolo - Saint Francis of Assisi - Leon Battista Alberti - Galileo Galilei - Gino Capponi - Giovanni Battista Niccolini - Vincenzo da Filicaia - Ottavio Rinuccini - D. H. Lawrence - Leon Battista Alberti - Niccolò Tommaseo - E.M. Forster

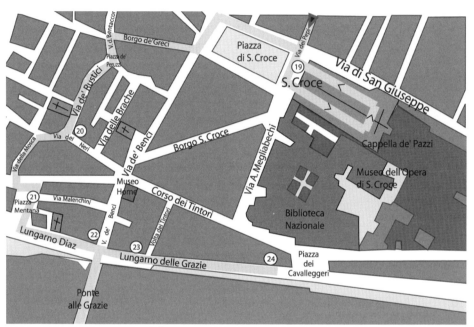

Piazza Santa Croce - Via de' Rustici - Piazza Mentana - Lungarno delle Grazie

19) DANTE ALIGHIERI   **Piazza and Church of Santa Croce**
MICHELANGELO BUONARROTI
VITTORIO ALFIERI
NICCOLÒ MACHIAVELLI
LEONARDO BRUNI
UGO FOSCOLO
SAINT FRANCIS OF ASSISI
LEON BATTISTA ALBERTI
GALILEO GALILEI
GINO CAPPONI
GIOVANNI BATTISTA NICCOLINI
VINCENZO DA FILICAIA

From Casa Buonarroti retrace your steps in Via Ghibellina and turn left into Via dei Pepi. Cross Via del Fico and continue for one more block. You will see the large Piazza Santa Croce on your right and the church on your left.

Statue of DANTE ALIGHIERI (1265-1321)

In front of the left side of the church's façade you will see Enrico Pazzi's 1865 statue of Italy's most important poet. Dante's severe downcast gaze accurately conveys the poet's perennial worry over the moral issues that fellow citizens, Tuscans and Italians faced – as well as his anger over being banished from the city in 1301. The eagle symbolizes the poet's longing for Italian unification under the Holy Roman Empire, while his toga recalls both ancient Roman dress as well as the simple tunic of a Christian pilgrim. During the 1966 flood, the Arno rose to the statue's feet so that Dante seemed to be walking on the water. Inside the church there is also a cenotaph dedicated to him. (For the entry on Dante, see Walking Tour 11).

MICHELANGELO BUONARROTI (1475-1564)

Enter the church. Michelangelo's tomb, by Giorgio Vasari, is built along the right-hand wall opposite the first pilaster on your right. The Latin inscription can be translated like this:

"To Michelangelo Buonarroti of the ancient family of the Simonis, known by fame to everyone as a sculptor, painter and architect. Leonardo had this plaque set here for his paternal uncle in the year of our salvation 1570 out of gratitude and deep affection for him. After he moved his bones from Rome he had them laid here in the church of his ancestors due to the sponsorship of the most serene Cosimo de' Medici, Granduke of Tuscany. Michelangelo lived eighty-eight years, eleven months and fifteen days." (See Walking Tour 3, sites 17 and 18).

Cenotaph of DANTE ALIGHIERI (1265-1321)

Continue along the nave on the right. Between the second and third altars is a monument to Dante. Although the Poet is buried in Ravenna where he died in exile, his importance to his city's past merits a place here in the church that is one of Italy's two pantheons. In English translation, the cenotaph reads:

"Honor the highest poet. To Dante Alighieri. In 1829 the people of Tuscany proudly erected this honorary tomb, which their ancestors had unsuccessfully intended to build three times." The cenotaph's first four words are Dante's own from Inferno, Canto IV, line 80 of the *Divine Comedy*, but the poet referred to is Virgil. The standing female figure on the monument pointing to the inscription represents Italy, while the crying statue leaning on the sarcophagus symbolizes Poetry. The words to the right of the cenotaph can be read in English like this: "On the seventh centenary of his birth. The National Association of Italian Municipalities. 1265-1965." The translation of those on the right: "On the seventh centenary of his birth. The Association of Dante Studies. 1265-1965."

VITTORIO ALFIERI
(1749-1803)

Continue to walk along the right-hand wall. Opposite the third pilaster on your right you will find Alfieri's tomb just before the third altar on the right. The neo-classical monument was created by Antonio Canova. The female figure represents Italy in grief. The Latin inscription can be read in English as:

"To Vittorio Alfieri from Asti. Louisa of the Princes of Stolberg, Countess of Albany, had this monument erected in 1810." The Countess of Albany was Alfieri's companion for almost twenty years and is also buried here in the Castellani chapel in the right arm of the transept. (For the entry on Alfieri see Walking Tour 6, site 35).

NICCOLÒ MACHIAVELLI
(1469-1527)

Continue walking along the right-hand nave. Opposite the fourth pilaster on your right you will come to Machiavelli's tomb. The translation of the Latin inscription reads: "So great is his name that no praise is sufficient. Niccolò Machiavelli died in 1527." The famous statesman and writer was buried here with other members of his family, and this monument was built later in 1787. (For the entry on Machiavelli see Walking Tour 5, site 27).

LEONARDO BRUNI
(1374-1444)

Continue along the right-hand nave past the fifth altar and the exit door on your right. The next large tomb is Bernardo Rossellino's monument to Leonardo Bruni, who was an historian, humanist and Chancellor of the Florentine Republic from 1369 until his death. His Latin epitaph reads thus in translation:

"After Leonardo left life behind him, History weeps, Eloquence is silent and it is said that both the Latin and the Greek Muses couldn't hold back their tears." Bruni was a profoundly cultured man whose literary education led him to write works of genuine civic-mindedness that were nurtured by the ideals of fifteenth-century Florentine humanism. He is known as a translator of Plato and Aristotle, but also wrote a *History of the People of Florence* and a "Praise of the City of Florence," which emphasized his city's autonomy and hegemony in the Italian peninsula. In 1436 he wrote biographies of Dante and Petrarch, and the former is a work that recognized the importance of Dante's insistence on using spoken Italian as a literary language instead of Latin.

UGO FOSCOLO
(1778-1827)

Past the last altar on your right you will see a niche with a standing statue of Ugo Foscolo atop a short pedestal. The inscription reads:

Le ossa di Ugo Foscolo morto a Londra	Ugo Foscolo's bones, who died in London
il X settembre MDCCCXXVII e sepolto	on September 10, 1827 and was buried
nel cimitero di Chiswick restituite	in the cemetery at Chiswick, were given back
dall'Inghilterra nel giugno del	by England in June of 1871
MDCCCLXXI e deposte in questo tempio	and laid to rest in this church.
che la poesia dei sepolcri aveva	His sepulcral poetry earned this church
consacrato alla memoria dei grandi	sacred memory among great Italians.
d'Italia trovano qui finalmente per	Hoping for worthy repose, his remains lie here
volontà del governo fascista e del	at last due to the wishes of the City of
comune di Firenze e auspicano	Florence and the Fascist government.
degno riposo XXVII aprile	April 27, 1939
MCMXXXIX XVII	17

Together with Leopardi, Foscolo is Italy's most important Romantic lyric poet, though his fame is also due to *The Last Letters of Jacopo Ortis* (1802), considered the first modern novel in Italian. The son of a Greek mother and a Venetian physician, Foscolo began to sympathize with European ideals of freedom and nationalism when he was a student at the University of Padua. Like many, he had looked to Napoleon to liberate northern Italy from Austrian domination but was deeply disappointed when the French ceded the Venetian territories to Austria under the Treaty of Campoformio in 1797. This political situation was what inspired him to write *Jacopo Ortis*, which is also loosely modelled on Goethe's *The Sorrows of Young Werther*. Foscolo's political enthusiasm was also reflected by his participation in battles against Austrian troops. Because of this he was sought as a subversive by the Austrian government – fleeing first to Bologna, and later to Milan, Florence and eventually France and England, where he lived the last fourteen years of his life in poverty. Some of his poetry is neoclassical, such as his odes and the unfinished poem *Le Grazie* – dedicated to Antonio Canova and inspired by his sculptural group *The Three Graces*. These are three poetic hymns that celebrate the Graces (Aglaia, Eufrosine and Talia) as civilizing forces and bearers of beauty and joy. His twelve sonnets (1799-1802) are more romantic in nature, while the long poem *Dei sepolcri* (*On Sepulchres*, 1807) is the work most closely associated with Florence. It is a protest against Napoleon's Edict of Saint-Cloud in 1804, which outlawed burials in churches in order to prevent the spread of disease. For Foscolo the Edict was an opportunity to celebrate the memory of the great Italians buried in this church. The poem was widely perceived as a declaration of historical, cultural and linguistic pride at a time when Italy was governed by foreign powers: Austria and France in the north and the Spanish Bourbons in the south. From a present-day perspective, the poem foreshadowed later revolutionary sentiment that preceded Italian unification in 1861. A part of *On Sepulchres* also exalts the city of Florence itself as the cradle of Italian literature and therefore the ideal burial place for the poets who created it: "And Florence, thou wert first to hear the song / That comforted the irate Ghibelline, / wandering in exile…". "Ghibelline" here refers to Dante. In this way, Foscolo intended Santa Croce to keep the memory of Italian letters alive for all time – especially the memory of those whom we have included here at this site.

SAINT FRANCIS OF ASSISI
(1182-1226)

Turning toward the central apse of the church, you will see that several chapels are aligned along the right transept. The first one to the right of the apse is the Bardi Chapel, which Giotto painted with scenes of the Saint's life. On the exterior wall above the chapel entrance is a depiction of the saint receiving the stigmata. Inside the chapel there are various other frescoes by Giotto. The ones most closely connected to the saint's life are episodes portraying: "Francis divesting himself of all worldly posses-sions before his father Bernardone and the Bishop of Assisi" and "the approval of the Franciscan order in 1210." Over the altar there is a panel by an anonymous thir-teenth-century Florentine artist that represents other scenes of his life.

More than any other religious figure from the 13th century, Francis' life seems com-parable to Christ's because of his genuine acceptance of the teachings contained in the Gospel. His strict vow of poverty also reflected Christ's choice to live simply. At the same time, it was an implicit criticism of the increasing secular power of the Catholic Church during his time. Moreover, Saint Francis' enormous love for nature in all of its forms was unusual and can be said to be a kind of ecological sensitivity. Indeed, Francis considered the creation of the natural world and all its creatures as products of divine love. From this point of view all natural entities, such as water, fire, wind and the sun itself exist in order to praise the divine. This mentality is explained in poetic form in his "Laudes creaturarum," also known as the "Cantico delle crea-ture"(Canticle of God's Creation*). It is one of the first texts in an Italic vulgar tongue (Umbrian), although it was dictated (and not written) by Francis two years before his death. Its language is striking because of its fresh spoken quality and spontaneity: "Blessed be Thou my Lord by our sister Mother Earth / who sustains and nourishes us / and produces many fruits, along with grass and colorful flowers."

Saint Francis was born in Assisi in 1182 to a wealthy merchant family. He led a care-free youth but fought in his town's battles against neighboring cities. When he was twenty-four he underwent a profound religious search, which some attribute to being imprisoned after a battle, others to a serious illness. Subsequently he lived alone for a few years and then began to attract disciples interested in his simple way of life and spiritual message. He died at age forty-four after receiving the stigmata and quickly became a legendary figure.

St. Francis is also the subject of others' literary attention. Dante celebrated his life in Canto Eleven of "Paradise" in the *Divine Comedy*. An anonymous Tuscan writer in the late fourteen century also penned a translation of fifty-three anecdotes about the life of Saint Francis and his followers: *I fioretti di San Francesco* (*The Little Flowers of Saint* Francis), based on a older Latin text entitled *Actus beati Francisci et sociorum eius* (*The Deeds of Saint Francis and his Followers*).

LEON BATTISTA ALBERTI
(1404-1472)

As you exit the Bardi chapel (facing Piazza Santa Croce), turn to your right past the apse. At the last pilaster that divides the central nave from the apse and from the left-hand nave there is a statue in honor of the great humanist Leon Battista Alberti, who is buried here. (The main entry on Alberti is matched to the location of his family home in this Walking Tour, at Site 22).

GALILEO GALILEI
(1564-1642)

From the Alberti's tomb return toward the church's main doors in the façade. In the next-to-the-last chapel off the nave on your right is Galileo's tomb.

The Latin inscription reads: Let Galileo Galilei, the Florentine patrician who was so great an innovator in the study of geometry, astronomy and philosophy as not to bear comparison to anyone of his time, rest here in peace. This monument, that Vincenzo Viviani ordered built in his will by ten Florentine patricians so that it would protect the master's and his own ashes, was erected most willingly in 1737 by his [Viviani's] heir, Giovanni Battista Clementi Nelli, son of Senator Giovanni Battista [Nelli].

The most revolutionary cosmological thinker of early modern Europe after Copernicus, Galileo is generally associated with the history of astronomy, but his works are also important in the evolution of Italian thought and language. He expressed himself in written prose that was remarkably concise and limpid for a period in which most writers of Italian couched their thoughts in complicated and indirect Baroque rhetoric. Moreover, most scientists of his time wrote in Latin, while Galileo bravely chose Italian, a modern language. As everyone knows, he was tortured and imprisoned by the Inquisition for his defense of heliocentrism, especially as he spoke of it in his *Dialogo sopra i due massimi sistemi del mondo*

(*Dialogue Concerning the Two Major World Systems, the Ptolemaic and the Copernican*, 1632). Among his many other works are his *Sidereus nuncius* (The Starry Messenger, 1610), announcing the discovery of four of Jupiter's moons and *Il Saggiatore* (The Assayer, 1623), on the nature of comets. He named the moons "astri medicei" or "Medici stars" in honor of Cosimo II de' Medici. In addition, Galileo's versatile mind lent itself to literary topics. In his youth he wrote on debates over the relative merits of Ariosto and Tasso, and on Dante's "Inferno." Born in Pisa, Galileo moved to Florence when he was ten years old, where his family had arrived two years earlier. He held the Chair of Mathematics at the universities of Pisa and Padua, but retired to his country home "Villa Gioiello" in Arcetri, not far from Florence. There, after the Inquisition condemned him to life in prison, he was able to live out the rest of his days under house arrest. Nearby is the Arcetri Observatory of Astrophysics, in Via del Pian dei Giullari 2, built in 1872. Buried with him here is his student Viviani and the body of a woman, perhaps his daughter Virginia (the nun Sister Maria Celeste). From the Convent of San Matteo in Arcetri she wrote her father many letters that have now been published. Their relationship has also been fictionalized in the novel *Galileo's Daughter* by Dava Sobel.

Vincenzo da Filicaia
(1643-1707)

As you walk toward the front of the church you will find Filicaia's tomb in the corner on your right, just to the left of the last altar on your right.

The plaque in Latin reads:

> *To God, the Best and the Greatest. To Vincenzo from Filicaia: Florentine Senator, son of Senator Braccio, who [Vincenzo] exceeded his ancestors' already uncommon nobility by bringing praise to his own creativity in writing elegant verse both in Latin and in Tuscan, with which he brought glory to the humanities for so many years. He was famous because Christina of Södermanland and queen of Sweden considered him her friend; he was celebrated for his writing and for the admiration it aroused in John V, King of Poland and in Leopold I of Hapsburg. Nonetheless, he surpassed the praise of these poetic accomplishments in his excellent government, first of Volterra and then of Pisa, and in the optimal fulfillment of other public appointments (among which was the office of senator) with lifelong honesty, prudence, modesty, self-control and humanity. His son Scipio, Knight of Saint Stephen, weeping and fraught with grief, erected this monument to his dearest father who left a strong desire to see him again in all those he knew. He [Vincenzo] died in the year of our salvation 1707, on September 24, at the age of 65. In the year of our Lord 1785, this cenotaph was moved to this venerable church from the ruins of the eminent church of San Pier Maggiore, where it had lain on the very noble tomb of the Filicaia family, so that it will not be lost but will be preserved for a long time.*

As you can see, very little needs to be added to the affectionate and lauditory language used by Filicaia's son Scipio! His friendship with Queen Christina of Sweden is almost proof of Filicaia's work in founding the "Arcadia" in 1690, because this literary movement arose in Rome after her death but in the social milieu she had frequented. The "Arcadia" came to be the first nation-wide literary academy in Italy, and sought to simplify Italian verse by freeing it from the encumberances of Baroque rhetorical excess. Filicaia's poetry dealt mainly with civic and patriotic themes in a grandeloquent style, and among his more important works are the poems: "Italia, Italia" (Italy, Italy) and the five "Canzoni in occasione dell'assedio e liberazione di Vienna" (Songs on the Occasion of the Seige and Liberation of Vienna, 1684). His collected works were published the year he died under the title *Poesie toscane* (Tuscan poems).

Gino Capponi
(1792-1876)

Turn to your left. There is a monument to Gino Capponi against the inner wall of the church façade between the main central door and the lateral door on your right.

Now remembered for his pedagogical ideas in *Frammenti sull'educazione* (Fragments on Education, 1845), which ran counter to Rousseau's ideas on education in *Émile* and on childhood development inherent in the concept of the "noble savage," Capponi believed instead in the efficacy of education as a component of social and civic relations and gave great importance to Italian women whose duty it was (he believed) to counterbalance dry didactic techniques with feminine affection. He set forth his economic opinions in *Cinque lettere di economia toscana* (Five Letters on Tuscan Economics, 1845) and wrote a *Storia della Repubblica di Firenze* (History of the Republic of Florence, 1875), although Capponi's career was principally concerned with politics. In this regard, he was generally in accordance with the liberal tendencies that led to Italian unification and was made senator of the Kingdom of Italy in 1860. The poet Giacomo Leopardi dedicated to him his "Palinodia al Marchese Gino Capponi" (To Marquis Gino Capponi: A Recantation, 1835), which is a pessimistic appraisal in verse of nineteenth-century Italian progressive liberalism and its optimism (see Walking Tour 3, Site 15). Capponi's home, the Palazzo Capponi by Carlo Fontana, is in Via Gino Capponi 26. Florence has named a secondary school in honor of him: the Istituto Socio Pedagogico Gino Capponi, in Piazza Frescobaldi 1, in Oltrarno just across the bridge of Santa Trinita.

Giovanni Battista Niccolini
(1782-1861)

The monument to this writer lies to the left of the main central door in the inner wall of the façade and the lateral door on your left.

Giovanni Battista Niccolini is known as the writer of the historical tragedies *Matilde* (1815), *Antonio Foscarini* (1827), *Giovanni da Procida* (1830), *Beatrice Cenci* (1838), *Arnaldo da Brescia* (1843) and *Filippo Strozzi* (1847). They are significant because they gave a cultural voice to the Italian struggle for independence and unification known as the "Risorgimento" (resurgence). At the same time, they provide manifest evidence of their author's ardent republican and anticlerical sentiment. The latter was directed especially at Vincenzo Gioberti's Neoguelph movement, which aimed at uniting a federation of Italian states under the guidance of the papacy. His sincere patriotism is also evidenced by his friendship with Ugo Foscolo, perhaps the most famous poet-patriot of the early nineteenth century (see the entry on Foscolo above).

20) OTTAVIO RINUCCINI   **Via dei Rustici, 2 (red)**
(1564-1621)

From the church of Santa Croce cross the square to its opposite side and walk down Borgo de' Greci to the corner of Via dei Bentaccordi. Turn left and then right almost immediately into Via de' Rustici. Just before the street is cut off by Via dei Neri you will see a plaque on the corner of a building on your left. It reads:

Ottavio Rinuccini, patrizio fiorentino,	The patrician Florentine Ottavio Rinuccini,
letterato illustre e gentile poeta	an illustrious man of letters and refined poet,
scrisse in questa sua casa la Dafne favola	wrote the pastoral fable Daphne in his home
pastorale primo de' suoi drammatici	here. The first drama of its kind, it was set
componimenti che messo in musica da	to music by Jacopo Corsi and Jacopo Peri
Jacopo Corsi e Jacopo Peri e rappresentato	and performed in Corsi's home in 1594
in casa Corsi con plaudente	to the amazement and acclaim of all.
universal meraviglia nel MDLXXXXIV	It breathed new life into art
spirò nell'arte un alito di nuova vita e fu	and initiated the birth of
nell'opera memorabile onde si	Italian opera for which
iniziò la riforma melodrammatica.	it is remembered.

Financed by Count Giovanni de' Bardi at the end of the sixteenth century, Rinuccini and the other members of the Florentine "camerata" hoped to recreate what they believed to be typical of ancient Greek music: a theatrical text set entirely to music. Among the Camerata's members was Vincenzo Galilei, father of Galileo and author of the "Dialogue on Ancient and Modern Music." A plaque in Via de' Benci, 5 identifies the site where the Camerata used to meet.

The imitation of classical models was a goal common to the Renaissance intelligentsia in Italy, and *Daphne*, with music (now mostly lost) by Jacopo Corsi and Iacopo Peri, was the first musical drama to do away with a text that was partially sung and partially spoken. Hence *Daphne* marked the birth of Italian opera and was followed by *Eurydice* in 1600, with music by Iacopo Peri. Among Rinuccini's librettos *Ariadne* (1607) and *Ballo delle ingrate* (Dance of the Ungrateful, 1608) may perhaps be the most poetically valid. A collection of his poetry (*Poesie*) was published posthumously in 1622. Several of its poems reflect the influence of Pierre de Ronsard and the French Pléiade school as a result of Rinuccini's stay in Paris from 1600 to 1602, but his language is particularly simple and unadorned with respect to elaborate pre-Baroque poetic tendencies already in fashion at the end of the sixteenth century.

21) D.H. Lawrence   Piazza Mentana 7
(1885-1930)

From Via de' Rustici turn right into Via dei Neri and then immediately left into Via della Mosca. This street empties into Piazza Mentana. The address you are looking for will be on your left, where Via Vincenzo Malenchini empties into Piazza Mentana.

The English novelist David Herbert Lawrence combined heightened naturalism with a treatment of sexual themes that was remarkably frank for its time. This author's most important novels analyze the intimate relationship between the sexes and the contrast between instinctual and rational thought: *Sons and Lovers* (1913), *The Rainbow* (1915) and *Women in Love* (1920). Lawrence's travels in Germany, Austria and Italy seem to reflect the alienation and restlessness of the early twentieth-century intellectual and therefore of modern consciousness itself. His search for the perfect "natural" environment unencumbered by the mechanization of modern life led him subsequently to Australia, Mexico and southern France, where he died of tuberculosis. Among Lawrence's many works, *Aaron's Rod* (1922) is the one that most closely reflects the author's own experiences in Florence. It is also a *roman à clef* containing many characters that stand in for members of the Anglo-American community then living in Florence, such as Norman Douglas, Bernard Berenson and Reginald Turner – as well as Lawrence and his German-born wife Frieda von Richthofen (cousin of the German flying ace known as the Red Baron). Lawrence and Frieda first went to Italy in 1914 before the outbreak of W.W. I, which Lawrence strongly opposed. In *Aaron's Rod* the protagonist undertakes an existential quest for what Lawrence later defined as "a powerful physicality." This was a quality that he recognized most of all in Etruscan civilization. Comparing England to Italy (assuming Aaron as Lawrence's alter ego) the narrator explains the protagonist's thoughts like this: "At home, in England, the bright grate and the ruddy fire… these had been inevitable. And now he was glad to get away from it all… He preferred the Italian way of no fires, no heating … The horrors of real domesticity. No, the brutal Italian way was better." Lawrence's wanderings also enabled him to write travel books full of evocative imagery such as *Twilight in Italy* (1916), *Sea and Sardinia* (1921), *Etruscan Places* (1932) and *Mornings in Mexico* (1927). In 1919 Lawrence and Frieda returned to Florence and stayed at the Pensione Balestri, in Piazza

Mentana 5. Today it is called the Albergo Balestri and is at number 7. Beginning in 1926 the Lawrences stayed for two years at the Villa Mirenda or "L'Arcipresso" in Scandicci outside of Florence, where he began to write *Lady Chatterly's Lover* (1928) and became a friend of Aldous Huxley. In a letter of March 26, 1926 Lawrence notes that it only took him half an hour to reach the Florence cathedral by tram from Scandicci. At this writing the city of Florence is now rebuilding the tram line of long ago. We wonder if the tram ride will take more or less time than it did in Lawrence's day.

22) LEON BATTISTA ALBERTI   Via de' Benci 1
(1404-1472)

From the Albergo Balestri in Piazza Mentana continue forward towards the Arno river but turn left into the street that flanks it: the Lungarno Generale Armando Diaz. Walk along the Arno until you reach the next bridge upstream, the Ponte alle Grazie. Turn left at the bridge into Via de' Benci, where number 1 is the first building on your left. This building is a nineteenth-century reconstruction of a Renaissance palace and sits atop the area once occupied by the Alberti family home. On the façade there are plaques showing designs of the site's former appearance.

In many ways Alberti embodies the Renaissance ideals associated with Florence during the fifteenth and sixteenth centuries. His interest in architecture displays a profound understanding of classical forms (discussed in theoretical terms in *De re aedificatoria* or *The Ten Books of Architecture*, 1450) and put into practice in the creation of Florence's Palazzo Rucellai and other important buildings. However, his literary reputation is based on the treatise *Della famiglia* (*On the Family*, 1433-41), in which he emphasizes the autonomy of the family as a civic and economic institution as opposed to the hegemony of the city-state. A treatise on the ideal organization of the bourgeois or noble family, it is divided into four parts: Book I - The Education of Children; Book II - Married Life; Book III - The Care and Management of Family Income and Investments; and Book IV - Friendship (a relationship Alberti esteems more than marriage or familial ties themselves). This work also provided the first theoretical definition of the "giardino all'italiana" or Italian Renaissance garden. It was written at a time when Renaissance humanism had returned Latin to stratospheric heights of literary prestige. Therefore it's remarkable that Alberti saw fit to write *Della famiglia* in Italian, becoming the first Renaissance intellectual to write a serious work in the vulgar tongue. Further evidence of his awareness that Italian would be an important written language outside of strictly academic circles is shown by the fact that he organized the "Certame Coronario" (1441): a contest to crown the writer of the best poetry in the vernacular. In *Della famiglia* Alberti also sought to defend his own interests, since his family had been exhiled from Florence even before he was born illegitimately in Genoa (a fact that made inheritance difficult for him). Ironically, he thus became his family's most fervid defender in spite of being illegitimate and having also taken vows to become a member of the clergy. It was in this latter capacity that he served in the chancelleries of Popes Eugene IV and Nicholas V and had the opportunity to travel throughout Europe uncovering ancient classical manuscripts (the most stereotypically humanist of the humanists' activities). Among other works in Italian are *De iciarchia* (*On Ruling the Household*, 1468), dialogues criticizing the "lifestyles of the rich and famous" during the reign of the Medici, which have a charming introduction describing Alberti's stroll down the hill from the church of San Miniato to meet his friends. *Teogeneo* is a stoic dialogue in which two imaginary interlocutors discuss virtue and fortune – topics that were to long interest Renaissance thinkers. At the same time, Alberti wrote a number of works in Latin too, such as the comedy *Philodoxeos fabula*. It's the tale of the young man Philodoxus (lover of glory) who woos Doxia (glory). The *Intercoenales* (*Dinner Pieces*, 1440) are short satirical stories and dialogues to be read over dinner and drinks. One describes a disgruntled intellectual who returns as a ghost to witness his own funeral and criticize the bishop's eulogy.

23) NICCOLÒ TOMMASEO (1802-1874) — Lungarno delle Grazie 14 (red)

From Leon Battista Alberti's home, return to the Arno but turn left into the Lungarno delle Grazie. Before you reach the next intersection, the narrow Volta dei Tintori, you will see the following plaque on your left:

Questo ricordo della casa	This plaque, in memory of the house
dove dimorò quattordici anni	where Niccolò Tommaseo
e nel 1° maggio 1874 morì	lived for fourteen years and
Niccolò Tommaseo	died on May 1, 1874,
poneva il Municipio di Firenze	was set here by the City of Florence.

This writer and patriot was born in Croatia to a family from the Venetian Republic. His strong sense of Italian identity expressed itself in an intense love for the Italian language and in his nostalgia for medieval civic and religious values. Many Italian Romantics re-interpreted these values as literary metaphors for a potential rebirth of populist culture and civic-mindedness that would lead to the emancipation of Italy from foreign domination. Indeed, this side of his personality inspired Tommaseo to produce his best work, the poems and songs published as *Canti popolari toscani, corsi, illirici, greci* or *Tuscan, Corsican, Illirian and Greek Folk Songs*, 1841.

After studying at the seminary in Split, Croatia, Tommaseo graduated in law from the University of Padua before going on to work as a journalist and writer in Milan and Florence. He became acquainted with Alessandro Manzoni in Milan and contributed articles to Giampietro Vieusseux's *Antologia* in Florence, where he lived from 1827 to 1834, and also became a friend of moderate revolutionary thinkers such as Gino Capponi (see Walking Tours 2, Site 13; and 4, Site 19). Because of his own political mind-set, Tommaseo couldn't stand the poet Giacomo Leopardi, who lived in Florence off and on during the same period (see Walking Tour 3, Site 15). Leopardi's profound pessimism and political disengagement repulsed him. When an anti-Austrian article by Tommaseo caused the authorities to shut down the *Antologia*, its author went into exile in France – though he returned to Italy in 1839 under the amnesty promulgated by the Austrian authorities and went to Venice. The 1830s were also very productive years for him. He published poems and theatrical works in verse under the title *Confessioni* (*Confessions*, 1836), a commentary on the *Divine Comedy* (1837) and his autobiography *Memorie poetiche* (*Poetic Memoires*, 1838). At the end of 1847 he was arrested there and imprisoned until March 1848 for his support of the reborn Venetian Republic. This he sought to maintain independent and keep from being annexed by Piedmont. When it fell, however, he fled to Corfu, where he married his wife Diamante but also went blind. Later he made his way to Turin and finally Florence, where he lived at this location from 1859 until his death.

In addition to his journalistic work, Tommaseo produced a number of literary works before losing his sight at age forty-six. Besides his *Dizionario dei sinonimi* or *Thesaurus* (1830), his *Nuovo dizionario della lingua italiana* (New Dictionary of the Italian Language), compiled from 1859 to 1879, is still considered important today. His only novel, *Fede e bellezza* (Faith and Beauty) (1838-40) is a sentimental work that traces the reciprocal declarations of love and emotional outpourings of its two protagonists: Giovanni and Maria. The book's alternation between religious morality and sexual tension also makes it a precursor of Decadent literature at the end of the nineteenth century. Tommaseo's *Diario intimo* (Intimate Diary), published only in 1938, presents a series of truly idiosyncratic details about the author's life: how much and how many times he chewed each mouthful, for example. Tommaseo is buried in the cemetery at Settignano outside Florence.

24) E. M. Forster   **Lungarno delle Grazie 2**
    (1879-1970)

From Tommaseo's lodgings proceed upriver along the Lungarno delle Grazie until you reach number 2, on your left.

London-born Edward Morgan Forster stayed at the Pensione Simi at this address when he first came to Florence with his mother in 1901. He stayed only for a few weeks, but returned to Florence again in the following two years for about the same amount of time. Two of his earliest novels are set in Tuscany: *Where Angels Fear to Tread* (1905) and *A Room With a View* (1908), the first half of which takes place right in Florence. Given the short period of time Forster spent in Italy, Francis King has observed that "it is remarkable that his two Italian novels … should have defined the Italian national character for so many English people of his generation and of two or three generations after." Forster himself stated that the Pension Bertolini in *A Room With a View* was modelled after the Pensione Simi here.

Like all of his novels, *Room With a View* is an analysis of interpersonal relations (a theme shared by many associated with the Bloomsbury Group) but also a study of Lucy Honeychurch's imprisoned sensibility and her struggle to express it. As in other works by Anglo Saxons, these two celebrate a love for Florence and describe a mentality typical of foreigners traveling in Italy. They also betray certain English stereotypes of Italians as irrational, impulsive and violent. To illustrate this, it's enough to recall that Lucy witnesses a quarrel between two Italians in Piazza della Signoria and faints after viewing the stabbing of one of them.

Lately, certain scholars have written about the so-called "Stendhal syndrome," which the nineteenth-century French novelist first described in *Rome, Naples et Florence* (1826) as a passionate psychological reaction to the profusion of artistic beauty in Florence. For Stendhal this reaction had sexual overtones, and Lucy Honeychurch experiences them as well. Graziella Magherini, a psychologist at the Hospital of Santa Maria Novella in Florence, analyzes this reaction as the result of a hidden but authentic sensibility that only occasionally manages to break through and overwhelm the mask of a secondary, superficial personality that normally assumes the task of engaging in all external relations. (We hope that the Walking Tours in this guidebook will help the visitor to Florence overcome any potential Stendhal syndrome attack without diminishing the impact of the city's beauty).

Forster published the novel *The Longest Journey* in 1907, just before *Room With a View*. It recalls his experiences in the British educational system and can be considered an attack against the English public schools. *Howard's End* (1910), a work of greater complexity, juxtaposes the lives of two sets of people: those who want money and the security that comes from social conformity and those who cultivate meaningful personal relationships. In 1914 he finished his novel on homosexuality, *Maurice*, which wasn't published until a year after his death. His masterpiece, *A Passage to India* (1924), is a study of the rapport between British colonials in India and that land's native peoples. More than an examination of social differences and injustice, the novel raises complex questions about the nature of human instinct, culture and one's relation to one's fellow man.

Walking Tour 5

Francesco Redi - Galileo Galilei - Niccolò Machiavelli - Francesco Guicciardini - Fyodor Dostoevsky - Elizabeth Barrett Browning - Anton Francesco Grazzini - Saint Catherine of Siena - Sir Walter Scott - George Gordon Byron

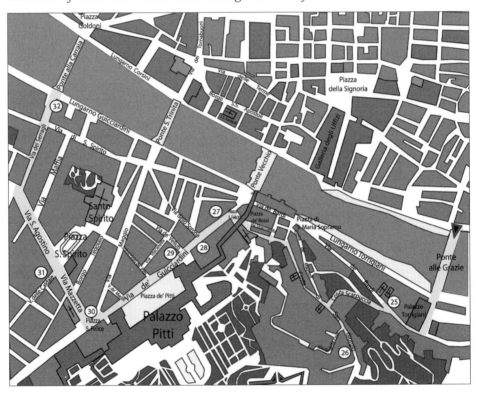

Via de' Bardi - Costa San Giorgio - Via de' Guicciardini - Piazza Pitti - Piazza San Felice - Via delle Caldaie - Lungarno Guicciardini

25) FRANCESCO REDI   Via de' Bardi 16
(1626-1698)

From Forster's ex-hotel in Lungarno delle Grazie, retrace your steps to the Ponte alle Grazie and turn left onto the bridge. On the other side of the river continue past the Lungarno Torrigiani on your right and the Lungarno Serristori on your left. Walk straight ahead past the Via dei Renai on your left and cross the narrow Piazza dei Mozzi. Turn right at the end of the Piazza into Via de' Bardi. Follow Via de'

Bardi to Costa Scarpuccia on your left, and there you will find the following plaque high up between the second and third floors at this address on your right:

In questa casa dimorò nel 1672	The eminent doctor, naturalist and poet
Francesco Redi	Francesco Redi (1626-1698)
Medico naturalista e poeta insigne 1626-1698	lived in this house in 1672.
In occasione del VII congresso	On the occasion of the Seventh International
Internazionale di storia della scienza	Convention on the History of Science

"Whoever drinks water will never hear thanks from me." These words, uttered by Bacchus, are taken from Redi's dithyramb *Bacco in Toscana* (*Bacchus in Tuscany*, 1685), considered the epitome of poetic praise of wine. Originally an ancient Greek form written to praise Dionysus (or Bacchus), it is used here in a comic vein. Redi imagines that the god of wine brought Ariadne to Tuscany after he had rescued her from the island of Naxos. The poem places Bacchus on the grounds of the Medici villa "Poggio Imperiale" where he sings the praises of some 500 Tuscan wines. Of course, he also drinks them and judges the red wine from Montepulciano to be the best. Redi was professor of Tuscan language in the Florentine "studio" (a private academy founded and supported by the Medici in the fifteenth century) and a member of the *Accademia della Crusca*, where he participated in writing the third edition of the academy's historic Italian dictionary (see Walking Tour 7, Site 38). Also an expert in Italian dialects, he compiled an important dictionary of the dialect of Arezzo, the city of his birth, which is still useful to Italian dialectologists. In 1692 he became a member of the Arcadia and was a friend of Vincenzo da Filicaia (see Walking Tour 4, site 19). But Redi was not just a man of letters. He was also a physician, scientist and naturalist and became the family doctor to the Medici after his father retired from that post. Redi was extremely attentive to his patients, and it's known that he believed in a process of healing based on intestinal purges. At the same time he continued to practice Galileo's tradition of scientific observation and left evidence of it in treatises such as *Le osservazioni intorno alle vipere* (*Observations on Vipers*, 1664) and *Esperienze intorno alla generazione degli insetti* (Experiences Concerning the Reproduction of Insects, 1668).

26) GALILEO GALILEI   **Costa San Giorgio 19**
    (1564-1642)

From Redi's home in Via de' Bardi, ascend Costa Scarpuccia, which you will see on your left. Follow Costa Scarpuccia till it empties into Costa San Giorgio, into which you should turn left. After you pass the Vicolo della Cava (Quarry Alley) on your right, you will see the following plaque above the door at this address on your right:

Qui ove abitò Galileo	Here, where Galileo lived,
non sdegnò piegarsi	the majesty of Ferdinand II de' Medici

alla potenza del genio	did not hesitate to bow
la maestà di Ferdinando II de' Medici	before his powerful genius.

The rather allusive language on this plaque refers to the aid and comfort that Galileo received from Ferdinand II Granduke of Tuscany when the great scientist was accused of heresy by the Holy Inquisition. In truth, all Ferdinand could do was protest in a generic way against Pope Urban VIII's accusations, since Ferdinand had control of only modest military forces and was afraid to use them. The Granduke only managed to delay Galileo's inevitable departure for Rome, where he was put on trial 1633 and forced to publicly recant his defense of heliocentrism. Later, when Galileo returned to Florence (*i.e.* Arcetri) under house arrest, Ferdinand continued to take an interest in him, even though Galileo had been publicly disgraced. When Galileo came to Florence in 1610, he lived at numerous addresses just outside the city. He lived here before moving to Arcetri at the end of his life (see the principal entry on Galileo in Walking Tour 4, Site 19).

27) NICCOLÒ MACHIAVELLI   Via Guicciardini 110 (red)
(1469-1527)

From Galileo's address retrace your steps to Costa Scarpuccia but continue past it, staying on Costa San Giorgio. Pass Costa de' Magnoli on your right. Follow Costa San Giorgio all the way down the hill as it bears left until it empties into Piazza de' Rossi. Proceeding in the same direction you will arrive in Piazza Santa Felicita. Turn left into the street on the far side of this square. It is Via Guicciardini. Cross it and after a few yards you will see the following plaque high up on a building on your right:

A Niccolò Machiavelli	To Niccolò Machiavelli,
dell'unità nazionale	daring precursor and prophet
precorritore audace e indovino	of national unification as well as
e d'armi proprie e non avventizie	founding father and teacher
primo istitutore e maestro l'Italia	of non-mercenary self-defense. Italy
una ed armata pose il 3 maggio 1869	armed and united placed [this plaque here]
quarto di lui centenario	on May 3, 1869, the 4th centenary of his birth.
Casa ove visse Niccolò Machiavelli e	The house where Niccolò Machiavelli lived
vi morì il 22 giugno 1527	and died on June 22, 1527 at the age of
di anni 58 mesi 8 e giorni 19	58 years, 8 months and 19 days.

Inside the groundfloor passageway lined with shops' display cases is another plaque on the wall on your right:

In questa casa dei Machiavelli poi	This house, belonging to the Machiavellis
dei Serristori dopo totale	and then to the Serristoris,
distruzione bellica oggi a nuova	has been restored to new life by

vita risorta per opera di Sofia Bossi	Sofia Bossi Pucci Serristori after
Pucci Serristori.	suffering total destruction during the war.
Trascorse i suoi giorni	Niccolò Machiavelli spent
Niccolò Machiavelli meditando	his days in contemplation
sulle umane vicende	of human events
e compose pagine immortali	and wrote immortal pages
di storia fiorentina	of Florentine history.

More studied worldwide by students of history and political science than by those of literature, Machiavelli was the first to separate political theory from the religious and moral fetters Medieval culture had imposed on it. Not only a thinker, Machiavelli was a man of action and served his city as a statesman and diplomat during the restoration of the Florentine republic from 1498 to 1512. This was an attempt to re-establish the bourgeois city state that had been the glory (off and on) of late medieval Florence. It became a reality when the Medici were driven out in 1494, and Machiavelli was put in charge of state correspondence. Later he oversaw the Republic's office of domestic affairs and served as Minister of War. In this capacity he was responsible for drafting Florentine citizens into the municipal army, which he strongly believed in. Indeed, the plaque above refers to the fact that Machiavelli's prescient defense of a citizens' militia ran counter to most Italian states' reliance on mercenary troops. When the Medici returned to power in 1512, Machiavelli was tortured, imprisoned and exiled for a year. From the Medici's viewpoint he had irreparably compromised himself, and they were never to trust him in their service – so he was forced to go into early retirement. It was then that he wrote all of his works, staying at a villa on his family's lands about seven miles southwest of Florence at Sant'Andrea in Percussina near San Casciano. The villa was called the "Albergaccio" because there was an inn attached to it, which is now a well-known restaurant called "Casa del Machiavelli" that serves country-style cuisine from the hills around Florence (Via Scopeti 64). Locally, people refer to the restaurant as "la fettunta" (the "fetta unta" or "the oiled slice of bread") because one of its best-known hors-d'oeuvres is day-old bread rubbed with garlic and dipped in extra-virgin olive oil. Machiavelli wrote about his life at the villa in a letter of December 10, 1523 to Francesco Vettori, the Florentine ambassador to Rome. He divided his time there between hunting, supervising the woodsmen on his estate and literary pursuits (among which was the writing of the "opuscolo De Principatibus" or *The Prince*). We can also glimpse in it the tragedy of Machiavelli's life: despite dedicating his life to public service and the city he loved, he was misunderstood and humiliated by the Medici. *The Prince* (1513) is the short treatise that has immortalized him, but its meaning is tied to the politically unstable and violent times its author lived in. The fact that Machiavelli looked to the ruthless and cruel Cesare Borgia as a leader capable of uniting divided Italian states may seem odd, but it illustrates his belief in the importance of seizing opportunities and having the courage to exploit them. These are the qualities that Machiavelli referred to as "virtue" in a statesman, which the cunning prince (alternately a lion or a fox) needed to counter the vagaries of Fortune (compared to a river that can overflow its banks). Among the earliest of Machiavelli's works are the *Decennales* (*Decades*) (1504-09), historical narratives in Dantean tercets about Florentine events after 1494. His most eye-stopping title is *The Description of the Way Duke Valentino Killed Vitellozzo Vitelli, Oliverotto from Fermo, Mr. Pagolo and the Duke of Gravina Orsini* (1503). The *Discourses on the First Decade of Livy* (1513-1517) contain reflections on Livy's history of the Roman republic, which Machiavelli looked to as a model for the ideal form of democratic government – as compared to the corrupt European states of his time. Because of its broad perspective, it is perhaps Machiavelli's most mature work. Other erudite (or non-literary) works are the *Art of War* (1521), in the form of dialogues, and the *Florentine Histories* (1525). Among his creative writing is the novella "Belfagor arcidiavolo o del demonio che prese moglie" ("Belfagor Archdevil or the Demon Who Took a Wife," 1518-1520), which can be read as a form of social satire. Most of all, however, this vein is crowned by his two plays *Clizia* (1524) and *La Mandragola* (*The Mandrake*, 1518) – the latter considered the best comedy of the Italian Renaissance.

28) FRANCESCO GUICCIARDINI (1483-1540)   Via Guicciardini 59 (red)

From the Machiavelli family home, continue walking down Via Guicciardini in the same direction, and pass Via dello Sprone on you right. Shortly afterwards you will see the following plaque high up over number 59 (red) on the left side of the street:

MDCCCXXI	1921
In queste case ab antico dei	In these houses belonging to the
Guicciardini si scrive a gloria	Guicciardinis since ancient times, the name
d'Italia il nome del grande storico	of the great historian Francesco is written
Francesco che i tempi da lui	for the glory of Italy – he who depicted the
politicamente vissuti	political times he lived through in immortal
affigurò in pagine sopravvissute immortali	pages that will survive forever.

To the right of the plaque above is the imposing entrance to this building, at number 15 (black). On the left side of the passageway behind the huge doors here is this plaque:

Fra le rovine delle più care strade	From the ruins of 1944, among the dearest
d'Oltrarno nel MCMXLIV	streets of Oltrarno,
ferito e pur saldo stette	Paolo di Francesco
questo sacro alla storia	restored and renovated worthily the

palagio de' Guicciardini nel MCML	Guicciardini's building, sacred to history,
Paolo di Francesco degnamente	damaged yet still standing,
restaurata l'avita dimora	and enlarged his ancestral dwelling
la rinnovò e l'accrebbe mentre	in 1950 just when the
il vecchio ceppo della sua stirpe	ancient stock of his bloodline,
anch'esso folgorato e percosso	battered and struck as well,
di nuova fronda si rinnovella	began to regrow new branches.
	(Roberto Ridolfi)

Like his contemporary Machiavelli, Francesco Guicciardini was a Florentine statesman and writer who lived through political upheavals that had direct impact on his personal life and the course of Italian history. In his *Storia d'Italia* (*History of Italy*, 1537-40) he points to the death of Lorenzo the Magnificent in 1492 as the beginning of a long period of crisis for Florentine and Italian stability. He began his career in 1512 under the restored Florentine republic as its amabassador to the court of Ferdinand of Aragon, King of Spain. Unlike Machiavelli, he was able to continue to serve his city when the Medici returned to power. In the years between 1516 and 1522 Pope Leo X (Giovanni de' Medici) made him governor of Modena, Reggio Emilia and Parma. The subsequent pope, Clement VII (Giulio de' Medici), placed him at the head of the papal forces in Romagna. Guicciardini was also the principal architect of the League of Cognac (1526), which established an alliance between the pope, the king of France and the Italian states against the hegemony of Charles V of Spain. Compared to Machiavelli, Giucciardini's political thought is certainly more skeptical, cautious and the result of an individualistic notion of history. His view of Fortune as the dominant force controlling human life is quite similar to Machiavelli's, but Guicciardini doesn't share Machiavelli's optimism about being able to intervene and control the direction of events. Consequently he never formulated a coherent political theory as Machiavelli did in *The Prince*. Instead he left a series of aphorisms and fragmentary reflections, the *Ricordi* (or *Memoires*, 1512-30) that are nonetheless quite striking – as they are obviously the result of a highly observant and intelligent mind. They don't relate personal experiences as such, but are the distillation of much critical analysis, and each "memory" offers a moral lesson. They range, for example, from the consideration that worldly success doesn't bring happiness to the idea (a mistaken one in his opinion) that a change in personal behavior can have a salutary effect on the future. Some are dryly practical while others are infused with a sense of melancholy, such as the following: "It's certainly true that we all know we have to die and [that we] live as if we were sure to live forever, but I don't think this is because we are more easily swayed by what we see and perceive with our senses than by things that are far away and can't be seen. After all, death is nearby and one could say that it is always close because of our daily contact with it. I think it derives from the fact that nature wants us to live according to the pace and order of the natural world – which nature doesn't want to appear dead and meaningless – and so gave us the ability to avoid thinking about death. If we thought about it, the world would be full of indecision and sluggishness."

29) FYODOR DOSTOEVSKY   Piazza de' Pitti 22
(1822-1881)

From the Guicciardini family home continue walking down Via Guicciardini in the same direction until it opens into the large Piazza de' Pitti. On the right side of the piazza on the building just past Via de' Velluti you will see the following plaque:

In questi pressi fra il 1868 e il 1869	In this area from 1868 to 1869
Fedor Mihailovic Dostoevskij	Fyodor Mikhailovich Dostoevsky
compì il romanzo "L'idiota"	completed the novel "The Idiot."

This plaque marks the spot where Dostoevsky probably lived with his second wife Anna Grigorievna Snitkina from the end of November 1868 through the first months of 1869. His address then was given as Via Guicciardini 8, but he was known to have lived at this location in front of Palazzo Pitti. We conclude that the house numbers in Via Guicciardini have changed since Dostoevsky's time. Fyodor and Anna arrived in Italy from Switzerland after having left Russia in 1867 to avoid creditors and start over after their first child had died. From mid-November to mid-December they stayed in Milan but left for Florence because of the cold rainy autumn and because Dostoevsky felt isolated having no contact with his native language even in written form. When he had been to Florence earlier (in 1861 or 1862) he used to go to the Gabinetto Vieusseux (see Walking Tour 2, Site 13) to read in Russian. In particular he almost certainly consulted the current issues of *Polar Star*, which was the voice of progressive Russians, printed in London but unavailable in Russia. The Gabinetto was located in Palazzo Buondelmonti in Piazza Santa Trinita, just a short stroll from his lodgings in the Pension Suisse (in Via Tornabuoni at the corner of Via della Vigna Nuova, opposite Palazzo Strozzi). He had gone to Florence the first time with his friend Nikolai Strakhov, who left the following description of Dostoevsky's habits: "Fyodor Mikhailovich was not a great master of travel, he did not pay much attention to nature or historic monuments, nor works of art, with the exception of the most important ones; he concentrated all his attention on people, interested only in grasping their temperament and their character and perhaps a general impression of street life. He explained to me heatedly how he hated the usual official way guide-books recommended the exploration of famous places. And in fact we did not look at anything but only strolled about chatting where most people were to be found." (Maybe he would have liked this guide, since his name appears here instead of a monument's.) In addition, Anna became pregnant, and because the doctor advised her to get exercise they used to walk daily in the Boboli gardens. Unfortunately, Dostoevsky wrote very little about his time in Florence, but Anna left valuable impressions in her letters and diary. She noted how isolated the two felt, which was the result of various causes. They had left Russia to escape Dostoevsky's gambling debts and it's unlikely that they spoke Italian very well. Still, Anna says in her *Reminiscences* that they were both moved by the beauty of the city around them. As stated on the plaque at this address, Dostoevsky completed *The Idiot* here, and during the same period came up with a new theme that was to lay at the heart of several subsequent works. He planned to write a triology entitled *Atheism* or *The Life of a Great Sinner* about a man who loses his faith and then undergoes a lengthy philosophical search leading him back to Christ, the Orthodox Church and a reverence for the land of Russia itself. This trilogy was never completed as such, but its theme is a significant part of *The Devils* (1873) and *The Brothers Karamazov* (1879-80), one of the most widely-read novels by subsequent European writers. Nearly all of his works hinge on the question of good and evil. They are tied at the same time to narrative realism used to further an analysis of existential values. Other important novels are *Crime and Punishment* (1866), *Notes from the Underground* (1865) and *The Gambler* (1867).

30) ELIZABETH BARRETT BROWNING (1809-1861)   Piazza San Felice 8

From Dostoevsky's flat, continue forward keeping the enormous Piazza Pitti on your left. Pass Sdrucciolo de' Pitti and Via de' Marsili on your right. As you leave Piazza Pitti behind you, Piazza San Felice opens on your right. There, at the intersection of Via Maggio and Piazza San Felice, is Casa Guidi. The plaque below, the words of which were written by Niccolò Tommaseo, is on the façade above the entrance:

Qui scrisse e morì	Here Elizabeth Barrett Browning
Elizabeth Barrett Browning	lived and died. She combined learned
che in cuore di donna conciliava	science and poetic spirit in a woman's heart
scienza di dotto e spirito di poeta	and made her verses a golden ring linking
e fece del suo verso aureo anello	Italy and England. Grateful, Florence
fra Italia e Inghilterra	erected this plaque
pone questa memoria	as remembrance.
Firenze grata 1861	1861

Elizabeth had grown up in the family castle, Coxhoe Hall, in Durham, England, where she was chronically ill due to respiratory and nervous problems. When she became subject to convulsions, fainting spells and attacks of hysteria, doctors prescribed a mixture of brandy and morphine as a sedative. As a consequence she became dependant on the drug for the rest of her life. In frail health and dominated by her father, she spent her youth studying the classics and writing poetry. Robert admired her poems, became her friend and then her husband, with whom she was finally able to achieve some personal autonomy. They left England soon after their wedding in 1846, passing through France, Genoa and Pisa before arriving in Florence in May 1847. Here the Brownings first rented an apartment in Via delle Belle Donne, near the Church of Santa Maria Novella before moving to this address, where their only child, Robert, was born in 1849. Elizabeth's health improved in Florence, and she appreciated the city's warm climate, social life and scenery – although she was disappointed by the state of Italian letters, which seemed backward to her in comparison to what writers were producing in France and England. In a sense she was right, since Italians' energies were largely devoted to their struggle for independence against their Bourbon and Austrian dominators during the first half of the nineteenth century. (Perhaps she didn't fully grasp the fact that Italy had suffered foreign occupation since the middle of the sixteenth century). Living in Florence, however, Elizabeth had the opportunity to observe Italian political events as they unfolded. In fact, one could say that her poetic output corresponds to the process of her personal and political maturation. She came to sympathize with the aims of many progressive Italians such Carlo Alberto of Savoy, Giuseppe Mazzini, Giuseppe Garibaldi, and Camillo Cavour. Perhaps for this reason one of her best works is the long narrative poem *Casa Guidi Windows* (1848-51), which celebrates the growth of Italian national consciousness. The title repeats the poem's first lines: "I heard last night a little child go singing / 'Neath Casa Guidi windows, by the church, / *O bella libertà, O bella!*" The first part of the poem expresses an optimistic enthusiasm for the revolutionary events of 1848, while the second part – showing disappointment in the outcome of events – criticizes the Church of Rome for failing to support the cause of Italian independence. In her words the poem was intended only to be "a simple story of personal impressions… as proving her warm attachment for a beautiful and unfortunate country." Her *Sonnets from the Portuguese* (1850) are love poems in the Petrarchan tradition, but written from a woman's perspective. Considered her most mature work, they seem to evoke the poet's husband as their object of affection, who chose the book's title, a reference to one of Elizabeth's early poems. In 1856 she published *Aurora Leigh*, a novel in blank verse, which is a remarkable assertion of women's rights in that the eponymous heroine renounces marriage in favor of a career as a writer. This novel offers a sympathetic view of prostitution and unmarried mothers too, but also includes common Victorian themes: education, patriarchy, the Crimean war, socialism related to the industrial revolution and the social relevance of art. Browning was so well-known and liked in Florence that the *Gazzetta del Popolo* (The People's Gazette) hailed her death as the loss of England's greatest woman poet and one of the most assertive defenders of the Italian cause (see also Walking Tours 2, Site 13 and 4, Site 23).

31) ANTON FRANCESCO GRAZZINI   Via delle Caldaie 4
(1503-1584)

From the Browning residence walk forward past Piazza San Felice and turn right immediately in Via Mazzetta. Follow it past Borgo Tegolaio and turn left into Via delle Caldaie. On the right side of the street you will find the following plaque at number 4:

Anton Francesco Grazzini da Staggia nell'Accademia Fiorentina detto il Lasca festoso scrittore di versi di novelle e commedie dimorò in questa casa di sua famiglia e vi morì il di XX febbraio MDLXXXIV	Anton Francesco Grazzini from Staggia, called the Roach by the Florentine Academy, was a lively writer of verses, tales and comedies who dwelled here in his family's house where he died on February 20, 1584.

Though he was known as "The Roach," we should say that Grazzini's nickname refers to a common, grey freshwater fish. He assumed this moniker as a member of the Accademia degli Umidi (the Damp Academy), a literary society that chose its name, of Latin derivation, to indicate all the good and fertile qualities associated with the humors (waters) of the earth. Other members had nicknames such as "The Cold," "The Damp" and "The Foamy." The society – one of the first to exist without the patronage of a famous writer – was formed to promote the use of Florentine as a literary language. Unlike other Renaissance academies, it aimed to free itself from pedantic classical culture in Latin and tried to foster informal social ties among its members. The famous but conservative Accademia della Crusca (the "Bran" or "Chaff" Academy) was much more formal (see also Walking Tour 7, Site 38). It aimed to assure the purity of the Florentine dialect and Grazzini was one of its founding members. Nowadays, however, Grazzini is principally remembered for the collection of folktales entitled *Le Cene* (*The Suppers*), some of which were already written before 1549. The book opens with an explanatory frame-story that is clearly modeled on Boccaccio's *Decameron*: five young men and five young women narrate the tales in front of the fire in the course of three evenings during Carnival. Unfortunately, we only have an incomplete version of it: the first two Suppers and the tenth tale of the third Supper. The narrators, who originally intended to read the *Decameron* aloud, decide to tell their own tales instead, which are generally more colorful and dramatic than Boccaccio's – though, as in the *Decameron*, they also relate stories about love, death, fortuitous events and adventure. D.H. Lawrence, who translated the last tale, ("The Story of Dr. Manente," 1929) considered Grazzini to have expressed the values and culture of Renaissance Florence better than any other writer of his time (see Walking Tour 4, Site 21). Grazzini was also a druggist and apothecary who ran a famous pharmacy that still exists: the Farmacia all'Insegna del Moro (Pharmacy of the Moor), which is across from the cathedral at the intersection of Piazza San Giovanni and Borgo San Lorenzo. It has been at this location since the first half of the fourteenth century and was taken over by Grazzini's family in 1521. Under his aegis it became a meeting place for intellectuals. There is also a plaque recognizing Grazzini inside the pharmacy:

In questa officina già del saracino or del moro fin dal M.D.XI fu farmacista A.F. Grazzini da Staggia leggiadro poeta commediografo e novelliere che quivi accolti a sua cura precipua Machiavelli Mazzuoli da Strada e lo Zanchino con altri di quei dotti in lieti convegni l'Accademia degli Umidi di poi fiorentina fondava le cui dette incruscate adunanze in quelle della celebre Crusca si tramutarono nelle quali tutte ei tolse il nome da impresa ove una lasca guizza dall'onda a ghermire l'incauta farfalla.

In this workshop, formerly called "the saracen's" and now "the moor's," A. F. Grazzini from Staggia was a pharmacist and excellent poet, playwright and short story writer beginning in 1511. Along with other learned men in the Florentine Damp Academy, he especially invited Machiavelli Mazzuoli from Strada and Zanchino here, where grain-filled meetings changed into the famous ones held by the Crusca Academy, in which he used the nickname inspired by a roach, that glimmers as it leaps up from the water to catch a butterfly unawares.

Besides *Le Cene*, Grazzini also wrote much burlesque and farcical verse in the tradition of Francesco Berni (1497-1535), whose works he edited. His plays include several farces and comedies. Among the former: *Il frate* (The Friar) and *La giostra* (The Joust); and among the latter: *La gelosia* (Jealousy), *La spiritata* (The Possessed Woman), *La pinzochera* (The Sanctimonius Procuress), *La strega* (The Witch), *La Sibilla* (The Sibyl), *L'arzigogolo* (The Quibbler) and *I parentadi* (Kinship) – all written before 1566. Grazzini's plays combine elements of ancient Roman comedy with Renaissance forms, but are most of all invaluable sources of information on everyday life and culture in Renaissance Florence. In addition they clearly indicate the author's great affection for this city, as when one character in *I parentadi* says: "There is no other city on the face of the earth where I would more willingly remain."

32) Saint Catherine of Siena   Lungarno Guicciardini 21
Sir Walter Scott
George Gordon Byron

From Grazzini's home in Via delle Caldaie, return to Via Mazzetta but turn left into Piazza Santo Spirito. Keeping the piazza on your right, walk past it into Via Sant'Agostino. Pass Via Maffia and turn right in Via dei Serragli, staying on this street past Borgo della Stella, Via di Santo Spirito and Piazza Nazario Sauro – beyond which you should turn right into the Lungarno Guicciardini. You will find the address above in the Palazzo Medici-Soderini on your right after just a few steps, but you will need to walk into the carriage entrance to see the following plaque on the left-hand side of the passageway.

In questo palagio che la storica casata dei Soderini eresse ed abitò soggiornava lungo l'anno MCCCLXXVII Santa Caterina da Siena ardimentosa zelatrice di pace

Saint Catherine of Siena, bold peacemaker between Pope Gregory II and the Republic of Florence, spent the year 1377 in this historic palace built

tra Papa Gregorio II e la repubblica di	and inhabited by the historic Soderini
Firenze qui stesso in più prossime età	family. In more recent times a ruler of
dominatori dell'arte e dei popoli	of peoples such as Napoleon I and
Raffaello, Napoleone I, Walter Scott,	masters of art such as Raphael, Walter
Lord Byron ebbero successiva	Scott and Lord Byron stayed here for
temporanea dimora	subsequent short periods of time.

Saint Catherine of Siena (1347-1380)

Born Caterina Benincasa, this mystic nun was the next-to-the-last of twenty-five children and felt a religious calling from the age of six, when she began penitential practices. Rebelling against her parents' desire to see her married, she joined the Dominican order at age twenty-four and spent her first years as a nun in solitary contemplation. Soon thereafter she spent most of her time helping the sick and aiding the inhabitants of a leper hospital. These activities did much to foster fame of her piety, although religious authorities were nonetheless suspicious of her sincerity. The Dominicans therefore insisted that she be formally interrogated so as to ascertain the orthodoxy of her faith, and she was placed in the tutelage of Father Raimondo from Capua, who became her spiritual mentor and confessor. At the same time, Catherine worked tirelessly for larger political goals, and it was only after a meeting with her that Pope Gregory II moved the papacy back to Rome in 1377. She was also instrumental in aiding Florence's difficult relations with Pope Urban VI in the following year when she was almost killed during the working-class insurrection known as the Ciompi Revolt. The Ciompi were underpaid wool carders excluded from the wool-workers' guild. When they rebelled in hopes of earning higher wages, their demands were suppressed by the Florentine nobility and bourgeosie. Catherine was born into a poor family but travelled widely for a person of her time and courageously approached the wealthy and powerful of her day. When she died in Rome she was buried in the church of Santa Maria sopra Minerva and canonized by Pope Enea Silvio Piccolomini (Pius II) in 1461. Soon afterwards her body was dismembered by Father Raimondo and parts of it reappeared here and there as holy relics. Her head and a finger are on display in the Church of Saint Dominic in Siena.

She left 381 letters addressed to popes, princes and common people but had to dictate them to male secretaries since she herself was illiterate. They are not only important evidence of spoken language in fourteenth-century Siena, but some of the earliest examples of Italian women's writing and epistolary prose. In addition to her letters, Catherine compiled a treatise entitled *Dialogo della Divina Provvidenza* (Dialogue on Divine Providence), also known as *Libro della divina dottrina* (Book of Holy Doctrine) in the form of a dialogue between the soul and God. It gives an especially good idea of the mystical and ecstatic elements of this saint's personality. Together with Saint Theresa of Avila, Saint Catherine is one of only two female Doctors of the Church. She is also the patron saint of Italy (along with Saint Francis of Assisi).

SIR WALTER SCOTT
(1771-1832)

Scott, who single-handedly invented the historical novel, began a legal and a literary career at the same time, initially publishing a series of epic poems steeped in Scottish folklore, such as *The Minstrelsy of the Scottish Border* (1802-05). After reaching commercial success with *The Lay of the Last Minstrel* (1805) he wrote a series of historical novels set in Scotland, such as *Waverly* (1805-14), that made him rich and brought him even wider fame. Moreover, Scott's fiction had enormous influence on the development of the novel throughout Europe. Alessandro Manzoni gave birth to this sub-genre in Italy, where it was widely cultivated – and even the first page of his novel *I Promessi sposi* (*The Betrothed*, 1827-42) makes it clear that Manzoni modeled its initial pages on the opening of Scott's novel *Ivanhoe* (1820), set in Medieval England during the time of Richard the Lionheart and the Crusades. Scott's literary success enabled him to invest in the publishing business and acquire Abbotsford, a large estate. An extremely prolific writer, from 1815 to 1819 he produced several novels set in Scotland, including *Guy Mannering*, *Rob Roy*, *The Heart of Midlothian*, *The Legend of Montrose*, and *The Bride of Lamermoor*. With *Ivanhoe* and *Quentin Durward* (1820) Scott established himself as a popular writer of historical novels, and went on to write *The Monastery* and *The Abbot*, both published in 1820 and set during the reign of Mary Queen of Scots. *Kenilworth* takes place during the time of Elizabeth I, while *The Fortunes of Nigel* (1822) has the reign of James I as its backdrop. These works are known for their attention to historical detail, their taste for the picturesque and their wealth of information about folklore. Because of this they outlined elements of Romanticism – such as the cultural identity of a people – and popularized them for readers throughout Europe. When Scott went bankrupt in 1826 as the result of the collapse of his publishing house, he was forced to take on a very heavy writing load to pay his creditors. Suffering from heart disease, he died at his estate after returning from a trip on the continent.

Florence was one of Scott's stops during that last trip across Europe in 1832, which he started after disembarking on the island of Malta. As he and his daughter Anne travelled up the Italian peninsula they stopped in Frascati south of Rome to visit the Villa Muti, owned by a fellow Englishman, Captain Edward Cheney. When the conversation made its way to literary matters, Scott said he admired Boiardo's and Ariosto's works so much that he reread the *Orlando innamorato* and the *Orlando Furioso* once a year. On the other hand, he said that Dante was "too obscure and difficult." He even complained to Cheney that: "It is mortifying that Dante seemed to think nobody worth being sent to hell but his own Italians, whereas other people had every bit as great rogues in their families…". Cheney replied that Scott had less of a right to complain about this than most, and proceeded to quote the tercet in the "Inferno" (Canto XX, line 117) where one of Scott's own family members is depicted among the sorcerers and seers: "Quell'altro che ne' fianchi è così poco, / Michele Scotto fu, che veramente / delle magiche frode seppe il gioco." (That other one whose thighs are scarcely fleshed / was Michael Scot, who most assuredly / knew every trick of magic fraudulence.) Michael had been a philosopher at the court of Frederick II in Palermo who translated Avicenna's Arabic commentary on Aristotle.

Later, on their way from Perugia to Bologna, the Scotts stopped in Florence for just two days. They only managed to visit the church of Santa Croce and the Pitti Palace, although Scott did consult the son of the Grand Duke's librarian about Italian historical facts for his literary research.

GEORGE GORDON BYRON
(1788-1824)

Perhaps the most fascinating of the English Romantic poets, Byron spent a lot of time in Italy, mostly in Venice, Ravenna, Pisa and Rome. Born a club-footed only child to an aristocratic family in London, he was sent to Harrow and was a student at Trinity College, Cambridge when he published his first collection of poems at age seventeen, *Fugitive Pieces* (1806). He gained notoriety after publishing *English Bards and Scottish Reviewers* (1809), which was perceived as an arrogant response to criticism levelled at his poems in *Hours of Idleness* (1807). A free spirit uncomfortable in English high society, Byron left England for several years to travel in Spain, Malta, Albania and Greece. When he returned in 1812, he published the first two cantos of *Childe Harold's Pilgrimage*, which depicts a mysterious and elegant Romantic hero modeled on Byron himself. This work made him famous and was followed by several others: *The Giaour* (1813), *The Corsair* (1814) and *Parisina* (1816). Byron wed Annabella Milbanke in 1815, and their union produced a daughter, Ada, but Annabella left him the year after. Hence, it could be said that his unhappy marriage is emblematic of his unstable emotional ties to women in general. During his short life he had numerous romantic liasons, and it seems that women found him fascinating. In Venice Byron had affairs with Marianna Segati and Margherita Cogni (known as "la Fornarina"). In Ravenna he fell in love with Countess Teresa Guiccioli and lived with her and her husband from 1821 to 1822. Indeed, Byron's energetic love life had long contributed to his reputation. His bisexual affairs at Cambridge may be seen as a point of departure, and the rumours that he was involved in an incestuous relationship with his half-sister Augusta Leigh probably sealed his decision to leave England for Geneva. In that city he lived with Percy Shelley, Mary Shelley and Claire Clairmont. Claire also bore a child by him, Allegra. In this context, even his long satiric poem *Don Juan* (1819-24) seems to have autobiographical resonance.

Byron passed through Florence in 1817 and visited the Medici chapel, which he called "fine frippery in great slabs of various expensive stones – to commemorate fifty rotten & forgotten carcasses". This same lack of appreciation characterized his thoughts about the tombs in the church of Santa Croce, the Italian version of Westminster Abbey. He said that "all of them seem to be overloaded – what is necessary but a bust & a name? – and perhaps a date? – the last for the unchronological – of whom I am one." However, he adored the Pitti Palace, "from which one returns drunk with beauty," where he preferred Raphael's and Titian's portraits, and Canova's statue of Venus. When he visited these galleries again in 1821 Byron complained about the crowds of tourists (a comment that seems to predict the conditions that visitors endure there today).

Although Byron understood little about Italy (which he saw mostly as a kind of museum), he shared certain points of view with the ideals of Italian patriots. He understood their longing to create a united, free nation, but took up Greece's struggle against the Ottoman Empire as his own. He arrived there to fight at the end of 1823 but fell ill and died at Missolonghi on April 19, 1824 after getting drenched in a rainstorm.

Walking Tour 6

Dino Compagni - Alessandro Manzoni - Vittorio Alfieri - Romain Rolland - Benvenuto Cellini

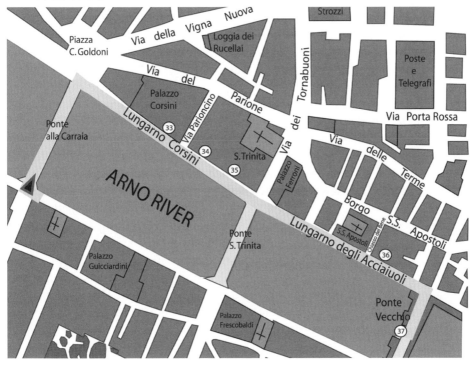

Lungarno Corsini - Lungarno degli Acciaiuoli - Ponte Vecchio

33) DINO COMPAGNI   Lungarno Corsini 8
    (1255 ca.-1324)

As you exit Palazzo Medici-Soderini turn left into the Lungarno Guicciardini the way you came. At the first corner cross the Carraia Bridge (Ponte alla Carraia) and turn right into the Lungarno Corsini. On your left is the enormous Palazzo Corsini. Walk along its façade until you come to number 8, where you will see the following plaque:

Che qui ebbero i Compagni le case   It's worth remembering that the Compagni
demolite alla fine del secolo XVII   family had its houses here, demolished at the
per dare luogo al palagio dei Corsini   end of the 17th century to make way for the

degno è si ricordi perché in esse	Corsini Palace, because here Dino Compagni,
Dino Compagni terzo confaloniere	third Supreme Magistrate of the Florentine
della repubblica con cuore di cittadino	Republic, realistically described his own
e mente di istorico descrisse dal vero	time and Dante's with civic pride and
i tempi suoi e di Dante.	historical understanding.

Along with Giovanni Villani, Dino Compagni is one of the two most important medieval chroniclers of Florentine events. His *Cronica delle cose occorrenti ne' tempi suoi* (*Chronicle of the Things Happening in His Time*) covers events in Florence from 1280 to 1310.

Compagni provides us with an impassioned and personal view of the civic unrest fomented by the White and Black Guelphs, the two political parties to which the wealthy merchant class belonged. The White Guelphs favored greater autonomy from papal hegemony, while the Black Guelphs preferred to curry papal protection as a hedge against the might of the Holy Roman Empire. When the Black Guelphs assumed control in 1301, important White Guelphs such as Dante were severely punished or forced into exile. Compagni, also a White Guelph, was able to avoid banishment because he was then Prior, Florence's highest municipal official. He shared Dante's well-known defense of civic values and condemnation of municipal corruption, and his love for Florence coupled with solid religious faith led him to consider history in terms of Good and Evil. For Compagni, goodness was the result of God's will and wickedness the effect of Satan's influence on civic affairs. His passionate views are particularly evident in the pages of the *Cronica* containing colorful political invective. In addressing prominent Black Guelphs one by one he calls them "harbingers of the destruction of [their] city." Compagni's work has also left us valuable portraits of historical figures such as Corso Donati, the leader of the Black Guelphs, and Charles of Valois, sent to Florence by Pope Boniface VIII to make peace between the two Guelph factions. When the Holy Roman Emperor Henry VII of Luxemburg led troops into Italy in 1310, many White Guelphs such as Compagni and Dante hoped for the establishment of a more balanced distribution of power between the two superpowers of the time. Indeed, Compagni's expectations were probably what inspired him to write the *Cronica* in the first place. Unfortunately, Henry VII's premature death dashed the hopes of many, and our writer was left so disappointed that he left the *Cronica* unfinished.

34) ALESSANDRO MANZONI   Lungarno Corsini 4
(1785-1873)

From Dino Compagni's address continue along the Lungarno Corsini and pass Via Parioncino on your left. After only a short distance you will find the following plaque high above the large entrance on your left:

Alessandro Manzoni qui nell'estate
del 1827 ebbe soggiorno di pochi
mesi sulle rive di questo Arno
"nelle cui acque risciaquai i miei
cenci." Volle scrivere egli dando
veste toscana al romanzo immortale
e dove la lingua il dolore le speranze
d'Italia trionfano. Questa memoria
il comune MCMXIX

Alessandro Manzoni stayed here during the summer of 1827 for a sojourn of a few months along the banks of the Arno "in the waters of which I rinsed my rags." He wanted to write giving Tuscan dress to the immortal novel in which the tongue, sorrow and hopes of Italy triumph. This remembrance, the City of Florence, 1919.

The word "rags" mentioned on the plaque here is a particularly Florentine one that Manzoni used to refer to the Italian language itself. When he came here in 1827, he had already completed the first edition of Italy's most important historical novel, *Fermo e Lucia* (*Fermo and Lucia*, 1821). The second edition, *I promessi sposi* (*The Betrothed*, 1827), represented a substantial revision, because Manzoni changed its language to conform to the dialect then spoken in Florence. Before this novel, most literature was written in an elitist Florentine dialect that existed only as a literary language for those outside Tuscany. It had been used as a lingua franca (*i.e.* Italian) ever since Dante, Petrarch and Boccaccio employed it in works of great subtlety and eloquence. In Manzoni's time all people in Italy still spoke local dialects and most of them outside Tuscany perceived Italian as an imposed language of learning. Manzoni wanted, however, to write a novel that all readers could appreciate and understand. This was a revolutionary concept at the time, and he was successful because he adopted the language of literary tradition but updated it by employing contemporary Florentine as spoken in his day. In this way he avoided writing only in his regional dialect and sidestepped the most difficult and antiquated aspects of Italian literary tradition. In addition, his successful search for a national language is matched by the decision to write a historical novel, which was the genre that best expressed the Italians' longings for national independence and unity. Indeed, Italian historical novels were read as political metaphors in which events from the past stood in for nineteenth-century oppression. This is why Manzoni set *The Betrothed* in seventeenth-century Lombardy when that region was a colony of the Spanish Empire. Its protagonists are two Lombard peasants engaged to be married but frustated by the arrogance of a Spanish nobleman who attempts to kidnap the bride-to-be. Even today, Italian readers find it ironic and funny to see typically Florentine expressions spoken by characters from Lecco and Milan. Due to Manzoni's novel, the so-called "language issue" became a topic of great importance in Italian culture, and Manzoni wrote several linguistic articles about it. Among them are: "Della lingua italiana" (On the Italian Language, 1830-1859); "Dell'unità della lingua italiana e dei mezzi di diffonderla" (On the Unity of the Italian Language and How to Promulgate It, 1868) and "Lettera intorno al libro *De vulgari eloquio* di Dante Alighieri" (Letter on the Book *On the Eloquence of the Vulgar Tongue* by Dante Alighieri, 1868). Manzoni's linguistic awareness actually led him to create a modern prose language for a popular (*i.e.* bourgeois) literary form: the novel. At the same time his poetry shows that he had one foot firmly planted in canonical poetic language as it had evolved from the Middle Ages to his own time. Among these works are: *Gli inni sacri*, (*The Sacred Hymns*, 1812-22); "Il cinque maggio" (May Fifth, 1821); "In morte di Carlo Imbonati," (On the Death of Carlo Imbonati, 1806) and the two tragedies *Il Conte di Carmagnola* (*The Count of Carmagnola*, 1820) and *Adelchi*, 1821.

Manzoni stayed here in Palazzo Gianfigliazzi for four months in 1827 in order to soak up as much knowledge of Florentine as he could.

35) VITTORIO ALFIERI   Lungarno Corsini 2
(1749-1803)

From Manzoni's lodgings continue forward a short distance in the same direction until you reach the address indicated on your left. The plaque there reads:

Vittorio Alfieri principe della tragedia per la gloria e rigenerazione dell'Italia qui con magnanimo ardire molti anni dettò e qui morì.	Vittorio Alfieri, princely tragedian, lived, died, and dictated his works here for many years with courageous generosity of spirit for the glory and rebirth of Italy.

"A man of senses and heart born free": with these words Alfieri began a poetic self-portrait of a man who never submitted to the will of tyrants. This is also how he is known to the readers of his works: disdainfully proud, individualistic, passionate, unyielding to authority, torn between anger and melancholy, but also one who felt superior to others even in his self-imposed isolation. For these same reasons he was caught between the Enlightenment and Romanticism. Alfieri was born a Count in Asti, Piedmont, when this region belonged to the Duchy of Savoy. As a young man he entered the military, which was expected of the sons of the Piedmontese nobility, but traveled all over Europe during military leaves – largely due to his restlessness and lack of direction. As he wrote in his autobiography *The Life of Vittorio Alfieri Written By Himself*, his youth "covered ten years of travels and debaucheries." After reading Plutarch's *Lives of the Noble Grecians and Romans*, Alfieri was inspired by the accomplishments of great men from the past and equally impressed by the moral and political problems with which they grappled. He visited Florence the first time in 1766 at age seventeen during a tour of Italy. It was the first city he liked after leaving Turin, and later in his autobiography he would admit having been unable to appreciate any of Florence's artworks except Michelangelo's tomb. As he put it, his "immense dissipation of mind" prevented him from having any idea of beauty. On top of this, he would "blush for eternity" for having studied English in Florence rather than Florentine. Eager to distinguish himself, Alfieri began to write and published his first tragedy, *Cleopatra*, in 1775. This was followed by twenty others, all based on biblical and historical personages from ancient and modern times. In 1776 he met the love of his life in Florence, Louisa Stolberg Countess of Albany, then still married to a pretender to the English throne, Charles Edward Stuart. Like Alfieri, she is now buried in the church of Santa Croce, though not next to him. After travelling together in Alsace and to Paris, they returned to Florence and settled at this address in 1792. As he recalls in his autobiography: "We finally arrived in Florence on the day of November 3rd, which we have never moved from and where I found again the living treasure of our language, which compensated me to no small degree for the many losses of every kind that I had to endure in France." Alfieri studied Latin and Greek only as an adult and reportedly tied himself to his chair in order to write. His tragedies, which are among the most important neoclassical works in Italian, often pit a doomed protagonist against tyrannical forces that suffocate his freedom. Consistent with this concept, Alfieri exchanged all claim to family lands in his native Piedmont for a life annuity. In this way, he was exempt from obedience to the monarchy of Savoy. Like many others, he first admired and then deplored the French revolution, which he exalted in the ode "Parigi sbastigliato" (Paris Freed of the Bastille, 1789) and later reviled in the *Misogallo* (The Francophobe, 1798), which is an assemblage of satiric epigrams, sonnets and prose. The *Rime* (Rhymes) gather together more than 300 poems echoing Dantean and Petrarchan themes, and many of them depict his love for Louisa Stolberg (see Walking Tour 4, Site 19, indicating Alfieri's tomb in the church of Santa Croce).

36) ROMAIN ROLLAND   **Lungarno degli Acciaiuoli 14**
    (1866-1944)

From Alfieri's residence continue in the same direction along the Arno. After passing the Santa Trinita bridge proceed along the left-hand side of the Lungarno degli Acciaiuoli. Just past the narrow alley Chiasso del Bene on your left you will come upon this plaque:

Romain Rolland insigne scrittore e critico d'arte qui soggiornò nel 1911.	The great writer and art historian Romain Rolland stayed here in 1911.

Rolland was a prolific writer and scholar of literature, philosphy and music who taught art history at the École Normale Supérieur and the history of music at the Sorbonne. His best-known work is the epic ten-volume novel *Jean-Christophe* (1904-12), whose protagonist represents the European intellectual at the beginning of the twentieth century. Rolland won the Nobel prize in literature in 1915 largely because of this novel, which empasizes ideals of universal brotherhood. During W.W. I Rolland, a pacifist, wrote ardently against the war in his essay "Au-dessus de la mêlée" (Above the Battle, 1914) and for this reason was accused of being a traitor. His pacifism was probably what led him to an interest in Indian mysticism later on, to his solidarity with Mahatma Gandhi and his friendship with Rabindranath Tagore. In 1919 he published his "Déclaration de l'Indépendance de l'Esprit" (Declaration of Spiritual Independence) in *L'Humanité*, which was signed by intellectuals such as Albert Einstein, Maxim Gorky, Bertrand Russell and Benedetto Croce. At the same time, Rolland was attracted to titanic personalities such as Michelangelo, Beethoven and Tolstoy, of whom he wrote biographies – in addition to several others that appeared in *Musiciens d'autre fois* (Musicians of the Past, 1908) and *Musiciens d'aujourd'hui* (Musicians of Today). Rolland came to Florence to lecture and recuperate after having been hurt when caught between two cars on the Champs-Elysées in Paris. He visited Italian acquaintances in Rome such as the novelist Grazia Deledda and the actress Eleonora Duse. In Florence he stayed in contact with Giuseppe Prezzolini, editor of *La Voce* (The Voice), one of the most avant-garde Italian literary journals of the early twentieth-century. Prezzolini later supported Italy's intervention in W.W. I while Rolland held fast to his pacifist ideals. The French writer also became acquainted with Gaetano Salvemini – the historian and socialist, then a professor at the University of Pisa. Salvemini, from Puglia, was an authority on the problems of southern Italy. In a letter written during the same year he came to Italy (1911), Rolland mentions *La Voce* and says that he "admir[ed] most of all its young editor: Prezzolini, and Salvemini, professor at the University of Pisa, an unhappy and courageous man who escaped from the earthquake in Messina after losing his wife and all his children in it and who – without being destroyed by it – work[ed] and struggle[d] with extraordinary energy for his dear Italian South." In fact, the character Bruno Chiarenza in *L'âme enchantée* (The Enchanted Soul, 1922-33) appears to be based on the description of Salvemini in that same letter. This seven-volume novel revolves around a female protagonist that is an analogue of Jean-Christophe. Rolland died in 1944 of tuberculosis, a disease that he had had since childhood.

### 37) BENVENUTO CELLINI					Ponte Vecchio
    (1500-1570)

From Romain Rolland's lodgings proceed forward and turn right at the next intersection onto the Ponte Vecchio. Halfway across the bridge there is an overlook on the river to your right. There you will see a fountain with a bronze bust of Cellini that carries this inscription:

> *A Benvenuto Cellini maestro*   To Benvenuto Cellini the master
> *Gli orafi di Firenze*   The goldsmiths of Florence

This monument to the great Renaissance goldsmith, sculptor and autobiographer was made by Raffaele Romanelli in 1900. It recognizes the fact that at the end of the sixteenth century the Archduke Ferdinand I de' Medici excluded all businesses but goldsmiths' shops from this bridge. Since that time it has been the traditional site of goldsmiths' stores in Florence. Before then, all manner of businesses, including butchers' shops, had been crowded onto it (for the complete entry on Cellini see Walking Tour 2, Site 11).

Walking Tour 7

Accademia della Crusca - James Russell Lowell - Ludovico Ariosto - Giampietro Vieusseux - Dino Compagni - Doney's - George Eliot - Caffè Giubbe Rosse

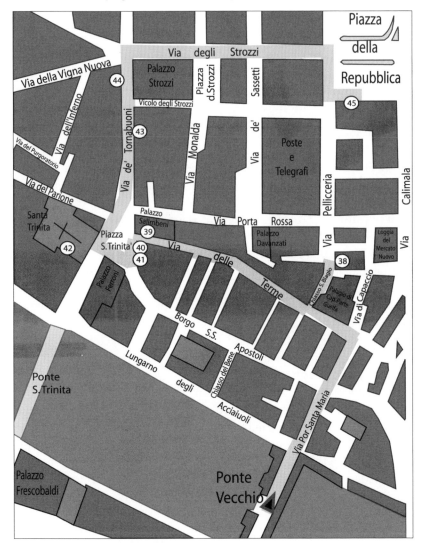

Via Pellicceria - Via delle Terme - Piazza Santa Trinita - Via Tornabuoni - Piazza della Repubblica

38) Accademia della Crusca   **Via Pellicceria 2 (red)**

From the bust of Cellini on the Ponte Vecchio retrace your steps to the Lungarno degli Acciaiuoli. Walk straight ahead in Via Por Santa Maria past Borgo SS. Apostoli on your left and turn left at the next corner into Via delle Terme. Continue past Via di Capaccio and turn right at the next corner, Chiasso di San Biagio. Skirt the building on your right (the Palagio di Capitani di Parte Guelfa) that sits in the tiny Piazza di Parte Guelfa and cross the next cross street, Vicolo della seta. On the corner of the building on your right is the following plaque:

Gli accademici della Crusca qui dal MDXC al MDCXII compilarono il primo vocabolario della lingua italiana. Il Municipio di Firenze poneva con delib del XXVII dic. MDCCCLXXXII	The members of the Academy of the Crusca compiled here the first dictionary of the Italian language from 1590 to 1612. Florence's Town Hall solemnly placed this [here] on December 27, 1882.

   This private society came into being in 1583 in the wake of friendly conversations between humanists and literary scholars. Anton Francesco Grazzini and Francesco Redi (see Walking Tour 5, Sites 25 and 31) were among its founding members, but Leonardo Salviati was the one who gave it its main purpose: compiling the first Italian dictionary. The Academy's name (the "Bran" or "Chaff" Academy) refers to the act of winnowing to separate wheat from its chaff (in this case, literary Florentine from the influences of other Italian dialects). The Preface to the first edition in 1612 explains that the dictionary was intended to be a compilation of archaic Florentine – or words used by the best writers of the fourteenth century – especially those used by Petrarch (1304-1374) and Boccaccio (1313-1375). These criteria had long been used by many writers throughout the peninsula, but Cardinal Pietro Bembo codified them in his *Prose della volgar lingua* (The Style of Written Italian, 1525). The Accademia della Crusca and its dictionary did much to standardize written Italian at a time when spoken Italian outside Tuscany varied enormously from place to place. Each entry carries examples of usage taken from writers of prose or poetry, and many include proverbs and idiomatic expressions. Subsequent editions of the dictionary were published in 1623, 1663, 1691, 1729-38, 1863 and 1923. Granduke Leopold of Tuscany tried to ensure that entries on scientific and nautical subjects as well as terminology concerning trades, professions and artisans' work would be included in the 1663 edition, but the members of the Academy repeatedly rejected this idea. The 1691 edition, however, made room for many entries taken from Torquato Tasso's works as well as new diminutives, augmentatives and superlatives. The Academy's decisions to include or exclude lexical choices were not always simple ones. At times important scholars – especially those from other Italian regions – protested against the dictionary's solely Tuscan focus. Since 1964 the Academy of the Crusca has been working on an edition written in accordance with modern linguistic theory.

39) JAMES RUSSELL LOWELL   **Via delle Terme 18**
     (1819-1891)

From the Academy of the Crusca in Via Pellicceria retrace your steps to Via delle
Terme and turn right. You will pass four narrow streets on your left (Chiasso del
Cornino, Via del Fiordaliso, Via delle Bombarde and Chiasso Ricasoli) before you
arrive in Piazza Santa Trinita. On the side of the last building on your right
(Palazzo Salimbeni) before you enter the Piazza Santa Trinita you will see the fol-
lowing plaque:

Qui nell'antico Hotel du Nord	Here in the old Hotel du Nord
James	the American
Russell Lowell poeta e critico	poet, literary critic and Dante scholar
americano	James Russell Lowell
studioso di Dante soggiornò	stayed during the winter
nell'inverno	of 1874
del 1874 traendo ispirazione	drawing inspiration
dalla bellezza	from the beauty
della città di Firenze.	of the city of Florence.

Born in Cambridge, Massachussetts, Lowell was a poet and literary critic who
wrote intelligently about his contemporaries Ralph Waldo Emerson, William Cullen
Bryant, Nathaniel Hawthorne and Edgar Allan Poe. He is associated with the group
known as the Fireside poets or the Schoolroom Poets, which included Henry
Wadsworth Longfellow, Oliver Wendall Holmes and John Greenleaf Whittier.
Because of his conservatism and his poetry's openly moral tone, his *Poems* (1844,
1846) fell out of favor with the public after the nineteenth century, although these
same qualities were the ones that appealed most to readers during his lifetime. His
best critical writing is in *A Fable for Critics* published in 1848. In the same year *The
Bigelow Papers* appeared, which brought him a degree of critical and popular success. Political and social satire in verse, *The Bigelow Papers* show Lowell's support of
the North in the Civil War and contributed to the discussions about antislavery at
the time. Lowell's poem *The Vision of Sir Launfal* (1848) provided an original twist to
Arthurian literature and the legend of the Holy Grail. While professor of Modern
Languages at Harvard University from 1855 to 1876, he was also the first editor of
the *Atlantic Monthly* from 1864 to 1872. Later Lowell became Minister to Spain and
then England from 1877 to 1885. He made his first trip to Italy with his wife Maria in
1851 when they rented Casa Guidi in Florence from Elizabeth and Robert Browning
(see Walking Tour 5, Site 30). After Maria's death in 1856 he came again and stayed
for two months at the Hotel Europe. He stayed at this address mentioned on the
plaque above in 1874. At that time Henry James was also in Florence, and it appears
that the two men did not get along very well together (see Walking Tour 1, Site 1).
Lowell's observations on his travels in Italy appear in "Leaves from my Journal in

Italy and Elsewhere" included in the first volume of his *Literary Essays*. There aren't many Florentine "leaves" in the Journal since he talks mostly about Rome, its region, and Naples, but it does contain comments about Italy in general. Some of these repeat stereotypes about Italy as a "beautiful woman" or its "slow" pace of life. Others are more perceptive: "Coming from a country where everything seems shifting like a quicksand, where men shed their homes as snakes their skins, where you may meet a three-story house, or even a church, on the highway, bitten by the universal gad-fly of bettering its position, where we have known a tree to be cut down merely because "it had got to be so old," the sense of permanence, unchangeableness, and repose which Italy gives us is delightful."

40) LUDOVICO ARIOSTO	Piazza Santa Trinita 2
(1474-1533)	Palazzo Buondelmonti

From Lowell's address in Via delle Terme enter Piazza Santa Trinita with its grandiose column and turn left. You will find the following plaque on Palazzo Buondelmonti on your immediate left:

In questa casa di Zanobi	In this house belonging to Zanobi
Buondelmonti	Buondelmonti
più volte ebbe grata dimora Ludovico	Ludovico Ariosto stayed and slept gratefully
Ariosto. Nel IV centenario della morte di	several times. The City of Florence placed this
lui il Comune di Firenze pose.	plaque here on the fourth centenary of his death.

The author of the greatest chivalric epic of the Italian Renaissance, *Orlando Furioso*, is known to have been in Florence in 1513 for the festivities surrounding the election of Pope Leo X, born Giovanni de' Medici. Ariosto probably arrived here in June when the celebrations reached their culmination, coinciding with the feast of the patron saint of Florence, Saint John the Baptist, on June 24th. Here he was able to see Alessandra di Francesco Benucci again, who was to become the love of his life. His encounters with her in Florence were merely fortuitous, but they actually reflect personal and literary themes that Ariosto would later develop in the *Orlando Furioso*. Its first canto opens with a recollection "[o]f ladies, cavaliers, of love and war, / Of courtesies and of brave deeds," which were also mirrored in the tournaments organized for the election of the Pope. Later on in the same work one of Ariosto's innovations was to make his hero Orlando go insane over the loss of his beloved, Angelica. Ariosto evokes Alessandra in much the same way by saying that he too has gone crazy over the woman he loves.

Ariosto recalls Florence and Alessandra during those days:

> In the Tuscan city, that honors this day most reverently, the news had brought people here
> from far and near to see the pagentry. Even I, desirous to witness it, came here. Of what else I
> saw, I remembered little and little do I care; I was left with just the immortal memory, that in
> all that fair city I saw no fairer thing than you... Doors, windows, streets, temples, theaters, I

saw full of ladies, bent on sport, on society, or hearing Mass; old and young, daughters and mothers, adorned in various robes; some at banquets, some gracefully dancing; but, in short, I saw no one, nor perceived that others saw, anyone who could equal you in beauty, in modesty, courtesy, and noble semblance, much less surpass you.

Alessandra was married at the time to the nobleman Tito di Leonardo Strozzi, who held a minor position at the court of Ferrara, then the administrative center of Emilia Romagna. After his death, Ariosto married Alessandra secretly in 1528.

Born the son of the captain of the citadel in Reggio Emilia, Ariosto was first pushed to undertake legal studies, but was then allowed to study literature and received a decent though incomplete humanistic education. After his father's death in 1500 he had to seek employment to support his nine brothers and sisters. In 1504 Ariosto was named secretary and advisor to Cardinal Ippolito d'Este, brother of the Duke of Ferrara, Alfonso d'Este, for whom the poet served as statesman and ambassador. Ludovico undertook several delicate (and sometimes dangerous) missions to the belligerent Pope Julius II, and later, from 1522 to 1525, was appointed governor of Garfagnana, a Tuscan region near the Ligurian border. Because of that area's many bandits and internal strife it was a difficult and dangerous post, but Ariosto was up to the task because of his common sense and ability to keep his balance even in difficult circumstances. This same capacity is evident in many of his works, in which he distances himself from situations and characters by means of irony that is free of sarcasm. In this way the poet is able to smile affably over weaknesses and shortcomings while gently making fun of them.

During his lifetime *Orlando Furioso* (1516, 1521, 1532) was widely read and translated throughout Europe. Its influence on other writers can hardly be underestimated and can be seen in many other works, such as Cervantes' *Don Quixote*. In addition, Ariosto produced seven *Satires* in verse (1517-1525) that criticize corruption and are inspired by Horace's classical ideals of moderation. His four comedies are some of the most important of the Italian Renaissance: *La Cassaria* (The Play of the Strong-box, 1508), *I Suppositi* (The Substitutes, 1509), *Il Negromante* (The Sorcerer, 1520) and *La Lena* (The Procuress, 1528).

41) GIAMPIETRO VIEUSSEUX (1779-1863)   Piazza Santa Trinita 2

From the plaque indicating Ariosto's lodgings turn to your right and you will find another one over the building's main entranceway:

In queste case già dei Buondelmonti abitò Gio=Pietro Vieusseux di Oneglia lungamente benemerito della civiltà italiana e qui moriva il di 28 aprile 1863. Il municipio di Firenze nel 2

In these buildings formerly belonging to the Buondelmonti family Giampietro Vieusseux from Oneglia lived and brought much benefit to Italian civilization through the years, where he died on April 28, 1863. The City of

| *maggio successivo decretava questa* | Florence honored the memory of this |
| *memoria all'inclito cittadino.* | illustrious citizen on the following May 2. |

Giampietro Vieusseux died here in his family home, but you can read the principal entry for him in Walking Tour 2, Site 13.

42) DINO COMPAGNI   Church Santa Trinita
(1255 ca.-1324)   Piazza of Santa Trinita

Standing in front of Vieusseux's home in Palazzo Buondelmonti, turn around to face the piazza and you will see the church of Santa Trinita opposite you on the other side of Via de' Tornabuoni.

The tomb of the 14th-century chronicler of Florentine history is here in the fourth chapel of the nave on your left. Look for it at the front of the chapel, at the base of the wall on your left (for the main entry on Dino Compagni, see Walking Tour 6, Site 33).

43) DONEY'S   Via Tornabuoni 8-10
(1858-1991)

Exit the church of Santa Trinita and turn left into Via Tornabuoni. On the right-hand side of the street at the address above is the former site of Doney's (pronounced "doan-AY" in Italian).

The Caffè Doney, opened in 1858 by Gaspero Doney, was located at this address for 133 years. It had marble tables and four columns that supported the vaulted ceiling of its main room, unofficially known as the café "delle colonne" or "the café with columns." The three-room interior was painted white with gold trim, where the waiters served lots of hot chocolate and ice cream, the products preferred by its clientele: aristocrats, politicians, the middle class and literary figures. Writers have also mentioned Doney's in their works: Elizabeth Barrett Browning in *Aurora Leigh* (1857), John De Forest in *European Acquaintances* (1858) and Lettice Cooper in her novel *Fenny*. Many tourists and foreigners (especially the English) also came to Doney's for tea in the afternoon because Via Tornabuoni has been one of Florence's most fashionable streets since the nineteenth century. Stendhal, Herman Melville, Ralph Waldo Emerson, James Russell Lowell and the Goncourt Brothers are all known to have come here regularly for breakfast. At that time flower girls also circulated among the tables selling bouquets and boutonnieres which they affixed to your buttonhole. In the morning the café hosted working-class customers too, when women from surrounding farms would stop by for coffee and rolls on their way to the Central Market from Porta al Prato or the Oltrarno. Coming to Doney's was a rare luxury for them, reserved for special occasions such as a child's First

Communion. Franco Zeffirelli's 1999 film *Tea with Mussolini*, an autobiographical recollection of childhood in Florence, includes a scene in which Fascist party members burst into Doney's and spoil a luncheon party. Another historic gathering place, the Caffè Giacosa on the corner of Via Tornabuoni and Via della Spada nearby, has recently undergone sweeping change and has reopened in radically altered form. An unfortunate trend, these changes represent the end of an era for places that were living pages of Florentine history.

44) George Eliot   **Via Tornabuoni 13**
   (1819-1880)

From Doney's proceed up Via Tornabuoni in the same direction. Cross the Vicolo degli Strozzi on your right and skirt the rear of Palazzo Strozzi. At the next cross street, Via degli Strozzi, cross Via Tornabuoni and return back in the same direction on the opposite side of the street for a short distance until you find the following plaque on your right:

In questa casa albergo preferito di musici sommi trascorse nel 1860 uno dei suoi primi soggiorni George Eliot (Anna Marie Evans) autrice della fiorentina "Romola" e di altri romanzi	George Eliot (Anna Marie Evans), author of the Florentine "Romola" and other novels, stayed in this house, the favorite hotel of great musicians, in 1860 during one of her first visits.

Journalist Mary Ann or Marian Evans was encouraged by the publicist George Lewes to switch from essays to fiction and publish in *Blackwood's Magazine* under the pseudonym George Eliot. She did so because: "a *nom de plume* secures all the advantages without the disagreeables of reputation." These pieces later appeared as *Scenes from Clerical Life* (1857). She met Lewes in 1852 at John Chapman's home in London when she collaborated with Chapman in issuing his radical *Westminster Review*, of which she gained virtual control from 1851 to 1853. Living with Lewes as his wife, Marian was one of the most scandalous figures in Victorian England and used a pseudonym to protect her real identity after her writing became better known. She went on to write many novels, including *Adam Bede* (1859), *The Mill on the Floss* (1860) – her best-known work, in addition to being semi-autobiographical – *Silas Marner* (1861), *Romola* (1863), *Felix Holt* (1866), *Middlemarch* (her masterpiece, published in installments from 1871 to 1872), and *Daniel Deronda* (also printed in serialized form from 1874 to 1876).

Her love for Italy dates from 1840, when she began studying Italian, and grew out of her sympathy for Italy's political subjugation. As you can tell from the date on the plaque above, this love lasted for twenty years and can be said to have paralleled Italy's own struggle for emancipation. In fact, one of the first books she read in Italian was Silvio Pellico's *My Imprisonments* (1832), which relates the experiences of a patriot persecuted by the Austrian authorities. Eliot made her first trip to Italy in 1849 after her father's death, when she traveled to various French cities before going on to Genoa, Lombardy and Como. Lewes was a member of the Society of the Friends of Italy in England founded by Giuseppe Mazzini, the revolutionary and political theorist. Eliot heard him speak in London and also admired his writing.

She traveled to Italy a second time in 1860 to do research for her Italian novel *Romola*. She stayed at the Pension Suisse, which was then located at this address. Eliot called *Romola* a "historical romance" set in Girolamo Savonarola's late 15th-century Florence. It tried to enliven the distant past at a time when Italians were famously rewriting their own history of oppression as *romans à clef* for their on-going problems. Included are interesting re-creations of literary history, as when the main male protagonist sings the first lines of one of Lorenzo de' Medici's *Carnival Songs*, or when a minor character quotes Luigi Pulci's poetry. It ends with Eliot's own prediction of Italy's future, imagined as a celestial tableau in which Petrarch's Laura, Dante's Beatrice, the Virgin Mary and the female personi-fication of Italy all nurture and protect their children.

Daniel Deronda's female protagonist makes a spiritual journey which some have likened to the one in Dante's *Comedy*. The novel also quotes Pietro Metastasio's poetry and poems by Giacomo Leopardi – and this at a time when Leopardi's romanticism was practically unknown in England.

45) Bar Caffè Restaurant Giubbe Rosse   **Piazza della Repubblica**
                                                                          13-14 (red)

From the site of George Eliot's hotel in Via Tornabuoni retrace your steps to the corner of Via della Vigna Nuova. Turn right crossing Via Tornabuoni into Via degli Strozzi and follow it past Piazza degli Strozzi and Via de' Sassetti on your right. Cross under the tall stone arch and you will find yourself in the large Piazza della Repubblica. Along the short right-hand edge of the square is the Bar Caffè Giubbe Rosse.

After all this walking you deserve a rest, and you couldn't find a more storied place to stop than this café. Similar businesses arose throughout Europe during the eighteenth century as venues to meet and discuss current events at a time when newspapers first became widely read. Later, when cafés differentiated them-selves from one another culturally, each appealed to a different kind of clientele: those with literary tastes being one of them. Famous cafés throughout the world still exist: Rome has Caffè Greco (established in 1760), where Goethe, Lord Byron, Franz Liszt and Richard Wagner were regular customers. In Venice, Caffè Florian (1720) was a meeting place for the likes of Giacomo Casanova, Jean-Jacques Rousseau, Carlo Goldoni, Madame de Staël, Alphonse de Chateaubriand, Charles Dickens, Marcel Proust and Gabriele D'Annunzio. Paris has not only Café Les

Deux Magots, where Jean-Paul Sartre and Ernest Hemingway often went, but also Café de Flore, that hosted Albert Camus and Simone de Beauvoir. Berlin's roaring twenties during the Weimar Republic are still associated with Café Adlon (1907), while Dorothy Parker's Round Table met at New York's Algonquin Hotel from 1919 to 1929. San Francisco has Caffè Trieste, where "Beatnik" writers such as Allen Ginsberg, Jack Kerouac, Lawrence Ferlinghetti and Gregory Corso gathered in the 1950's. Florence is known for the Giubbe Rosse (Red Jackets). Founded by the Swiss Reininghaus brothers in 1900, it carried their name until 1933 when it acquired the present one. Until 1910, it catered mostly to the wealthy, as did most of the cafés in the city's center, but its customers began to be of a different sort in wake of the social and economic crises after the turn of the century. Writers, artists and poets started coming here who were also supporters of artistic and political movements, and they met at Caffè Giubbe Rosse in part to organize protests and meetings. It was a place to chat, write, express yourself, argue, proclaim your ideas in public and sometimes leave without paying the bill. Some customers wrote for Florentine literary magazines such as *Leonardo* (founded in 1902) or, later, for *La Voce* (The Voice). The former promoted the diffusion and discussion of recent international trends and forms of irrationalist thought then just emerging. The latter was not strictly literary since it was concerned with social and political issues such as the underdevelopment of Southern Italy, the Italian invasion of Libia, the movement to reclaim Friuli Venezia-Giulia and Trentino-Alto Adige from Austria as well as the struggle to give women the vote. Some of the Giubbe Rosse's famous customers were Giuseppe De Robertis, Federico Tozzi, Marino Moretti, Benedetto Croce, Ottone Rosai, the Hermetic poets Eugenio Montale and Giuseppe Ungaretti, and Mario Luzi. After founding the Futurist movement, Filippo Tommaso Marinetti came to Florence in 1910 for a friendly meeting and exchange of ideas. Since Futurism aimed at the destruction and consequent death of traditional culture, a fight broke out at the meeting, but Marinetti's friend Aldo Palazzeschi managed to coax everyone over to the Giubbe Rosse where they made peace and began shouting "Death to death!" From then on the Giubbe Rosse became known as a futurist hangout for writers such as Giuseppe Prezzolini, Giovanni Papini and Ardengo Soffici as well as for painters such as Umberto Boccioni, Carlo Carrà, Gino Severini and Giacomo Balla. After the outbreak of W.W. I in 1914, fights erupted here again between the vast majority of those in favor of intervention in the war and the pacifist minority. Many intellectuals who left for the front came back to the Giubbe Rosse when they were on leave, but many never returned at all: Scipio Slataper, Ugo Tommei and Carlo Stuparich (brother of the writer Giani Stuparich). Other writers who came here later were Arturo Loria, Carlo Emilio Gadda and Elio Vittorini, the neorealist. Today, the Giubbe Rosse basks in the glory of its history and is still an important downtown bar. Enjoy your espresso!

Walking Tour 8

Caffè Paszkoswski - Gabriele D'Annunzio - André Gide - Leigh Hunt - Carlo Collodi

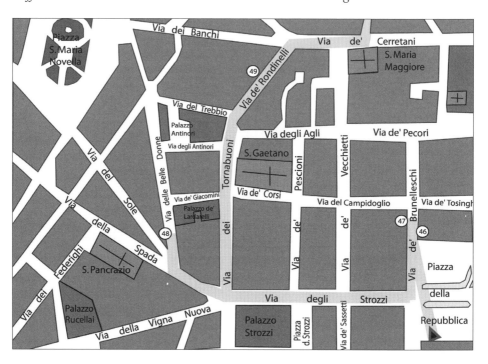

Piazza della Repubblica - Via de' Brunelleschi - Via delle Belle Donne - Via Rondinelli

46) Caffè Paszkoswski   **Piazza della Repubblica 6 (red)**

With the Giubbe Rosse behind you and the square's large arch on your left, cross the square and head for its corner on your left. Caffè Paszkoswski is located at the corner where Via de' Brunelleschi empties into the square.

Founded in 1846 by a Pole, Caffè Paszkoswki started life as a beer hall when the present-day Piazza della Repubblica was occupied by Florence's Jewish ghetto. It was inaugurated in its current form in 1907 after the creation of this square, which was then known as Piazza Vittorio Emanuele II in honor of Italy's first king. The column on the opposite edge of the square, a monument to Abundance, marks the site of the city's original Roman colony and the approximate location of the Forum and the temples. Like the Giubbe Rosse, Paszkoswski's clientele was comprised of writers, artists and musicians and therefore didn't identify with either the working class or the aristocracy. Unlike the Giubbe Rosse, however, its customers did not come here as members of a single literary movement or political group. Still, it was a literary café and writers for Giuseppe Prezzolini's magazine *La Voce* (1908-1910) were known to come here, as well as those who published work in the futurist magazine *Lacerba*, founded at the beginning of 1913 by Giovanni Papini and Ardengo Soffici. *Lacerba* was at times an experimental magazine while at others it came out openly in favor of W.W. I. After 1914 *Lacerba* tried to define and promote a specifically Florentine kind of Futurism that concentrated primarily on literary issues. Other customers later helped found an anti-futurist magazine *La Difesa dell'Arte* (The Defense of Art). In the 1930's the poets associated with what is known as Florentine hermeticism frequented this café: Mario Luzi, Piero Bigongiari, Alessandro Parronchi and Alfonso Gatto. These poets aimed at writing evocative poetry that wasn't merely communicative. Indeed, the label "hermetic" refers to the fact that their compositions are not easily understood because they need to be interpreted rather than just read. The Hermetics found inspiration in preceding work by the French Symbolists and hoped to offer an alternative to the poetry of Gabriele D'Annunzio. They published primarily in Florentine magazines such as *Il Frontespizio* (The Frontispiece) and *Campo di Marte* (The Parade Ground), which is also the name of a Florentine neighborhood. Numerous other writers came here too: the literary critics Silvio Ramat and Oreste Macrì, the poet Umberto Saba as well as Romano Bilenchi and the neorealist writer Vasco Pratolini (see Walking Tour 10, Site 58). Paszkoswki is renowned for its large "whiskeyteca" (whiskey collection) and for its "schiacciata con l'uva" (bread with grapes).

47) GABRIELE D'ANNUNZIO   Bar Gambrinus
ANDRÉ GIDE   Via de' Brunelleschi 1

From Caffè Paszkoswski, turn the corner into Via de' Brunelleschi and cross the street into the arcade covering the sidewalk on the other side. Walk half a block to your right and you will see the Caffè Cinema Gambrinus near the corner of Via del Campidoglio.

GABRIELE D'ANNUNZIO
(1863-1938)

Gabriele D'Annunzio often came to the Caffè Gambrinus when he was in Florence. Born in Pescara in the region of Abruzzo, Italy's best-known exponent of Decadentism spent his adolescence in Tuscany from 1874 to 1881 at the "Collegio Cicognini" boarding school in Prato, just outside of Florence. He started his career as a journalist but gained fame and fortune as a poet and novelist who appealed to the Italian bourgeoisie, which was bored and disappointed in the wake of Italian unification. Sensual thoughts typically dominate the emotions of his quasi-aristocratic protagonists. They perceive all experiences as aesthetic ones and express them in binary motives such as love and death or pleasure and suffering. In their absurd attempt to imitate Nietzsche's superman they show instead that they have abandoned the moral values of the nineteenth century, and in this they embody fin-de-siècle Decadentism. His novels are: *Il piacere* (*The Child of Pleasure*, 1888), *Giovanni Episcopo* (1891), *L'innocente* (*The Innocent*, 1892), *Il trionfo della morte* (*The Triumph of Death*, 1894), *Le vergini delle rocce* (*The Virgins of the Rocks*, 1895), *Il fuoco* (*The Fire*, 1900) and *Forse che sì forse che no* (*Perhaps yes perhaps no*, 1910). In addition to *Il poema paradisiaco* (*The Poem of Paradise*, 1893), some of D'Annunzio's best poetry lies in "Maia," "Elettra" and "Alcyone," the first three books of *Laudi del cielo, del mare, della terra, degli eroi* (*Praises*, 1903). Among the most noteworthy are: "La pioggia nel pineto" (The Rain in the Pine Forest), "La sera fiesolana" (Fiesole in the Evening), "Meriggio" (Midday) and "Stabat nuda aestas" (Summer Stood Naked). D'Annunzio's choice of words, rhyme and rhythm in evoking landscape imagery helped reinvigorate Italian poetry at the end of the nineteenth century by giving it a different musicality. His tragedies, based on themes such as incest and violent sexual desire, include *La città morta* (The Dead City, 1896) and *La figlia di Jorio* (The Daughter of Jorio, 1907). From 1898 to 1910 D'Annunzio owned the Villa La Capponcina in Settignano (a hill located just beyond Florence's city limits). The villa was not far from the home of the actress Eleonora Duse, who performed in his play *La Gioconda* (1899) and brought it success. *Il fuoco*, however, caused a scandal because it supposedly revealed details of the author's love affair with Duse. His books also made him wealthy, but when creditors had the villa repossessed to pay for the debts he incurred with his lavish lifestyle he fled to Paris. D'Annunzio lived in France until the outbreak of W.W.I. A fervid interventionist and someone who saw himself as a protagonist on the world stage, he flew his own plane over Vienna and dropped tricolor leaflets in favor of regaining Italy's former northeastern territories from Austria. After the war he led a small contingent of soldiers on a march from Ronchi to Fiume, which he occupied and governed for two years as its sole regent. The villa he owned on Lake Garda at the end of his life "Il Vittoriale degli italiani," extravagantly furnished, is now a museum.

　　The French writer André Gide knew D'Annunzio, and described in his journal a conversation he had with him here on December 28, 1895: "Together we go to the Gambrinus; d'Annunzio indulges with obvious greediness in little vanilla ices served in small cardboard boxes. He sits beside me and talks gracefully and charmingly without, it seems to me, paying any special attention to the role he is playing. He is short; from a distance his face would seem ordinary or already familiar, so devoid is he of any exterior sign of literature or genius. He wears a little pointed beard which is pale blond and talks with a clearly articulated voice, somewhat cold, but supple and almost caressing. His eyes are rather cold; he is perhaps rather cruel, but perhaps it is simply the appearance of his delicate sensuality that makes him seem so. He is wearing a black derby, quite unaffectedly. He asks questions about French writers... Ibsen displeases him by 'his lack of beauty.' 'What do you expect?' he says as if to excuse himself; 'I am a Latin.' He is preparing a modern drama of classical form and observing the 'three unities.' "

ANDRÉ GIDE
(1869-1951)

Born into a wealthy family in Paris with a Protestant Huguenot past, Gide publicly declared his homosexuality in his 1924 short story "Corydon" even though married to his cousin Madeleine. He spent New Year's Eve 1895 in Florence while travelling with his wife in Italy in 1895 and 1896 and recorded his impressions in his journal, a part of which is entitled "Feuilles de Route" (Leaves Gathered by the Wayside), that covers the period from December 15, 1895 to January 6, 1896. He toured the city's major attractions including the Cathedral, the churches of Santa Maria Novella, San Miniato and the cloister of the church of San Marco (about which he has left his own comments on Fra Angelico's frescoes). At the Galleria Palatina in Palazzo Pitti Gide was particularly struck by Giorgione's "Concert" and its depiction of a young man's head on the left-hand side of the painting, but he also appreciated the Raphaels in the Tribuna of the Uffizi gallery, and was impressed most of all by Donatello's "David" in the Bargello. Going up the hills above the city, he took Viale dei Colli up to Piazzale Michelangelo to look out over the valley, but spent most of his time in Florence alone – since Madeleine was ill and had to stay in her room. On several occasions Gide met D'Annunzio and a minor Italian writer, Roberto Gatteschi.

Gide's most important novels are *L'immoraliste* (*The Immoralist*, 1902) and *Le Caves du Vatican* (*The Vatican Cellars*, 1914). Among his literary criticism is his study *Dostoevsky* (1923), an author whose influence can be seen in the two novels just mentioned. In 1908 Gide founded the *Nouvelle Revue Francaise* (New French Revue), which became the most important French literary journal between the two world wars. After travelling to the Congo in 1925 and 1926, Gide's moral conscience was politicized and he turned towards communism (although never a member of the French Communist Party). He received the Nobel Prize in 1947.

48) JAMES LEIGH HUNT   Via delle Belle Donne 1 (red)
    (1784-1859)

From Caffè Gambrinus, walk back along Via de' Brunelleschi into Piazza della Repubblica and turn right under the large arch into Via degli Strozzi. Follow it past Via de' Sassetti and Piazza degli Strozzi on your left. After you cross Via Tornabuoni, bear right into Via della Spada and, at the next intersection, bear right again into Via delle Belle Donne (the street of beautiful women). The first address on your left is the one above.

Editor of the weekly *Examiner* for 13 years, Hunt first brought Keats' and Shelley's poems to the public's attention in that publication. That he was also interested in Italy is shown by his narrative poem *The History of Rimini* (1816), which is a version of the love story between Paolo Malatesta and Francesca da Rimini (recounted most famously in Canto V of Dante's "Inferno"). Leigh Hunt arrived in Italy in November 1820 with his wife and several children. Shelley and Byron had invited him many times to come here, but he decided to make the trip only after the radical *Examiner* had such serious financial problems that he thought it would be worth a try looking for financial backers in Italy for a new publication expressing revolutionary ideals. The Italian climate was also warmer than England's and would help Mrs. Hunt's tuberculosis. After arriving in Livorno where they met with Shelley, the Hunts ended up staying in Pisa with Byron. Following Shelley's accidental death in 1822 the Hunts moved to Genova and then to Florence in 1823, where they first stayed at this location. They changed addresses constantly and finally found semi-permanent lodgings at a villa in Maiano, near Fiesole. Hunt's *Autobiography* (1850) contains a number of references to Florence, of which he was very fond. Hunt "loved the fine arts and the old palaces" and "the good-natured, intelligent inhabitants, who saw fair play between industry and amusements," although he was critical of the Grand Duke's policies. Rightly so, as it turns out, because the government's censorship was ultimately the reason why he was never able to find Italians to finance or print his publications. Perhaps because the first Italian words he heard in Florence were "fiore" (flower) and "donna" (woman), Hunt "loved the name" of the city and its implied meanings: "flourishing" and "flower."

49) CARLO COLLODI   Via Rondinelli 7
(1826-1890)

From Hunt's address in Via delle Belle Donne return to Via della Spada and turn left. After a few steps turn left from Via della Spada into Via Tornabuoni, which you should follow past Via de' Giacomini, Via degli Antinori and Via del Trebbio on your left. Via Tornabuoni ends here, and if you bear to your right you will find yourself in Via Rondinelli. Halfway along this block you will find the following plaque on your left:

Qui Carlo Lorenzini dettosi Collodi	Carlo Lorenzini, who called himself Collodi,
visse gli anni della sua maturità di	lived the years of his adulthood here
uomo e di scrittore adoperandosi	as a man and writer working
con arguta vena di sensi artistici e	with acute artistic and civil sensibilities
civili a educare i ragazzi e gli uomini	to bring up the children and adults

dell'Italia unita e qui finalmente con tenera amara virile fantasia raccontò loro la immortale favola dell'uomo burattino. Il comitato per le manifestazioni del centenario di Pinocchio. 1981.

of unified Italy. Here he finally told them the immortal tale of the puppet man, with tender, bitter and virile imagination. The Committee for the Celebration of Pinocchio's Centenary. 1981.

Carlo Lorenzini spent his childhood at another address, where you can read the principal entry on him (see Walking Tour 1, Site 9).

Walking Tour 9

Lorenzo de' Medici - Michel de Montaigne - Giuseppe Mazzini - Leonardo Da Vinci - James Fenimore Cooper - Marsilio Ficino - Salomone Fiorentino

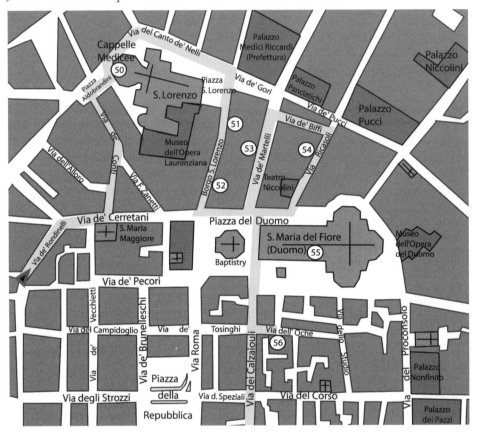

Piazza Madonna degli Aldobrandini - Borgo San Lorenzo - Via Martelli - Via Ricasoli - Duomo - Via dell'Oche

**50) LORENZO DE' MEDICI
(1449-1492)**

**Medici Chapels (Cappelle medicee),
Piazza Madonna degli Aldobrandini**

From Collodi's adult home continue forward in Via Rondinelli and turn right at the end of the block into Via de' Cerretani. Follow it almost to the next corner, where there is a traffic light and crosswalk on your left, which you should take to cross the very busy Via de' Cerretani to its opposite side. Continue in the same direction and turn left into Via de' Conti on your left. Follow Via de' Conti to a small intersection, bear left, and continue on to Piazza Aldobrandini. Bear right around the square and you will see a large round, domed structure on your right: the Medici Chapel and tombs. After visiting the crypt, ascend the stairway at its opposite end on your right. At the top of the stairs you will find the Cappella dei Principi (Princes' Chapel) on your left. If you continue to bear right along the hallway you will come to the Sagrestia Nuova (New Sacristy), Michelangelo's first work of architecture, begun in 1521 and completed by Giorgio Vasari and Bartolomeo Ammannati. Against the wall opposite the altar is a simple box-like marble sarcophagus surmounted by three statues (a Madonna and child flanked by Saints Cosma and Damiano). The remains of Lorenzo de' Medici, called "the Magnificent" and his brother Giuliano are inside it. The plaque on the floor in front of the sarcophagus states:

> *The bones of Lorenzo the Magnificent and his brother Giuliano were brought here from the old church sacristy in 1559. Florence wanted to remember this on the fifth centenary of Lorenzo's birth.*

Lorenzo's fame is rightly attributed to his ability to govern Florence, mediate relations between the Italian superpowers of his day (Milan, Venice and Naples) and thus maintain peace throughout all of Italy during the second half of the fifteenth century. For this he was known as "the fulcrum" of Italian politics. Because he had studied Greek and Latin as an adolescent and humanism with Marsilio Ficino (one of the principal Florentine Neoplatonists) he was also appropriately poised to participate in the cultural life of his city and be an important patron of the arts. His sickly father Piero di Cosimo was called "Piero the Gouty," but his mother Lucrezia Tornabuoni had enormous influence on him and arranged his marriage to the Roman noblewoman Clarice Orsini – even if he had already given his heart at a young age to Lucrezia Donati, a married woman. They were lovers: he competed in tournaments carrying a banner in her honor and wrote Petrarchan sonnets for her included in the collection of his *Rime* (*Poems*). Andrea Del Verrocchio's marble bust of the "Lady of the Primroses," now in the Bargello Museum, may be a portrait of her.

Lorenzo's youthful intensity is expressed in Verrocchio's terracotta bust (in the National Gallery, Washington D. C.), and Giorgio Vasari's portrait of him is in the Uffizi Museum. Another portrait of Lorenzo is in the Sassetti Chapel in the right arm of the transept of the church of Santa Trinita, where the lunette at the top of the center wall was painted by Domenico Ghirlandaio to represent "St. Francis receiving the rule of order from Pope Honorius," and on the extreme right are four grouped figures, of which Lorenzo is the second from the left (see the entry on Poliziano in Walking Tour 2, Site 10).

What is now called the Palazzo Medici Riccardi is the building Lorenzo and his family called home: at the intersection of Via Cavour and Via de' Gori (just around the corner from here). Lorenzo counted Florence's most prominent intellectuals and writers among his friends: the philosopher Giovanni Pico della Mirandola, Angelo Poliziano (of course), Luigi Pulci (author of the narrative comic poem *Il Morgante*, 1478-83 – a new twist on the Roland legends) and Bernardo Rucellai, Lorenzo's brother-in-law, who held literary gatherings in his gardens. Under Lorenzo's aegis, Ficino's Platonic Academy held meetings at the Medici's villa in Careggi, outside Florence. As a scholar, the "Magnificent" was a dilettante, but his writings embody many Renaissance ideals, one of which was a defense of the vernacular tongue against the greater prestige then accorded to Latin. His *Comento de' miei sonetti* (*Comment on My Sonnets*) is a collection of poems followed by commentary in the style of Dante's *Vita nuova* and *Convivio*. Remarkably, they are written examples of everyday spoken Florentine. In 1476 Lorenzo sent a compilation of Tuscan poetry to the Aragonese court in Naples at the request of Ferdinand of Aragon. Now known as the *Raccolta aragonese* (Aragonese Collection), it includes two hundred years' worth of poetry from Dante up to and including work by Lorenzo himself. It may be the first anthology of its kind. His narrative poetry before 1470 includes *L'uccellagione di starne* (The Partridge Hunt), the *Simposio* (Symposium) – also known as *I beoni* (The Heavy Drinkers) – and the hilarious rustic love poem *La Nencia da Barberino* (Nencia from Barberino), which is a country bumpkin's praise of his beloved, a barnyard wench. In the rustic but classically-inspired narrative poems *Corinto*, *Ambra* and the *Selve d'amore* (Woods of Love) we can see Angelo Poliziano's influence, while *Giacoppo* and *Ginevra* are prose tales reminiscent of Boccaccio's *Decameron*. In addition he penned a religious play in the vernacular, the *Rappresentazione di san Giovanni e Paolo* (Representation of Saints John and Paul, 1491) and his most famous work, the *Canti carnascialeschi* (Carnival Songs). One of them, the hedonistic "Triumph of Bacchus and Ariadne" echoes Horace's famous words "carpe diem" while also evoking a melancholic awareness of the brevity of youth – and life itself.

51) MICHEL DE MONTAIGNE   Borgo San Lorenzo 14
(1533-1592)

Exit the Medici Chapels and turn right into Via del Canto de' Nelli (which will be called Piazza di San Lorenzo after you pass one cross street) . It flanks the left side of the church of San Lorenzo and is usually filled with the stalls of the San Lorenzo Market. Turn right past the large white statue of Giovanni delle Bande Nere in front of the unfinished façade of the church of San Lorenzo and continue into Borgo San Lorenzo at the end of the Piazza. On the second story of the building at the address above is this plaque:

| *In questa casa dove era l'antica locanda dell'Agnolo nel 1580 e nel 1581 soggiornò Michel de Montaigne.* | In this house, where the old Inn of the Lamb once was, Michel de Montaigne stayed in 1580 and 1581. |

Montaigne arrived in Florence the same year that the first two books of his *Essais* (*Essays*) were published. Masterpieces of rationalist skeptical thought, they contain anecdotes, reminiscences, maxims and reflections on antiquity that are also deeply human. He wrote and revised them till the end of his life, and they were issued in definitive form only in 1595. He also translated the very substantial *Theologia naturalis* (Natural Theology) by the Catalan writer Ramon Sabunde. During his travels he kept a journal, the *Journal de voyage en Italie par la Suisse et l'Allemagne* (*Travel Journal*), that was only printed after his death in 1774. It differs stylistically from the *Essays* since Montaigne never meant to publish it. For this reason it includes a variety of interesting personal, cultural, social and historical observations. He even wrote short parts of his journal directly in Italian: the only foreign language in which Montaigne ever expressed himself. In his words: "[a]ssaggiamo di parlar un poco questa altra lingua" (let's try to speak this other language a little). Written Italian was highly regarded in sixteenth-century France, where it was considered a third classical literature. The reason for Montaigne's travels was to find a cure for his kidney stones, which he treated by visiting the spas, first in Germany and then in Italy. But as we read his notes on the condition of his health we gain insight into his mind's lively curiosity and his interest in the mores of a foreign culture (*i.e.* "This morning at daybreak I had the colic in my right side. It afflicted me for about three hours. Then I ate my first melon. Cucumbers and almonds are eaten in Florence from the beginning of June.") Montaigne was also in Florence on June 24 for the Feast of Saint John, Florence's patron saint. Ariosto before him witnessed these festivities in 1532 and Leopardi was to remark on them later in 1827. Literary tourism in Italy thus attests to the strength of this holiday in Tuscany's capital city. The contemporary visitor to Florence may be able to sympathize with Montaigne's thoughts too, as when he complained about the weather: "The heat did not seem to me more violent than in France. However, to escape it in these hotel rooms, I was forced to sleep at night on the dining room table, putting mattresses and sheets on it; not having found here any comfortable lodging to rent, for this city is not a good one for strangers; also to escape the bugs, with which the beds are most thickly infested." (June 21-August 13, 1581) While here, Montaigne also met important local people, such as a member of the Piccolomini family, and was interested enough in Florentine prostitutes to take a look at several of the city's brothels: "…I went alone for fun to see the women who let themselves be seen by anyone who wants. I saw the most famous: nothing exceptional." Montaigne, a judge who was born into a wealthy commercial family in Bordeaux that had recently acquired a noble title, received an extremely liberal education – and learned as a child to speak Latin as a living language.

52) GIUSEPPE MAZZINI   **Borgo San Lorenzo 4**
   (1805-1872)

From Montaigne's hotel continue walking down Borgo San Lorenzo in the same direction till you reach the address above on your left. The plaque there above the entrance door reads:

In questa casa dove abitò il popolano	In this house where the working man
Giuseppe Dolfi convennero patrioti	Giuseppe Dolfi lived, generous patriots
generosi da ogni parte del mondo	from every corner of the civilized world
civile e Giuseppe Mazzini e Giuseppe	gathered. Both Giuseppe Mazzini
Garibaldi vi ebbero fida ospitalità	and Giuseppe Garibaldi found
in vario tempo 1860-1866-1867	sanctuary here in 1860, 1866 and 1867
a promuovere la feconda armonia	while promoting fruitful cooperation
del pensiero e dell'azione	between thought and action.

Above this plaque to the right is another one, surmounted by a bronze bust of Dolfi:

Qui abitò Giuseppe Dolfi e vi morì	Here Giuseppe Dolfi lived and died on
il di 26 luglio 1869 Per onorare	July 26, 1869. To honor the
la memoria del virtuoso popolano	memory of this virtuous working man,
che la modesta vita dedicò alla	who with his modest life
causa della libertà la fratellanza	dedicated the brotherhood of artisans
artigiana il municipio di Firenze	to the cause of liberty. Florence's Town Hall
annuente questa lapide	approvingly placed this plaque here on
poneva il di 3 luglio 1870.	July 3, 1870

Giuseppe Dolfi (1818-1865) was a Florentine baker active in nineteenth-century revolutionary events. As political head of the Florentine working class, he was instrumental in liberating Florence from the grasp of Grand Duke Leopold II of Hapsburg Lorraine by helping to find common political ground for the working class, the aristocracy, the bourgeoisie and the Grand Duke's soldiers. As the first plaque above implies, it was his doing if Garibaldi and Mazzini both found safe harbour here as well (for the principal entry on Garibaldi see Walking Tour 1, Site 4).

The phrase "thought and action," together with "Dio e popolo" (God and the common people) were slogans coined by the Genoese Giuseppe Mazzini, one of the most original political theorists of the nineteenth-century movement for Italian independence and liberation. "Thought" refers to Mazzini's concept of Christian devotion to the Italian fatherland and his belief in bettering the physical conditions of life for the Italian working class. "Action" indicates that for Mazzini the true patriot had to be ready to sacrifice even his life in order to create a national republic. Mazzini also founded the first organization for workers in Italy, the "Unione degli operai italiani" (Union of Italian Workers), the goals of which foreshadowed the birth of socialism later. His political ideas are set forth primarily in *Fede e avvenire* (Faith and the Future), first published in French in 1835 and *I doveri dell'uomo* (The Duties of Man, 1861). He is best known for founding the first nation-wide political party, *La giovine Italia* (Young Italy), that had as its motto: "Independent Italy: A Unified Republic." Unfortunately this had to remain a clandestine organization in order to avoid persecution from the Austrian authorities. Mazzini's literary ideas largely reflect his political ones. In his opinion writers needed to educate their readers and instruct them morally since he considered literature to have a primarily ethical function. Among Italian writers he admired Dante most of all as a prophet of moral rectitude and Ugo Foscolo because his novel can be considered a fusion of political action and personal ideals. *Del dramma storico* (On Historical Drama, 1830) explains what characteristics Mazzini valued most in historical plays. He tought they needed to present a philosophical analysis of history and be faithful to the spirit of the past while not necessarily referring to actual events. In nineteenth-century Italy the most successful historical dramas were set to music and became opera. Mazzini addressed this question in *Filosofia della musica* (The Philosophy of Music, 1836), in which he wrote that it was composers' duty to inspire civic ideals for the development and improvement of civilization itself. In *Ai poeti del secolo diciannovesimo* (To the Poets of the Nineteenth Century, 1832) Mazzini criticized those who complained that the poetic ideals of prior times were either no longer valid or no longer respected. He argued instead that each generation needed poetry in which its own history and institutions are reflected. Other works are *Byron e Goethe* (1840) and *Genio e tendenze di Thomas Carlyle* (Thomas Carlyle's Genius and Tendencies, 1843).

Mazzini came to Florence in 1849 when a popular insurrection dethroned the Tuscan Grand Duke. He spoke in front of enthusiastic crowds here and was cautiously welcomed by his former comrade Francesco Guerrazzi, who favored keeping Tuscany independent. This event was also rewarding for him in a personal way because he was able to see Giuditta Sidoli again, a titled Lombard woman to whom he had been engaged during his exile in Marseille and by whom he fathered a child who died in infancy. (Not surprisingly, Mazzini's published correspondence includes a number of letters to her that reveal not only his passion for patriotic ideals but his love for a woman). Later, after Garibaldi's invasion of Sicily in 1861, Mazzini came to Florence again to prepare an attack against papal Umbria to coincide with Garibaldi's subsequent occupation of Naples.

53) LEONARDO DA VINCI **Via Martelli 7**
   (1452 -1519)

From Giuseppe Dolfi's home continue forward in Borgo San Lorenzo in the same direction until you reach the Piazza del Duomo. Turn left at the corner and you will see the Baptistry and the Cathedral in front of you on your right. At the next corner cross the street first and then turn left into Via Martelli. Just before your reach the next cross street on your right, Via dei Biffi, you will see the address above across the street on your left. The plaque there is high up between two second-story windows to the right of the entrance door at number 7. For this reason you will only be able to read the plaque if you view it from the opposite side of the street.

In queste che furono case dei Martelli Leonardo Da Vinci coabitò nel MDVIII con Giovanfrancesco Rustici scultore e qui dava a lui consiglio e norma pel gruppo in bronzo il Battista il Fariseo il Levita che sopr'una delle porte del nostro bel San Giovanni è fiorentina memoria consacrata dal pensiero e dalla mano dell'artefice universale. Il maggio MCMXIX quarto centenario della morte	In these houses, formerly belonging to the Martelli family, Leonardo Da Vinci lived with the sculptor Giovan Francesco Rustici in 1508. He offered him both advice and instruction for his bronze figures "John the Baptist, the Pharisee and the Levite," above one of the doors of our Saint John, which has been immortalized in the memory of the Florentine people by the mind and hand of the Creator of the Universe. May 1919 on the fourth centenary of his death.

Born the illegittimate son of a notary in Anchiano (near Vinci) in the Province of Florence, Leonardo took an interest in painting as a boy and was sent to Florence to study it in Andrea Del Verrocchio's workshop. Being inquisitive he also did what he could to learn about music, mathematics and physical and natural sciences. For a while he enjoyed Lorenzo de' Medici's patronage in Florence, but worked from 1483 to 1499 for the Duke of Milan, Ludovico Sforza, who hired him for his mechanical and engineering expertise. Leonardo designed the locks for Milan's extensive system of canals and painted the fresco of Christ's "Last Supper" in the refectory of the church of Santa Maria delle Grazie. When Ludovico was overthrown, Leonardo sought employment elsewhere: in Venice, Mantua, Florence (again), in the territory of Romagna (as Chief Engineer for Cesare Borgia), Milan (but this time in the service of Louis XII of France), and in Rome, from 1513 to 1516. From 1517 to the end of his life Leonardo was employed by Francis I of France, who appointed him his highest-ranking royal painter, architect and engineer. He died in the castle at Cloux, the residence assigned to him by the king.

As a writer Leonardo admitted being uncultivated (in his words "omo sanza lettere"), but left almost 5,000 pages of notes. Since he wrote entirely in what was then largely an unwritten idiom, these notes are an important step in the spread of Italian as a written language and also distinctly expressive in rendering the details of minute scientific observation. At his death, the manuscripts were saved by his ex-student Francesco Melzi. They are written in specular script from right to left, and many contain marvelous illustrations. The best-known is the Atlantic

Codex, now in the Ambrosian Library in Milan, which contains 1,119 pages on mathematics, geometry, astronomy, zoology and military arts. In the same city the Sforza Castle holds the 55-page Trivulziano Codex on military and religious architecture (and includes literary exercises). The seventeen-page Codex on Bird Flight is in the National Library in Turin. In Paris the Institut de France has the two Ashburnham codices: Codex A, (on painting) and Codex B (on architecture) – as well as Codices C and M (964 pages) on military arts, optics, geometry, bird flight and hydraulics. The Arundel Codex (283 pages) contains studies on physics, mechanics, optics, Euclidean geometry, weight and architecture and is in the British Museum in London. In addition, the three Forster Codices (on geometry, weight and hydraulic devices) are in the Victoria and Albert Museuem. Six hundred drawings of anatomical parts, horses, geographic sites, and caricatures are kept in the Royal Library at Windsor. In 1994 Bill Gates purchased the thirty-six-page Leicester Codex on hydrodynamics, astronomy and geology, which is now in Seattle. In 1966 two codices were discovered in the National Library in Madrid: the first (on mechanics) is 192 pages long, and the second (on geometry) contains 157 pages. After Leonardo's death many short notations, known as "Thoughts," were organized into categories such as *Allegories, Fables, Witticisms, Thoughts on Nature* and *Thoughts on Art*. Based on the description of plants, animals, objects and other natural phenomena, the *Fables* are interesting because they combine aspects of scientific prose with moral observations. The town of Vinci, west of Florence, maintains a library and museum containing models of Leonardo's inventions, including a bicycle, a self-propelled wagon and a helicopter. Three kilometers away, in Anchiano, you can also visit his boyhood home. Da Vinci never married, but cohabitated with his student Giacomo Caprotti (called "il Saladino") for twenty-six years. Among his maxims are the following:

Men wrongly complain of time's passing when they say that it goes by too quickly – not noticing that it's neither slow nor fast; but with the good memory that nature has given us we can bring things back to the present that happened in the past.

Acquire in your youth all that you need to relieve your old age. If you think that wisdom is the food of maturity, try your best during your youth to assure that your golden years lack nothing to eat.

Just as a day well spent leads to tranquil slumber, a life well lived leads to a peaceful death.

54) JAMES FENIMORE COOPER   **Via Ricasoli 9**
(1789-1851)

From Da Vinci's lodgings in Via Martelli turn right into Via de' Biffi on your right. Turn right again at the next corner into Via Ricasoli. You will find the address above on your right.

Cooper stayed here in 1828 with his wife Susan De Lancey after staying at the English York Hotel in Via de' Cerretani. They arrived here from England, passing through Belgium, Holland, Germany and Switzerland during a trip abroad that lasted from 1826 to 1833. He left impressions of his travels in *Gleanings in Europe: Italy, By an American* (1838), which is a compendium of letter-like entries. (He also penned two other eponymous volumes that treat England and France, both published in 1837). Arriving from the north, he observed that "the city of Florence appeared, seated on a plain, at the foot of hills, with the dome of its cathedral starting out of the field of roofs, like a balloon about to ascend." Besides attributing a sense of lightness to the cathedral's massive shape, this comment reveals Cooper's interest in technology and the hot-air balloon, invented by the French Mongolfier brothers in 1783. During Cooper's lifetime Italy was fertile ground for revolution, and this city (still under Austrian control) was a hotbed of conspiracy, as were most major Italian cities. Nonetheless, Cooper found Florence to be amazingly tolerant. He wrote that "the natives of half the civilized countries of the world appear to have met on neutral ground in this little capital, the government having the liberality to tolerate even men or political opinions that are elsewhere proscribed ... This is the age of cosmopolitism, real or pretended; and Florence, just at this moment, is an epitome both of its spirit and of its representatives." He noticed that "the policy of the Tuscan government encourage[d] diplomatic appointments, and [he believed that] all the great courts of Europe ha[d] ministers here." Among them were "French, Russians, English, Austrians, and Prussians." His landlord at this address was the young Baron Bettino Ricasoli, who due to his liberal and moderate ideas would later become Tuscan Minister of the Interior in 1859 (after Grand Duke Leopold II was toppled) and then Prime Minister of Italy from 1861 to 1862 and from 1866 to 1867. During Cooper's stay, however, the Grand Duke, then about thirty years old, was still very much in power, and Cooper, being a notable foreigner, was presented to him at court where they conversed for five minutes in French. Being observant, Cooper took notes about all sorts of things in Florence. One of these was the fact that he saw people come every day around eleven a.m. and knock on a shuttered opening on one side of the gated entrance to Palazzo Ricasoli. A family servant would then retrieve an empty flask from each customer and replace it with a full bottle of wine for a cost of ten cents. Cooper concluded: "In this manner, I understand, most of the great families of Florence now dispose of the products of their vines! It would be curious to learn if the Medici carried on this trade." In short, Cooper thought very highly of Italy and couldn't help comparing Florence to American cities, which he felt had "a certain absence of taste, a want of leisure and of tone; a substitution of bustle for elegance, care for enjoyment, and show for refinement." These words are remarkable if we compare them to the fact that Cooper's novels are remembered for their protagonists' escape from civil society in order to live in contact with nature: *The Pioneers* (1823), *The Last of the Mohicans*

(1826), *The Prairie* (1827), *The Pathfinder* (1840) and *The Deerslayer* (1841). These novels, known collectively as *The Leather-Stocking Tales*, differ from earlier maritime fiction admired by Herman Melville and Joseph Conrad such as *The Pilot* (1823), *The Red Rover* (1828) and *The Sea Lions* (1849) – as well as from Cooper's historical novels: *Satanstoe* (1845), *The Chainbearer* (1845) and *The Redskins* (1846). After being expelled from Yale and having spent time as a sailor, Cooper began to write at the age of thirty. His first novel, *Precaution* (1820) was somewhat tentative, but he achieved success with his second, *The Spy* (1821).

55) MARSILIO FICINO   Duomo (Cathedral of Santa Maria del Fiore)
(1433-1499)

From Cooper's address in Via Ricasoli continue straight forward into Piazza del Duomo and, turning right, enter the cathedral from the front. Walk along the right-hand nave and in the fourth bay on your right you will find a white-marble bust of Marsilio Ficino set in an alcove above a large plaque. The bust was sculpted by Andrea Ferrucci in 1521. On the plaque, in Latin, are the following words:

En hospes hic est Marsilius sophiae pater platonicum qui dogma culpa temporum situ obrutum illustrans et atticum decus servans latio dedit fores primus sacras divinae aperiens mentis actus numine vixit beatus ante cosmi munere lauriq medicis nunc revixit publico _ S _ P _ Q FAN. M. D. XXI.

This tomb hosts Marsilio, father of philosophy, who, by illustrating Plato's dogma wrongly forgotten by time, and to conserve the decorum of the Greeks, delivered it to Rome [*i.e.* by translating it in Latin]. Inspired by God, he was the first to open the sacred doors of divine intelligence. Formerly he lived happily thanks to the protection of Cosimo and Lorenzo de' Medici, though now he has been resurrected to new life due to support of the entire city. The Senate and the people of Florence. 1521.

Ficino, the philosopher and humanist, studied in Pisa and Florence and completed an enormous amount of original research under the patronage of Cosimo de' Medici, who gave him a villa at Careggi, at that time just outside Florence. Rereading Plato, Ficino wanted to reconcile the Greek philosopher's thought with Christianity: an approach that led to what would later be called Neoplatonism. Under Cosimo's aegis Ficino founded the Neoplatonic Academy in 1459, which met at Careggi. Among its members were Giovanni Pico della Mirandola, Angelo Poliziano, Leon Battista Alberti, Coluccio Salutati, Cristoforo Landino and Giovanni Argyropoulos. After Cosimo's death the Academy reached its peak under Lorenzo the Magnificent, when Niccolò Machiavelli was a member. Besides translating all of Plato's works into Latin, Ficino also collected and translated from Greek works by Plotinus, Porphyrius, Archimedes, Hypocrates and Hermes Trismegistus. Like nearly all the fifteenth-century humanists he wrote his own works in Latin, which were meant to transcend the limits of medieval scholasticism as based on Aristotelian models. Ficino's works include the treatises *De voluptate* (On Sensual Pleasure, 1457), *De Christiana religione* (On Christian Religion, 1474), *Theologia Platonica de immortalitate animorum* (*Platonic Theology*, 1482) and *De Triplici Vita* (*Three Books On Life*, 1489). These treatises did not interpret Plato's works as models to be imitated blindly, but rather as a theoretical corpus one could use to arrive at a less austere form of Christianity: a form of religion that would recognize the potential of human initiative and creativity. In this context Ficino's ideas had enormous influence on subsequent Renaissance writers, on treatises concerned with Platonic love and on new ideas about love poetry. Ficino wrote: "I believe that human love is not only blameless, but an almost necessary thing: …a true source of refinement and greatness of spirit. Above all it is the reason [we are] mov[ed] to [undertake] worthy and excellent deeds." A priest, Ficino also inherited certain misogynistic ideas common in the Church at that time, which unfortunately cast a certain shadow on his otherwise innovative thought. There is a portrait of Ficino by Domenico Ghirlandaio on the right wall of the apse in the church of Santa Maria Novella. It is in the bottom-most scene on your right in the fresco showing the angel who appeared before Saint Zachary. The first figure in the lower left-hand corner is Marsilio Ficino.

56) SALOMONE FIORENTINO   Via dell'Oche 19
(1743-1815)

As you exit the Duomo turn left into Via dei Calzaiuoli and then left at the first cross street into Via dell'Oche. Just past the corner you will see the following plaque on your right:

Salomone Fiorentino, distinto poeta,	Salomone Fiorentino, distinguished poet,
probo cittadino, abitò molti anni	upright citizen, lived many years
in questa casa e vi cessò di vivere	in this house and died here on
il dì IV febbrajo MDCCCXV.	February 4, 1815.

Salomone ("Solomon") Fiorentino, a merchant, was the first Jew recognized as an Italian writer, although there were in fact others before him. Both of his names clearly identify him as Jewish and his family name in particular was long associated with Jewish communities in both Livorno (Leghorn) and Arezzo. He was born in the town of Montesansavino in the Province of Arezzo where a Jewish population existed since the Middle Ages. Indeed, after 1593 Jews enjoyed more civil rights in Livorno, where the Medici had built a port. In that year the Granduke Ferdinando de' Medici liberalized relations between Jews and Gentiles in a law known as "la livornina," which exempted Jews in Livorno from living in a ghetto as they had to in Florence. When the Neapolitan Republic was formed in 1799 the working class in Naples was organized by the clergy into an "Army of Holy Faith" in opposition to the Republic. Salomone found himself the object of this kind of clerical persecution by the so-called "sanfedisti" even in Tuscany, because it also existed as a political party, but he was fortunate enough to obtain the protection of the Tuscan Granduke Pietro Leopoldo, who then awarded him a Chair of Literature at the Jewish University in Livorno. Being a Tuscan poet, he wrote in the vernacular about public life (civic issues) and private sentiments (love poetry), and his work reflects a transitional period in Italian letters between the end of the Enlightenment and the beginning of the Romantic period. The poet Giovanni Fantoni, one of his contemporaries, called him: "His first wife's mournful minstrel / Pride of the scattered children of Israel." Among his works are narrative poems such as *La notte d'Etruria* (The Night of Etruria) – celebrating Pietro Leopoldo's reforms – and *La spiritualità e l'immortalità dell'anima* (The Spirituality and the Immortality of the Soul), which attempts to counter forms of rationalist thought in Enlightenment philosophy. He wrote a number of sonnets known for their vivid visual descriptions of the sort developed earlier by Carlo Innocenzo Frugoni, such as the poem *Lodi di Galileo Galilei* (In Praise of Galileo Galilei) in blank verse and his *Elegie* (Elegies), considered to be his best work. One of these, entitled *Per il suicidio di Neera* (For Neera's Suicide) relates the story of a young woman who killed herself after she was seduced. Three other elegies lament his wife's death and some of them commemorate events in friends' lives, such as weddings. These are imitative literary exercises in the style of Dante and Petrarch. As a whole, his works are also permeated by undeniable references to Judaism and moral concerns. In 1802 he published *Daily Prayers for the Use of Spanish and Portuguese Jews*, which he translated from Hebrew because so many Italian Jews had little or no knowledge of that language. Although there is no written proof, many scholars believe that Salomone was a friend of Vittorio Alfieri and remained in contact with other important writers of his time such as Melchiorre Cesarotti, Pietro Metastasio and Vincenzo Monti.

Walking Tour 10

Dino Compagni - Vasco Pratolini - Leonardo Da Vinci - Girolamo Savonarola - Benvenuto Cellini - Giorgio Vasari - Francesco Petrarca

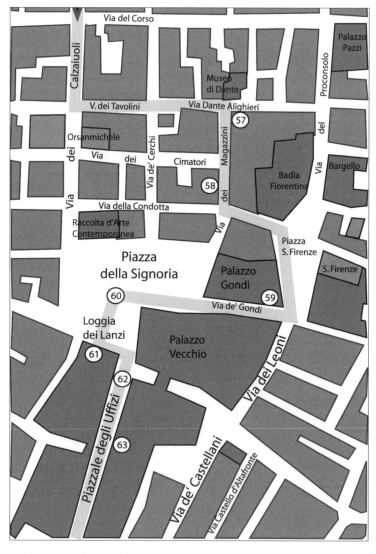

Piazza San Martino - Via dei Magazzini - Via de' Gondi - Piazza della Signoria - Piazzale degli Uffizi

57) DINO COMPAGNI   **Piazza San Martino 1**
    (1255-1324)

Turn left into Via dei Calzaiuoli and follow it past Via del Corso on your left. Turn left at the next corner into Via dei Tavolini. Follow this past Via de' Cerchi and Piazza de' Cimatori to Via Dante Alighieri. At the next corner turn right into Via dei Magazzini. You will find the Torre della Castagna (Chestnut Tower) facing you at this intersection on the opposite side of the square. The plaque there states:

... E chiamaronsi Priori dell'Arti:	... And they were called Guild Priors:
E stettono rinchiusi nella torre	and they stayed shut up in the Tower of the
della Castagna appresso alla	Chestnut near the Church of the Badia, so
Badia, acciò non temessono le	that they wouldn't fear the threats of the
minacce de' potenti ...	powerful ...
Dino Compagni *Cronica* 1. IV	Dino Compagni *Chronicle*, Book I, IV

If you walk around the tower to its left side you can read these words on another plaque:

Questa Torre della Castagna	This Tower of the Chestnut
unica resta delle sedi	is all that remains of the many places
onde i Priori delle Arti	from which the Guild Priors
ressero Firenze prima che la forza	governed Florence before the strength
e la gloria del fiorente comune	and glory of this flourishing city
facesse sorgere	led it to build the Palazzo Vecchio
il Palazzo della Signoria	(Old Palace).

For the principal entry on Compagni see Walking Tour 6, Site 33. The Chestnut Tower was the first public structure built in Florence for the elected Magistrates (Priors) who governed the city's guilds after 1282. These organizations formed the economic and political base that allowed the city to largely free itself from the hegemony of both the Papacy and the Holy Roman Emperor. Because of the guilds Florence became wealthy, powerful, and one of the first self-governing city states in central Italy. The seven most important were: the Wool Workers' Guild, the Wool Merchants' Guild, the Silk Workers' Guild, the Money Changers' Guild, the Judges' and Notaries' Guild, the Doctors' and Pharmacists' Guild, and the Fur Workers' Guild. After these, there were other minor ones: the Butchers' Guild, the Cobblers' Guild, the Master Stone Masons' Guild, the Blacksmiths' Guild, and the Used Goods Dealers' Guild. The city's own monetary unit, the gold Florin, gained great importance at the same time because it was used as a means of exchange by the largest Florentine banks and commercial enterprises that established branch offices in France, Belgium, Holland, England and in the Middle East. Meanwhile, due to Dante and the poets of the Dolce Stil Novo, the Florentine dialect was also being used more and more frequently as the most important written lingua franca after Latin. Compagni's style, while often full of harsh criticism, can also well up with his affection for Florence as if it, and not Rome, were *caput mundi*. As he himself wrote: "The above-mentioned city of Florence is well populated and productive due to its healthy air; the citizens are well behaved, and the women are beautiful and well dressed; its buildings are very handsome and full of every kind of business you could need – more than the other cities in Italy. For these reasons many come from far away to see it, not because they have to, but because of the quality of its tradesmen and the city's adornments and beauty."

58) VASCO PRATOLINI   Via dei Magazzini 1
(1913-1991)

From the Chestnut Tower continue to your right in Via dei Magazzini. Just past Via dei Cimatori you will see the following plaque on your right:

In questa casa dell'antico centro nacque il 19 ottobre 1913 Vasco Pratolini che a narrare una storia italiana trasse perenne alimento dall'amore per la sua Firenze. Il Comune di Firenze nel quinto anniversario della morte. *12 gennaio 1996.*	Vasco Pratolini, who drew on his perennial love for Florence in order to recount an Italian story, was born in this house of Florence's ancient historic center on October 19, 1913. The City of Florence on the fifth anniversary of his death. January 12, 1996.

Pratolini is identified with Florence to the same extent that Dante is. His works evoke the streets, houses and neighborhoods of working- and middle-class Florentines in tangible, identifiable ways that are evidence of a real sense of attachment to this city. Not having a university degree Pratolini was essentially self-taught, although he was a methodical reader of Italian and German philosophy as well as of medieval Italian history (Compagni) and folktales (Boccaccio and Sacchetti). He took night classes in French and occasionally audited lectures at the university. As a young man he worked as an errand boy, hotel porter and printer but eventually taught Art History at Florence's Academy of Fine Arts. Through his friendship with the painter Ottone Rosai, Pratolini also knew some of the most important Florentine writers of his generation, such as Romano Bilenchi, Dino Garrone and Aldo Palazzeschi. After contracting tuberculosis in the 1930's Pratolini spent two long periods of time in sanatoriums but managed to write for the journal *Il Bargello* and found another (*Campo di Marte*) together with the poet Alfonso Gatto. He moved to Rome in 1939 to work for the Ministry of Education, continued to write for Roman magazines, and was head of the Resistance during W.W. II for a large portion of Rome. Pratolini's novels are important for their "choral" view of a social group. Among them are: *Via dei Magazzini*, (1941 – the address of this site), *Le amiche* (The Girlfriends, 1943), *Cronaca familiare* (*Family Chronicle* or *Two Brothers*, 1947), *Il Quartiere* (*The Naked Streets*, 1943), *Cronache di povere amanti* (*A Tale of Poor Lovers*, 1947) and *Le ragazze di San Frediano* (The Girls of San Frediano, 1949). Three subsequent novels – *Metello* (*Metello: A Novel*, 1955), *Lo scialo* (The Waste, 1960) and *Allegoria e derisione* (Allegory and Derision, 1966) – form a trilogy in which Florentine characters and places stand in for national political and social changes. Pratolini's best work is identified with Neorealist writers, who employed a simple, populist style and lexicon accessible to anyone. With these means they hoped to inspire a national social consciousness in their readers. Bilenchi, one of Neorealism's theorists, believed in the use of a documentary-like style ("cronaca") to represent realistic Italian environments that were faithful to actual customs and spoken language. Pratolini's works succeed in reaching this goal and are unique in this sense because the peasants and working class characters in the works of other Neorealists are generally not associated with Florence. Still, after W.W. II Florence began to lose its national prominence as a cultural stage, giving way to Rome as the site of national identity, to Turin and Milan as industrial centers, and to Naples, which continued to be the cultural capital of the South. Several of Pratolini's novels were also made into films, and he himself co-authored screenplays for other ones: Rossellini's *Paisà*, Visconti's *Rocco and His Brothers*, Nanni Loy's *Le quattro giornate di Napoli* (The Four Days of Naples) and Mauro Bolognini's *La viaccia* (*The Love Makers*). Pratolini was also a poet, and his poetry is collected in *Il Mannello di Natascia* (Natasha's Spool, 1985). The first lines of the following poem nicely sum up Pratolini's literary, intellectual, political and human development, linking it to his love for Florence and nostalgia for his youth:

The City Formed My First Thirty Years

The city formed my first thirty years / my voice in vernacular forecasts my future. / And its river is my blood / galloping under its bridges towards its outlet.

At night the cafes were open / and one cigarette after another / a cappuccino a glass of wine, / the luckiest paid or a prostitute.

At the break of dawn you could hold / the sky in your hand. On the threshold of the / Cathedral from the first light of day / there was an array of flowers.

We used to like Bach as much as pop songs. / We would fall asleep when mothers went out to do the shopping.

Even Petrarch was a song / even the New Life and Dora Markus and the Dancer / Who captured Esenin, / the nymphs of the Après-Midi / the expulsion in the Carmine. / The Bandolero who offered his rose . . . .

59) LEONARDO DA VINCI   **Via de' Gondi 2**
                                                    (1452 -1519)

From Pratolini's childhood home continue along Via dei Magazzini in the same direction and then turn left into Via della Condotta. Pass Vicolo dei Gondi on your right and you will find yourself in Piazza San Firenze, where you should turn right. Skirt the piazza along its right side and turn right at the next corner into Via de' Gondi. Enter through the arched doorway at the address above. The words below appear above the tall arched entry at the end of the passageway that leads from the street to the building's internal courtyard:

Leonardo Da Vinci visse la beneaugurata giovinezza in una casa dell'arte dei mercatanti che da Giuliano Gondi fu compra e disfatta nel murare questo palagio al quale dandosi perfezione nel MDCCCLXXIV il Comune e il Signore concordi vollero che la memoria di tanto nome al nobile e vago edificio accrescesse decoro.	Leonardo Da Vinci lived his auspicious youth in a building belonging to the Merchants' Guild that Giuliano Gondi bought and demolished in order to construct this palace, which was remodeled in 1874, when the City of Florence and God agreed that the memory of such a great name should augment the dignity of this noble and beautiful building.

For the principal entry on Da Vinci see Walking Tour 9, Site 53.

60) GIROLAMO SAVONAROLA   **Piazza della Signoria**
    (1452-1498)

Follow Via de' Gondi forward into Piazza della Signoria. As you enter it the imposing Palazzo Vecchio with its crenellations and tower will be on your left. Walk forward toward the large white statue of Neptune just to the right of the Palazzo Vecchio. Florentines have always called it "il Biancone," or "the big white statue." About five yards beyond it you will find a round red-granite plaque imbedded in the piazza's pavement:

Qui dove con i suoi confratelli Fra Domenico Buonvicini e Fra Silvestro Maruffi il XXIII maggio del MCCCCXCVIII per iniqua sentenza fu impiccato ed arso Fra Girolamo Savonarola. Dopo quattro secoli fu collocata questa memoria.	On this very spot with his brothers Friar Domenico Buonvicini and Friar Silvestro Maruffi on May 23, 1498 Friar Girolamo Savonarola was hanged and burned after being unjustly sentenced. This inscription was set here four centuries later.

Savonarola rose to political power in Florence at the end of the fifteenth century and wanted to establish an austere religious republic at the expense of the Medici. He was eventually excommunicated by Pope Alexander VI, hung and then burned at the stake in Piazza della Signoria.

Girolamo was born in Ferrara and studied medicine before turning to theology. The fact that he suffered a devastating disappointment in his youth may have caused him to choose a religious vocation, since his deep love for Laudomia Strozzi was thwarted by her titled family. Perhaps he was also influenced by his grandfather Michele, doctor to the Duke Niccolò III d'Este, who advised him to stay away from public life at Italian courts if he wanted to be religious. Joining the Domenican order in Bologna in 1476, he moved to the convent of San Marco in Florence in 1482. By the time he was convent prior in 1491 his sermons on the Books of Genesis and Revelation were famous even outside of Tuscany. Savonarola had plainly internalized the art of religious oratory that the Domenicans instilled in its adherents and preached that a whole series of apocalyptic disasters were to about to rain down on Florence and all of Italy as punishment for their sins. His public burnings of "vanities" and sermons in the Florence cathedral (Santa Maria del Fiore) gained him enormous favor with the populace, but as his power continued to grow he also began to criticize the Medici. His followers held real political power and were known as "piagnoni" or whiners. The painter Sandro Botticelli is the most famous of these, who became an adherent at the age of 60 and radically changed his style as a consequence. Lorenzo de' Medici managed to keep the "piagnoni" in check until his death in 1492. For his part, Savonarola looked to the people of Florence to establish a republic based on a renewal of Christian values in opposition to the Medici's humanistic culture and explained his political platform in his *Trattato circa il reggimento e governo della città di Firenze* (Treatise on the Control and Organization of the City of Florence, 1498).

Savonarola's best works are his sermons. Published postumously as *Prediche*, they give a good idea of the fire and brimstone that was a staple of his dramatic and prophetic oratory. His religious philosophy is espoused in his *Compendio delle rivelazioni* (Compendium of Revelations, 1495), the *Epistola della sana e spirituale lezione* (Epistle of Sound Spiritual Teaching, 1497) and the *Trionfo della Croce* (Triumph of the Cross, of uncertain date). Savonarola also left at least 14 individual poems as well as formal religious compositions in verse known as "laude."

After Lorenzo de' Medici's death in 1492, Florence went through a profound political crisis aggravated by famine. Medici rule was seriously destabilized by the arrival of Charles VIII of France, who attempted to occupy the Italian peninsula as far south as Naples. Savonarola supported Charles VIII, but had antagonized Pope Alexander VI by openly criticizing him. The friar's support was then further weakened in general when the Florentine bourgeoisie recoiled from him when it became clear that a papal threat of excommunication and interdiction would have legally permitted debtors to default on payment to Florentine banks. In 1497 Savonarola was excommunicated, but was eager to prove that God was on his side by submitting to public torture by fire. When he was kept from doing so for legal reasons, the superstitious masses still on his side withdrew from him too and he was burned at the stake here with the two other Domenicans friars mentioned above.

61) BENVENUTO CELLINI (1500-1570)

Loggia dei Lanzi
Piazza della Signoria

After reading the plaque indicating the spot of Savonarola's execution turn to your right so that you are facing the large Loggia dei Lanzi with its three large arches. In the center of the left-hand arch is the bronze statue of Perseus that is Cellini's masterpiece (the principal entry on Cellini is in Walking Tour 2, Site 11).

An important figure in Greek mythology, Perseus was the son of Zeus and the Princess of Argo, Danae. He is remembered for having liberated and married Andromeda the Princess of Ethiopia from the rock to which she had been chained by the God of the Sea, Poseidon. This divinity took revenge on Andromeda after her father had bragged that she was more beautiful than the Nereids, female sea nymphs. Perseus freed Andromeda by wresting her from the clutches of the giant Atlas, who kept her enslaved. To do so he decapitated the monster Medusa, who had snakes for hair and turned to stone anyone who gazed upon her. This statue recreates the moment when Perseus held Medusa's head aloft so that Atlas would look at it and remain petrified. Perseus slew Medusa with his sword while watching her reflection in his highly polished shield. Cellini's statue shows the hero with a downcast gaze for this reason. It was commissioned by Cosimo I de' Medici Grand Duke of Florence in 1545 to celebrate the consolidation of the Medici's control of Florence. After the Sack of Rome in 1527 by Spanish forces of the Imperial Army, the Florentines banished the Medici, who then returned to power in 1531. Perseus represents the authority of Cosimo I and his ability to oppose Florence's enemies. This hero also symbolizes the force of justice and courage in opposition to injustice and evil, which petrify freedom. For all of these reasons this statue sits in Florence's most important civic space close to Michelangelo's David, which also represents Florentine liberty and strength. Cellini's *Vita*, or autobiography, describes the making of this statue in great detail. His narration makes it clear that the creation of Perseus was an extremely laborious and difficult process that tried him physically, emotionally and artistically. In the middle of casting what Cellini repeatedly calls "my Perseus," the passionate sculptor ran into obstacles that almost kept him from completing his task. His workshop caught on fire and he came down with a sudden high fever that made him delirious. The fact that he persevered in the face of these odds places Cellini in the guise of Machiavelli's "virtuous" man, who was capable of exploiting all of his talents and wits to achieve an end in spite of obvious difficulties, identified by Machiavelli with Fortune. Read the following passage from the *Vita* as you study the male hero's beauty and the beheaded monster's female sensuality:

I promised myself, with assurance, that once I had completed the work on the Perseus I had already begun, all my tribulations would be transformed into the highest satisfaction and glorious prosperity. In this way, having regained my vigour, with all my pow-

ers – both of my body and my purse, though little money remained to me – I began to search for several loads of pine-wood, which I procured from the Serristori pine forest near Monte Lupo; and while I waited for the wood I clad my Perseus in those clays that I had prepared several months before, so that they might be properly seasoned. After I had made this clay tunic – they call it a tunic in our craft – and had properly strengthened and enclosed it very carefully with iron supports, with a slow fire I began to draw out the wax, which came out through the many air-vents that I had made: for the more one makes, the better the moulds will fill … I then confidently told them [i.e. helpers] to light the furnace. By putting in that pine-wood, which exudes an oily resin that the pine tree produces, and having built my little furnace so well, it worked so perfectly that I was obliged to check it, now on one side and now on the other, with so much exertion that it was unbearable; and yet I forced myself to do it. And to add to my problems the workshop caught fire, and we were afraid that the roof would collapse upon us; on the other side of the workshop, toward the orchard, the heavens were driving so much rain and wind against me that it cooled off the furnace. And so, fighting against these perverse occurrences for several hours, I made an effort even greater than my robust constitution could withstand, so that I was seized by a sudden attack of fever, the worst that could ever be imagined, and for this reason I was forced to go and throw myself on the bed … As I was suffering these boundless tribulations, I saw a certain man entering my room; his body seemed to be as twisted as a capital S; and he began to speak in a particular tone of sorrow or affliction, like the men who give comfort to those who are condemned to death, and he said: "Oh, Benvenuto, your work is ruined, and there's no way out of it at all!" As soon as I heard the words of this wretched man I let out a cry so loud that it could have been heard from the sphere of flame; and getting out of bed, I grabbed my clothes and began to dress; and to the servants, my shop-boy, and everyone who drew near to help me I gave either kicks or punches, and I complained, saying: "Ah! You jealous traitors! This is a deliberate betrayal; but I swear by God that I'll get to the bottom of it, and before I die I'll give such a proof of my worth to the world that I'll leave more than one person astonished."… As soon as I had found the remedy for all these great disasters, with the loudest cries I was shouting now to one person and now to another: "Bring it here! Take it there!", so that, when they saw that the cake was beginning to liquefy, the entire troop obeyed me with such good will that each man did the work of three. Then I had a half-bar of pewter brought, which weighed about sixty pounds, and I threw it onto the cake inside the furnace, which, along with the help caused both by the wood and by stirring it, now with iron pokers and now with iron bars, in a short space of time became liquid. Now when I saw that we had brought a corpse back to life, contrary to the opinion of all those ignorant workmen, I regained so much energy that I no longer realized whether I still had any fever or any fear of death.
(Translation by Julia Conaway Bondanella and Peter Bondanella)

62) GIORGIO VASARI   **Piazzale degli Uffizi**
     (1550-1568)

From the left side of the Loggia dei Lanzi walk into the enclosed courtyard of the Uffizi museum just to the right of the main entrance to Palazzo Vecchio.

This building, that now houses the Uffizi museum, was begun by the writer, architect and painter Giorgio Vasari (1511-1574) and completed by Alfonso Parigi and Bernardo Buontalenti. The long narrow courtyard enclosed by the building's two wings is an astonishing urban space that draws the eye toward the elegant covered arch at the opposite end overlooking the Arno river. Above the surrounding columns are two floors of windows, behind which lies the Uffizi Gallery. As you look up at the Uffizi's roof, compare its height to the courtyard's length: one almost has the impression of standing in a roofless gallery. Cosimo I de' Medici commissioned the construction of the Uffizi to house the offices ("uffici" in modern Italian) of Florence's city government (*i.e.* its administration, courts and files). If we consider his writing alone, Vasari is known most for his *Vite de' più eccellenti architetti, pittori e scultori italiani da Cimabue insino a' tempi nostri* (*Lives of the Most Eminent Italian Architects, Painters and Sculptors from Cimabue to the Present Day*, 1550). These three categories of artists define the way Vasari's book is organized and also reflect the Classical division separating the arts they pursued. While it is in large part a work of art history, the second edition, enlarged and issued in 1568, includes many of Vasari's own contemporaries, such as Titian. Vasari's work provides an analysis of the artists' styles, gives an account of their life stories, and is still a valid source of information about historical curiosities – besides being very entertaining. The biographical sketches hark back to the medieval tradition of oral storytelling and are therefore reminiscent of the Italian "novella" or folktale. Vasari highly valued the quality of artistic spontaneity, which can be compared to natural unselfconsciousness or the lack of affectation called "sprezzatura" by Baldesar Castiglione in "*Il cortegiano*" (The Book of the Courtier, 1528), his treatise on Renaissance courtly behavior. According to Vasari, Michelangelo embodied both artistic spontaneity and perfection more than any other.

As you gaze down the length of the Uffizi courtyard from Piazza della Signoria, face the arch at the courtyard's opposite end. Around the periphery of the Piazzale (and along the Arno) there are twenty-eight statues of eminent Tuscans in niches. Starting from those on your left are many of the same authors included in this volume: 3) Lorenzo il Magnifico (under the colonnade, to the right of the first door on your left), 7) Leon Battista Alberti, 8) Leonardo Da Vinci, 9) Michelangelo Buonarroti, 10) Dante Alighieri, 11) Francesco Petrarca, 12) Giovanni Boccaccio 13) Niccolò Machiavelli and 14) Francesco Guicciardini. When you reach the opposite end of the Piazzale, return towards Piazza della Signoria walking along the opposite colonnaded portico where there are statues of: 16) Galileo Galilei, 18) Francesco Redi and 24) Benvenuto Cellini. Here, as you observe the assembly of writers personified in sculpture it is almost as if they are watching you, reversing the traditional role between reader and writer.

Left: Corner of via della Scala and Piazza Santa Maria Novella, near where Henry James may have stayed in 1874
Right: Via del Giglio 29 (red), John Milton's address

Church of Santa Maria Novella, mentioned in Boccaccio's Decameron

Entrance to the English Cemetery, also known as the Protestant Cemetery

The English Cemetery's central pathway

Tomb of Elizabeth Barrett Browning

Tomb of Giampietro Vieusseux

Michelangelo Buonarroti's childhood home

Statue of Dante in front of the Church of Santa Croce

Church of Santa Croce: Michelangelo's tomb

Church of Santa Croce: Niccolò Machiavelli's tomb

Church of Santa Croce: Vittorio Alfieri's tomb   *Church of Santa Croce: Ugo Foscolo's tomb*

Piazza San Felice: Casa Guidi   *Piazza Pitti: Fyodor Dostoevsky's lodgings*

Lunagarno Guicciardini: Palazzo Soderini

IN QUESTO PALAGIO
CHE LA STORICA CASATA DEI SODERINI
ERESSE ED ABITÒ
SOGGIORNAVA LUNGO L'ANNO MCCCLXXVII
SANTA CATERINA DA SIENA
ARDIMENTOSA ZELATRICE DI PACE
TRA PAPA GREGORIO II E LA REPUBBLICA DI FIRENZE
QUI STESSO IN PIÙ PROSSIME ETÀ
DOMINATORI DELL'ARTE E DEI POPOLI
RAFFAELLO, NAPOLEONE I, WALTER SCOTT, LORD BYRON
EBBERO SUCCESSIVA TEMPORANEA DIMORA

Palazzo Soderini: Saint Catherine of Siena,
Sir Walter Scott, George Gordon Byron

Lungarno Corsini: Vittorio Alfieri's home

Lungarno Corsini: Alessandro Manzoni's address

Ponte Vecchio: bust of Benvenuto Cellini

Lungarno Acciaiuoli: building where Romain Rolland lived

Piazza Santa Trinita, Palazzo Salimbeni and Palazzo Buondelmonti: plaques for James Russell Lowell, Ludovico Ariosto and Giampietro Vieusseux

Piazza della Repubblica: Caffè Giubbe Rosse

Piazza della Repubblica: Caffè Giubbe Rosse

Piazza della Repubblica: Caffè Paszkowsky

Piazza della Repubblica: Bar Gambrinus

Via dell'Oche: Salomone Fiorentino's house

Via Martelli: temporary home of Leonardo da Vinci

Courtyard of the Uffizi Gallery:
statue of Dante Alighieri

Courtyard of the Uffizi Gallery:
statue of Giovanni Boccaccio

Courtyard of the Uffizi Gallery:
statue of Francesco Petrarca

Courtyard of the Uffizi Gallery:
statue of Lorenzo the Magnificent

Courtyard of the Uffizi Gallery:
statue of Benvenuto Cellini

Courtyard of the Uffizi Callery:
statue of Michelangelo Buonarroti

Courtyard of the Uffizi Gallery:
statue of Niccolò Machiavelli

Courtyard of the Uffizi Gallery:
statue of Francesco Guicciardini

Piazza San Martino: Torre della Castagna

QVI
DOVE CON I SVOI
CONFRATELLI FRA DOMENI
BVONVICINI E FRA SILVEST
MARVFFI IL XXIII MAGGI
DEL MCCCCXCVIII PER INIQ
SENTENZA FV IMPICCATO ED A
FRA GIROLAMO SAVONAROL
DOPO QVATTRO SECOLI
FV COLLOCATA QVESTA
MEMORIA

Piazza della Signoria: site where Girolamo Savonarola was burned at the stake

Dante Alighieri's house

Ponte Vecchio: Dantean plaque

San Pier Scheraggio: site of the church where Dante and Boccaccio spoke

63) FRANCESCO PETRARCA   **Piazzale degli Uffizi**
    (1304-1374)

Directions to Petrarch's statue are included above at the end of the entry on
Vasari.

Together with those of Dante and Boccaccio, Petrarch's works established
Florentine Italian as the tongue that would forever after be Italy's literary language.
Ironically, however, Petrarch never lived in Florence until he was an adult. His
father was a White Guelph banished from this city along with Dante during a
tumultuous period of civic political unrest: that's why Petrarch was born in
Arezzo. While he was still a boy his family moved to Pisa and then Avignon in
Provence, where his notary father found employment at the papal court, though
later they lived in Carpentras. After studying law in Montpellier and Bologna,
Petrarch returned to Avignon and dissipated his small inheritance in pursuit of
the attractions offered by that city's elegant high society. To assure himself a liveli-
hood he turned to the Church and became the family chaplain in Avignon to the
powerful Colonna family from Rome. On April 6, 1327 he saw Laura De Sade for
the first time in the church of St. Clare in Avignon. She was to become the object
of most of his 366 poems, collected in *Rerum volgarium fragmenta*, also known as
his *Canzoniere* (collected lyrics). These poems mirror the changes in Petrarch's
passion for Laura, a married woman, but also moral and religious feelings: guilt,
shame and remorse for his own desire – for it was this that led him astray from the
true path of love for God. This internal conflict makes of Petrarch's poetry a body
of work that examines the self as an object of poetic study. For this reason the
Canzoniere marks a very significant shift away from a medieval mentality and a
turn toward a new sensibility for individual experience and what would later be
termed Humanism. Indeed, Petrarch's poetry is one of the first and most eloquent
examples of the emergence of literary introspection and psychological self-analysis
in a modern Western language. These innovations distance Petrarch's work signif-
icantly from Dante's, since Petrarch's is no longer concerned with solely moral or
didactic issues. Among its novelties are sudden emotional outbursts and a new
emphasis on memory: recalling Laura in younger days as well as the greatness of
ancient Rome. In contrast to this, Petrarch held Latin studies in the highest
esteem (having himself rediscovered several lost works by Cicero) and was
crowned poet laureate in Rome in 1341 for his long Latin narrative poem *Africa*
(on the second Punic War). This event took place largely because Petrarch had
organized it, though he first had to submit to a three-day formal examination in
Naples by King Robert of Anjou. It was an occasion that indicated the poet's thirst
for fame and glory, even though he himself recognized the vanity and ultimate
transience of these goals. Indeed, a situation of perpetual internal conflict lies at
the heart of the poet's consciousness, a state of affairs reflected in the fact that he
never really established a permanent place of habitation. Petrarch became famous

during his own lifetime, in contrast to which he sought periods of solitude in order to meditate. In doing so he implicity attributed greater importance to individualism and the self than had been previously customary and at the same time presaged the future development of consciousness in the West. His *De vita solitaria* (On Solitary Life) contains his reflections on the intellectual's need to isolate himself from public and social life. Nonetheless, the poet spent many years employed as an ambassador in the service of different prelates and princes. Thus, in a professional capacity Petrarch was able to travel all over Europe during a time when most people lived circumscribed lives in places they rarely strayed from; and he stayed at different times in Mantua, Padua, Ferrara, Florence, Naples, Milan, Venice, Paris and Prague. He would also return periodically to a home he kept after 1353 in Vaucluse (Provence) on the banks of the Sorgue, where he went to meditate and write. One of his most famous and sensual poems is set there: "Clear, fresh and sweet waters." In addition to the *Canzoniere*, the works that best display Petrarch's tortured inner life are the *Secretum* (My Secret), also known as *De secreto conflictu curarum mearum* (On the Secret Conflict of My Worries, 1342-1358), and *I Trionfi* (Triumphs, 1353-1374). The *Secretum*, in Latin, was never intended for publication. It is an impassioned dialogue that the poet imagines with Saint Augustine, as a female figure (Truth) looks on. In it the poet defends his all-too-human passions and faults, and he contrasts them with more important spiritual concerns and the meaning of death within the context of a truly Christian life. The *Trionfi*, a poem in Florentine triplets, are a collection of six typically medieval, allegorical tableaux in which each Triumph is supplanted by the moral superiority of the subsequent one. Hence, Love is followed by Modesty, Death, Fame, Time and Eternity.

Toward the end of his life, Petrarch donated his library to the City of Venice in exchange for housing and subsequently built a home at Arquà outside Padua, where he died. Although Petrarch wrote numerous other works not mentioned here, in both Florentine and Latin, he is probably Italy's greatest and most prolific author of early love poetry. Making use of a variety of forms, he raised the development of the sonnet and the "canzone" to new heights. His poems were considered the standard by which all Italian love poetry was judged for hundreds of years, giving birth to what is called "Petrarchism," and his magisterial control of the sonnet led to its adoption by poets in English, French and Spanish. As a creative force, Petrarch's influence can be detected even in the works of twentieth-century poets such as Eugenio Montale, and its importance continues to be felt today.

Walking Tour 11

Dante Alighieri

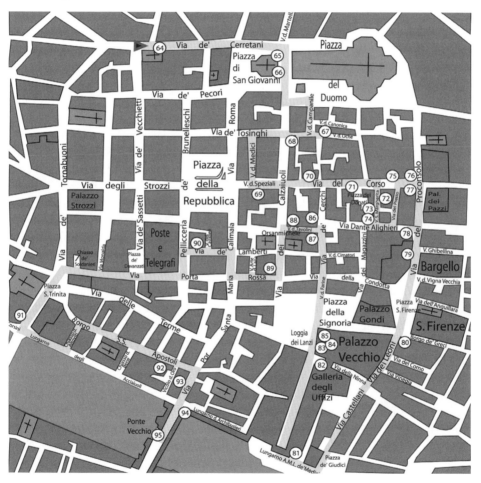

Via de' Cerretani / Piazza San Giovanni / Via dell'Oche / Via del Corso / Via Santa Margherita / Via Dante Alighieri / Via del Proconsolo / Borgo de' Greci / Via della Ninna / Palazzo Vecchio / Via dei Cerchi / Via dei Tavolini / Via dei Calzaiuoli / Via dei Lamberti / Via dei Tornabuoni / Borgo SS. Apostoli / Via Por Santa Maria / Ponte Vecchio

DANTE ALIGHIERI
(1265-1321)

This native son of Florence is Italy's most famous author even though he spent
much of his adulthood in exile. His reputation is justly deserved: he is the father
of Italy's national language, the man who perfected medieval Italy's most refined
school of courtly love poetry, the author of the most original religious allegory of
the Middle Ages, a visionary writer about national political consciousness, and an
imaginary creator of fantasy literature. His works reflect both the medieval culture in which he was educated as well as the intellectual, moral and ethical objec-
tives he hoped to attain by writing them. Dante's fame derives mostly from the
Divine Comedy, an allegory on religious, political and historical themes that is
elaborated in terms that are at once personal, civic, and national. Its title indicates that it ends in a non-tragic way – with the salvation of Dante's soul – while
the word "Divine" was not incorporated into the title until 1555, long after
Boccaccio used this adjective to praise Dante's masterpiece. Written entirely in
rhyming interlocking tercets, the *Comedy* is a voyage into the Christian afterlife
through Hell, Purgatory and Heaven; yet in talking about death Dante examined
the meaning of life profoundly. His moral vision, moreover, led him to create a
highly organized view of the human soul's existence beyond the grave in concrete
terms. For this reason, those he portrays in Hell and Purgatory suffer punishments that match the gravity and nature of their sins, while the souls in Heaven
are blessed by divine grace to a degree that is equal to the good works they carried out in life. While those who were educated in his time habitually wrote only
in Latin, Dante was the first to write a serious and ambitious work in Florentine:
the spoken language of his native city. That the outcome of his efforts resulted in
a work of astonishing complexity and subtlety also means that the *Divine
Comedy* in Italy carries all the weight of an epic: the story of a nation's struggle for
statehood and ethnic as well as linguistic identity. Equal parts of medieval religious scholasticism and courtly love poetry also contribute to this work – Dante
having been the one to bring the *Dolce stil novo* (Sweet New Style) to its fullest
flowering. On the one hand Dante's poems for his beloved Beatrice announced
themselves most openly as love lyrics in the collection entitled *La vita nuova* (*The
New Life*, 1290-95). In this work, comprised of both prose and poetry, the
medieval tension between the sacred and the profane is resolved by creating an
angelic female love object that purifies the poet who loves and makes him worthy
of divine grace. The name "Beatrice" in fact means "she who beatifies." On the
other hand the *Divine Comedy* realizes the religious ramifications of the *Dolce stil
novo* in ways that are only implicit in *The New Life*, since it is in the *Divine
Comedy* that Dante ascends to heaven in Beatrice's presence. In this sense
Dante's love for Beatrice can be said to be sublimated in the *Comedy*, which he
only began after being exiled from Florence in 1301 (sometime between 1306 and

1308) and completed shortly before his death. As one of his city's most prominent citizens Dante was elected Prior (Supreme magistrate) in 1300, a year that coincided with the greatest animosity between the Black and White Guelphs: the latter faction being the one with which Dante sided. (For an explanation of the conflict between the Florentine Guelphs see Walking Tour 6, Site 33). The poet's commitment to civic service is an expression of his moral and political values, which he refers to frequently in the *Divine Comedy* through references to his own career, his future, and the political history of Florence and Italy. For this reason his exile, although a bitter experience, offered him the chance to meditate on Florence as a literary, political and spiritual theme: a lost homeland to be recaptured only in a celestial vision of Florence's past. Indeed, he never returned to Florence again because he was sentenced to perpetual exile under penalty of death and all of his property was confiscated.

Dante was born to a Guelph moneychanger and lost his mother at an early age. He married Gemma Donati in 1285 and perhaps fathered four children, although none of them are mentioned in his works. His son Pietro, however, became one of the *Divine Comedy*'s first commentators. As a young man Dante studied under the Franciscan friars at the church of Santa Croce where he read Latin classics, philosophy and theology , but was exposed to the ideas of the *Dolce stil novo* in 1287 after going to Bologna. During his exile Dante found refuge at various courts in Italy to whom he sometimes offered his services as ambassador. Staying mostly in Tuscany and Emilia Romagna, the host he remembered most fondly was Can Grande della Scala, lord of Verona. It is to him that Dante dedicated "Paradise" in the *Divine Comedy*. For the rest of his life Dante moved from place to place, and for this reason died in Ravenna, where he is still buried. All of Dante's other works were written mostly during his exile: the *Convivio* (1304-07), *De vulgari eloquentia* (1303-04), *Monarchia* (1313-18), his Latin *Eclogues* (1319-20), *Questio de aqua et terra* (1320), thirteen Latin *Epistole*, and his uncollected poetry, known as *Rime*.

The *Convivio* is a collection of four treatises (although the poet originally meant to write fifteen of them) supposed to make academic ideas accessible to those who hadn't formally studied philosophy. This intent is furthered by the fact that the *Convivio* was written in Italian rather than Latin, and therefore shows that Dante also took the opportunity to promote Italian as a written language. In addition, the word "convivio" means "banquet," which is a metaphor for an intellectual meal to which everyone is invited. A kind of Italian encyclopedia in prose and poetry, it is also a statement of self-defense in which Dante explains why he was unjustly exiled from Florence.

Ironically, Dante's treatise on the eloquence of the vulgar tongue (*De vulgari eloquentia*) was written in Latin. He provides a history of world languages in this book, includes a review of Italian dialects and gives his own definition of Italian (a literary spoken language – Florentine or Sicilian – that could also include words from other dialects).

His *Rime* (rhymes) include poems written over a period of twenty-five years and bring together compositions typical of the *Dolce stil novo* (such as "Per una ghirlandetta ch'io vidi"), poems about friendship (such as "Guido, i' vorrei, che tu e Lapo ed io") and the harsh so-called "rime petrose," written about the insensitive and unreceptive woman Petra (stone), that include poems such as "Così nel mio parlar voglio esser aspro."

In the Latin treatise *Monarchia* Dante explained what he thought the proper relationship should have been between the two superpowers of his day: the Papacy and the Holy Roman Empire. Because the tensions between them had vitiated peace in medieval Europe since the eleventh century, Dante delineated a utopian situation in which the Papacy was to be deprived of all political power while the Emperor was to be excluded from any spiritual matters. This division of power might seem idiosyncratic to the contemporary reader because we know that Dante's political sympathies lay with the republican ideals espoused by the White Guelphs, but his deeply felt religious convictions and his wish for a politically disinterested Church led him, perhaps paradoxically, to this conclusion. At the same time, all the ideas that Dante developed at length in his treatises are also an integral part of the *Divine Comedy*. This work had immediate and enormous success, which has only grown throughout the centuries. Its oral narrative character made it an easy text to recite and popularize, and it has been translated in countless languages. Recently there has also been a revival of interest in it, and Florentines organize dramatic readings of it and performances of different cantos, especially during the summer.

Walking Tour 11 leads you to plaques throughout the city's center with verses from the *Divine Comedy*. Each plaque indicates a place in Florence that Dante mentioned in his masterpiece, although the plaques do not offer a comprehensive idea of Dante's long and complicated work. We have provided an explanation of each site's significance and its relation to the *Divine Comedy* and hope that by following the walking tours presented below Florence's present-day cityscape will become a voyage through the *Divine Comedy* itself and the streets of this city during the Middle Ages.

64) *Inferno* XV, 82-85   Via de' Cerretani 39 (red)

Just beyond the wall supporting the left side of the church of Santa Maria Maggiore you can read:

...in la mente m'è fitta, e or m'accora,	within my memory is fixed – and now
la cara e buona imagine paterna	moves me – your dear, your kind paternal image
di voi, quando nel mondo ad ora ad ora	when, in the world above, from time to time
m'insegnavate come l'uom s'etterna	you taught me how man makes himself eternal;

Dante's meets his former teacher here in the Second Zone of the Third Ring of the Seventh Circle of Hell, the place reserved for those condemned for the sin of violence against Nature: sodomy. Along with all the others here, his mentor Brunetto Latini is obliged to walk in an endless circle on coal-hot sand under a rain of fire. Latini, one of the most important Italian intellectuals of the thirteenth century, was author of the *Trésor*, an encyclopedic-like treatise, and the *Tesoretto*, a long allegorical didactic poem in Florentine. Surprised to see him, Dante recognizes and speaks to Latini as he passes by, but never explicitly mentions his teacher's sin. Rather, he shows him great respect and reminds the reader that it was Latini as father figure and scholar who taught him that those who write great literature continue to be remembered after their deaths. Brunetto Latini was buried inside this church, where, along the right side of the wall of the apse on the left, a single column marks what remains of his tomb.

65) *Inferno* XIX, 17   Baptistry, Piazza San Giovanni

From site 64 in Via de' Cerretani continue in the same direction, walking towards the center of Florence. When you see the octagonal baptistry of San Giovanni on your right, walk around it till you reach the side opposite Via de' Martelli, which enters Piazza San Giovanni diagonally. There, at the base of the Baptistry is the following plaque:

>   *... nel mio bel San Giovanni*   ... in my handsome San Giovanni

This is an affectionate reference to Florence's baptistry, where Dante himself was baptized. It recalls the baptismal fonts that at one time were buried in the building's floor, so that the faithful were lowered into them. Dante recalls the baptistry as he passes through the Third Pouch of the Eighth Circle of Hell, a place set aside for those guilty of simony (the sale of spiritual goods or the fraudulent acquisition of ecclesiastical office). The simonists are buried in holes headfirst so that only their feet stick out. Tongues of flame protrude from the soles of their bare feet and torture them.

66) *Paradise* XXV, 1-9   Baptistry, Piazza San Giovanni

Keeping the Baptistry to your right continue around it till you reach the side of it opposite the bell tower (campanile). There, at the base of the Baptistry are the words:

> *Se mai continga che il poema sacro*   If it should happen ... If this sacred poem –
> *al quale ha posto mano e cielo e terra*   this work so shared by heaven and by earth
> *sì che m'ha fatto per più anni macro*   that he has made me lean through these long years
> *vinca la crudeltà che fuor mi serra*   can ever overcome the cruelty
> *del bello ovile ov'io dormii agnello*   that bars me from the fair fold were I slept
> *nimico a' lupi che gli danno guerra;*   a lamb opposed to wolves that war on it,

> *con altra voce omai, con altro vello*   by then with other voice, with other fleece,
> *ritornerò poeta, ed in sul fonte*   I shall return as poet and put on,
> *del mio battesmo prenderò il cappello*   at my baptismal font, the laurel crown;

Upon arrival in the Eighth Heaven, the Sphere of Fixed Stars, Dante is examined by Saints Peter, James and John on the meaning of the three theological virtues: faith, hope and charity. His words here precede part of his definition of the meaning of hope, which he places in a personal context. Since he wrote the *Divine Comedy* in exile, he fervently hoped to return to Florence one day as its famous author and be crowned poet laureate here at the Baptistry. The "fair fold" refers to Florence; "other fleece" to the gray hair that Dante would probably have; and "wolves" to the cruel Florentines who exiled him.

67) *Paradise* XVI, 112-114   Via dell'Oche 20 (red)

Walk from the Baptistry toward the cathedral bell tower and cross the square, where a small street (Via del Campanile) empties into it from the buildings that surround the square just behind the bell tower. Take Via del Campanile past Via della Canonica on your left and turn left at the next corner into Via dell'Oche. After a few steps you will come across this plaque on your left:

> *Così faceano li padri di coloro*   such were the ancestors of those who now,
> *che, sempre che la vostra chiesa vaca,*   whenever bishops' sees are vacant, grow
> *si fanno grassi, stando a consistoro.*   fat as they sit in church consistories.

The central figure in cantos XV, XVI and XVII of Paradise is Dante's ancestor Cacciaguida. Since the Fifth Heaven, the Sphere of Mars, is full of those who fought and died for the Faith, Cacciaguida is among its blessed souls because he probably died in the Second Crusade (1147-1149). He recalls the strong sense of civic virtue that Florentines felt during his lifetime and compares it to the lassitude of civic moral values in Italy during Dante's lifetime. Cacciaguida refers in particular to the Visdomini and Tosinghi families, who formerly held jurisdiction over Florence's archdiocesan land whenever there was no bishop and abused this right in order to amass wealth. The Visdomini lived in this medieval tower-house. Dante sees the militant spirits, such as Cacciaguida, as bright-red points of light that form a Greek cross. Each point spins as it sings in praise of Christ's resurrection while the luminous figure of Christ on the cross flashes. From his place on the right horizontal arm of the cross Cacciaguida moves to its center and then descends to its base to meet Dante.

68) *Paradise* XVI, 115-117   Via dell'Oche 19

Retrace your steps to Via del Campanile but continue past it. Proceed forward past an arched passageway on your left where there is the following plaque just before you reach the intersection of Via dell'Oche with the very busy Via dei Calzaiuoli.

L'oltracotata schiatta che s'indraca	The breed – so arrogant and dragonlike
dietro a chi fugge, ed a chi mostra il dente	in chasing him who flees, but lamblike,
o ver la borsa, com'agnel si placa,	meek to him who shows his teeth or else his purse –

As in the previous plaque, these are Cacciaguida's words. He denounces another arrogant and corrupt Florentine family: the Adimari clan, that had lived in houses built at this location. He accuses them of acting aggressively with those who fled but being submissive with those who were combative or willing to pay. Cacciaguida's accusation also functions as an indirect form of revenge for Dante, whose home and belongings were seized by the Adimari family when he was exiled in 1301. The Adimari coat of arms is also attached to the wall here just below the quotation above.

69) *Paradise* XVI, 40-42   Via degli Speziali 3

From Via dell'Oche continue in the same direction and cross Via dei Calzaiuoli into Via de' Tosinghi. Turn left at the next corner into Via de' Medici and follow it one block, where it empties into Via degli Speziali. When you reach this street, cross it to the opposite side where you will see this plaque in the middle of the block to the left of number 3.

Gli antichi miei ed io nacqui nel loco	My ancestors and I were born just where
dove si trova pria l'ultimo sesto	the runner in your yearly games first comes
da quel che corre il vostro annual giuoco.	upon the boundary of the final ward.

In this tercet Dante's ancestor Cacciaguida refers to the administrative divisions that defined Florence in his lifetime. He recalls that his own forebears always lived in this neighborhood, which contestants ran through in the yearly race ("palio") that took place during the Feast of Saint John, Florence's patron saint. At that time Florence was divided into four quarters (or "wards") named after the city gates next to them: Porta del Vescovo (around the present-day Piazza del Duomo), Porta San Piero, Porta San Pancrazio and Porta Santa Maria. The Eliseis (Cacciaguida's family) lived here in Via degli Speziali, while the Alighieri family home was in the quarter of Porta del Vescovo. By Dante's time these neighborhoods had been changed, and Florence was divided into six different neighborhoods (or "sestieri") subsequent to the construction of the second ring of city walls. This is why Dante uses the word "sesto" in the second verse of the tercet above.

70) *Inferno* VIII, 61-63   Via del Corso 18

Turn to your left in Via degli Speziali and cross Via dei Calzaiuoli, where you will find yourself in Via del Corso. Follow Via del Corso a short way to the address above, which you will find on your left. The plaque there reads:

Tutti gridavano: "A Filippo Argenti!"	They all were shouting: "At Filippo Argenti!"
e 'l fiorentino spirito bizzarro	At this, the Florentine, gone wild with spleen
in sé medesmo si volgea co' denti.	began to turn his teeth against himself.

In the Fifth Circle of Hell Dante crosses the swamp in the River Styx, in which those damned for their anger (the Wrathful) are immersed up to their necks in mud. These souls fight amongst themselves for eternity. Dante hears them yell and turn against one of their own: Filippo Argenti. This man's actual family name was "Cavicciuoli," a family related to the Adimari (mentioned in Site 67) who owned houses at this site too. Because Filippo was so eager to show off his wealth that he had his horse shoed with silver, he was nicknamed "Argenti" (silver). Filippo Argenti was also one of Dante's many enemies because he opposed the poet's return to Florence. Thus Dante expresses pleasure in this tercet to see Filippo attacked by his angry peers in Hell.

71) *Purgatory* XXIV, 79-84   Via del Corso 31 (red)

Keep walking in the same direction. Pass Via Sant'Elisabetta on your left and Via dei Cerchi and Piazza de' Donati on your right. The plaque at this address will be on your right.

... il loco u' fui a viver posto,	– because the place where I was set
di giorno in giorno più di ben si spolpa	to live is day by day deprived of good
e a trista ruina par disposto.	and seems along the way to wretched ruin."
... che più n'ha colpa	"Do not be vexed," he said, "for I can see
vegg'io a coda d'una bestia tratto	the guiltiest of all dragged by a beast's
inver' la valle ove mai non si scolpa.	tail to the valley where no sin is purged".

This plaque is placed on the towerhouse of the Donati family, once one of Florence's most powerful and principally responsible for Dante's exile. As he passes through the Sixth Terrace of Mount Purgatory, Dante encounters Forese Donati, his friend but also the brother of Corso Donati, Dante's main enemy. Around 1290 the two friends wrote a series of satirical sonnets in question-and-response form known as a "tenzone." In the verses above, Dante speaks first and then Forese answers him (though there is no tenzone in this case). Dante again laments Florence's decline and corruption, while Forese forecasts the death of his brother Corso: dragged into Hell by a demon's tail. In reality Corso died in 1308 in a series of events after being found guilty of treason. He fled the city and was brought back by force tied to a horse. (Traitors were traditionally punished by being paraded through the streets tied to the tail of a horse). Forese, who spends time in this part of Purgatory for his gluttony, must expiate this sin by suffering hunger and thirst. Those punished are so emaciated that Dante compares them to the Jews during the siege of Jerusalem.

72) Chiesa di Santa Margherita de' Cerchi   Via Santa Margherita 4 (red)

Keep following Via del Corso in the same direction. Turn right after only a short distance under the arched passageway into Via Santa Margherita. After only a few steps you will come across the church of Santa Margherita on your left.

This small church, built presumably in 1032, was restored in 1973 and was probably the one attended by Beatrice Portinari, Dante's beloved. A plaque set beneath the altar along the left interior wall mentions both Beatrice and her father Folco Portinari:

Sotto questo altare Folco Portinari costruì la tomba di famiglia. L'8 giugno 1291 vi fu sepolta Beatrice Portinari. Pietra tombale di Beatrice Portinari.	Beneath this altar Folco Portinari built his family tomb. On June 8, 1291 Beatrice Portinari was buried here. Tombstone of Beatrice Portinari.

Below the altar on the right there is a reproduction of Monna Tessa's tombstone. The plaque there reads:

Monna Tessa ispiratrice di Folco Portinari Fondatrice delle Oblate ospitaliere di Santa Maria Nuova. Morta il 3 luglio 1327.	Miss Tessa, who inspired Folco Portinari, founded the Hospital Oblates of Santa Maria Nuova. She died on July 3, 1327.

Tessa was Beatrice's nanny and a trusted as well as longtime household retainer. She held a valuable position in the Portinari family looking after the twelve children born to Beatrice's mother Cilia de' Caponsacchi as well as keeping house. As if this weren't enough, Monna Tessa became well known because of the charity and aid she brought to the poor. Indeed, Folco was said to have been so inspired by her that he financed the construction of a hospital in 1288. Tradition holds that Dante was also wed here to Gemma Donati in an arranged marriage that had been agreed upon by the parents of them both when they were still children.

To the left of the entrance door is a painting entitled "Dante meets Beatrice Portinari accompanied by her mother Cilia de' Caponsacchi and Monna Tessa," by Mario D'Elia (1991). On the right-hand wall of the nave is the oil painting "Beatrice Portinari's Wedding" (1928) by Raffaello Sorbi, in which Beatrice is shown in front of this church. Some scholars believe that Beatrice may have existed only as a literary invention, but it is interesting that several sources note that she was born in 1266 and was the wife of Simone de' Bardi.

73) Casa di Dante   Via Santa Margherita 1

Follow Via Santa Margherita till you come to the address listed here, which will be on your right.

According to tradition Dante was born in one of the houses built on this site. What stands here now was built in 1875 over the remains of a medieval tower and then restored again by the City of Florence in 1910 in order to evoke the atmosphere of the medieval cityscape. For this reason, what you see does not reflect a historical reconstruction of Dante's actual birthplace. All the same, in the years between the two dates above a number of studies were undertaken to establish the exact site of Dante's birth, but they could only determine with certainty that it was in one of the buildings next to or on this site. The building is now a museum organized in the following way: Room 1: Florence in Dante's Time; Room 2: Dante's Early Years; Room 3: Dante's Public Life in Florence; Room 4: Dante's Life in Exile from 1301 to 1311; Room 5: Dante's Life in Exile from 1311 to his Death; Room 6: Dantean Iconography Through the Centuries; Room 7: Dante's Legacy Through the Centuries.

74) *Inferno* XXIII, 94-95   **Via Dante Alighieri 2**

As you exit Dante's house turn right into the little square next to it and then right again into Via Dante Alighieri. The plaque holding a quotation from the Inferno is attached to the side of Dante's house just around the corner to your right:

> ... *'I' fui nato e cresciuto*   I answered: "Where the lovely Arno flows
> *sovra 'l bel fiume d'Arno a la gran villa"*   there I was born and raised, in the great city ... "

Here in the Sixth Pouch of the Eighth Circle of Hell, Dante passes through the zone where he speaks to two Jovial Brothers condemned as Hypocrites, who weep and walk slowly under the weight of hooded cloaks that are gilded externally but lined with lead. The weight of the cloaks represents the effort that hypocrites expend to maintain false appearances, while their golden color indicates a virtue that is only apparent. The weight of the lead stands for the vice that hypocrites nurture and hide within themselves. When the two ex-priests talk to him, Dante identifies himself with the words above.

75) *Purgatory* XXX, 31-33   **Via del Corso 6**
Palazzo da Cepparello (formerly Portinari Salviati)

Take Via Dante Alighieri past Via Santa Margherita and turn left at the next corner into Via del Presto. Pass Piazza dei Giuochi on your left and proceed until it empties into Via del Corso, where, on the far side of the street and slightly to your left, is the address above:

> *sovra candido vel cinta d'uliva*   a woman showed herself to me; above
> *donna m'apparve, sotto verde manto*   a white veil, she was crowned with olive boughs;
> *vestita di color di fiamma viva.*   her cape was green; her dress beneath, flame-red.

A plaque appears at this address because Beatrice's family occupied buildings on this site. After reaching the top of the Mountain of Purgatory, Dante arrives at Earthly Paradise, where he witnesses an allegorical procession representing the Church triumphant. At the end of the procession Dante recognizes Beatrice atop a cart. She is wearing a red gown with a green cape and a white veil held in place by an olive garland. These are the colors of the three Theological Virtues: hope (green), faith (white) and charity (red). The olive garland is a reference both to peace and to Minerva, the goddess of wisdom, to which it was sacred. Virgil is Dante's guide through Hell and Purgatory, and he represents human reason, but as soon as Dante sees Beatrice, Virgil is nowhere to be found. Thus human reason gives way to the superiority of illuminating grace, represented by Beatrice.

76) *Paradise* XVI, 94-96   **Via del Corso 4**

Return to the intersection of Via del Presto but walk past it in the opposite direction. The address here is on the left side of Via del Corso just before it intersects with Via del Proconsolo, the next cross street.

... la porta ch'al presente è carca	... the gate that now is burdened with
di nova fellonia di tanto peso	new treachery that weighs so heavily
che tosto fia iattura de la barca	that it will bring the vessel to shipwreck

As in the plaques at sites 66 and 67, this one refers to words spoken to Dante by his ancestor Cacciaguida, who points out the names of powerful litigious families in Florence and notes that the city was once peaceful and free of those who greedily sought political power. He mentions the Cerchi family in this instance, which was known to be fiercely partisan and disloyal, because it had its houses on this spot. Their treachery is "new" because the Ravignani family had previously owned this property (as well as many others up to the Gate of San Piero) before it passed to subsequent owners. It was eventually acquired by the Cerchi family (originally from the countryside) whom Dante here bemoans – though he supported the Cerchi politically because they led the faction of White Guelphs. The word "vessel" is a metaphor for the city of Florence.

77) *Paradise* XV, 112-114   **Via del Corso 1 (red)**

Look across Via del Corso to the opposite side of the street. The plaque is located just before Via del Corso intersects with Via del Proconsolo.

Bellincion Berti vid'io andar cinto	I saw Bellincione Berti girt
di cuoio e d'osso, e venir da lo specchio	with leather and with bone, and saw his wife
la donna sua sanza il viso dipinto;	come from her mirror with her face unpainted;

Dante's forebear Cacciaguida evokes Florentine history during the twelfth century. His is a nostalgic look back at former times in which men such as Bellincion

Berti (the patriarch of the Ravignani family) were famous for dressing simply ("with leather and bone") and for the fact that his wife wore no makeup. Berti, who was a knight, held a position of importance in society and would have dressed in an ostentatious way during Dante's lifetime. (In addition, many fourteenth-century writers remarked on Florentine women's excessive use of makeup at the time. In one of his poems, Franco Sacchetti called the use of makeup "alchimia maladetta" or "damned alchemy.") As mentioned at the previous site, the Ravignani family owned property at this location, and indeed Bellincion Berti is also mentioned in Giovanni Villani's *Chronicle*. Berti's daughter Gualdrada, renowned for her honesty and goodness, married into the family of the Counts Guidi, whose descendants gave sanctuary to Dante at the Castle in Poppi near Arezzo in 1310.

78) *Paradise* **XV, 97-99**   **Via Dante Alighieri 1**

From the previous site turn right into Via del Proconsolo and then right again into Via Dante Alighieri. After walking about fifty feet, you will find the plaque here on the left-hand side of the street just to the right of a large entrance to the Badia fiorentina.

Fiorenza, dentro dalla cerchia antica,	Florence, within her ancient ring of of walls –
ond'ella toglie ancora e terza e nona,	that ring from which she still draws tierce and nones –
si stava in pace sobria e pudica.	sober and chaste, lived in tranquillity.

The verses on this plaque precede those indicated at the previous site and mark the beginning of Cacciaguida's remembrance of Florence during the twelfth century. He recalls that the city was still surrounded then by its first ring of walls built in the ninth and tenth centuries, and that Florentines regularly heard church bells of the Badia (Abbey) mark the canonical hours of "tierce" and "nones" (nine o'clock in the morning and three o'clock in the afternoon). These hours signaled the beginning and end of the normal working day for a medieval artisan. Two subsequent rings of walls were later built encircling this initial one as the city grew: the second in 1173 and the third, begun in 1284, was still unfinished in 1300. These were demolished shortly after 1864 when Florence became the capital of Italy (1865-1871). They were located on the site of the present-day boulevards ("i viali") that surround the city center: Viale Fratelli Rossselli, Viale Filippo Strozzi, Viale Spartaco Lavagnini, Viale Giacomo Matteotti, Viale Antonio Gramsci and Viale della Giovine Italia.

79) *Paradise* **XVI, 127-130**   **Via del Proconsolo 19**

Return to Via del Proconosolo and turn right into it. The plaque at this site is located on your right after you turn the corner. It faces Via Ghibellina, which ends here, and is located just to the right of the main entrance to the Badia fiorentina (Florentine Abbey).

Ciascun che de la bella insegna porta	All those whose arms bear part of the fair ensign
del gran barone il cui nome e il cui pregio	of the great baron – he whose memory
la festa di Tommaso riconforta,	and worth are honored on the feast of Thomas –
Da esso ebbe milizia e privilegio,	received knighthood and privilege from him,

Cacciaguida recalls here Hugh the Great of Brandenburg, Marquis of Tuscany and Imperial Vicar General of Holy Roman Emperor Otto III. He notes that all the Florentine families allied with Hugh incorporated part of his coat of arms into their own and were either knighted or rewarded with noble titles because of it. The fact that many powerful Florentine families were tied to the Holy Roman Emperor in this way testifies to Florence's strong Ghibelline past. Hugh died on December 21, 1001 and is buried here in the Badia (a Benedictine abbey), founded by his mother Villa in 978. If you enter the Badia from Via del Proconsolo, turn left into the church. Hugh's fifteenth-century tomb, Mino da Fiesole's masterpiece (1469-1481), is on the left side of the nave.

80) *Paradise* XVI, 125-126   Borgo de' Greci 29

Continue down Via del Proconsolo in the same direction but cross the street to walk on the opposite side. Pass Via della Vigna Vecchia and Via dell'Anguillara on your left as you walk through Piazza San Firenze. The large brown sandstone edifice on your left is known as San Firenze, a Baroque building that now houses Florence's municipal courthouse. Gray sandstone steps lead up to its entrance from street level. As you cross the next street on your left, Borgo de' Greci, look into it, where you will see a plaque just where Borgo de' Greci empties into the square.

Nel piccol cerchio s'entrava per porta	... The gateway through
che si nomava da que' della Pera.	the inner walls was named for the della Pera.

Cacciaguida recalls that near this spot there was once a city gate in the first circle of city walls. It may have taken its name from the Italian word for pear "pera," or from either the "della Pera" or the "Peruzzi" families. Perhaps the point that Cacciaguida (*i.e.* Dante) wishes to make is that a family that at one time was so important as to have a city gate named after it had by Dante's time completely died out and been forgotten.

81) *Inferno* X, 22-27   The arch of the Uffizi facing the Arno

From Borgo de' Greci continue straight ahead into Via dei Leoni and pass Via del Corno and Via Vinegia on your left. The rear of Florence's huge City Hall (Palazzo Vecchio) will be looming over you on your right. Proceed past Piazza del Grano and walk down Via de' Castellani till you reach Piazza dei Giudici. Cross the street overlooking the Arno, Lungarno Anna Maria Luisa de' Medici, and turn right, walking along the narrow sidewalk. After just a few steps you will see the grey and white Uffizi gallery from the rear, with four statues set in niches. The first one on your right represents Farinata degli Uberti.

There is no plaque with a quotation from the *Divine Comedy* here, but the verses below are intimately linked with this famous man:

> *"O Tosco che per la città del foco*   "O Tuscan, you who pass alive across
> *vivo ten vai così parlando onesto*   the fiery city with such seemly words,
> *piacciati di restare in questo loco.*   be kind enough to stay your journey here.

As Dante walks through the Sixth Circle of Hell, which is set aside for the Heretics, he comes across the Epicureans. Their materialistic philosophy, first espoused by Epicurus (342-270 B.C.), denied the immortality of the soul, and in effect his medieval followers could be considered the first atheists (even if the concept of atheism is in itself a modern one). They are punished by being buried in red-hot stone tombs that torment them with the same ardor that they attributed to a false belief. This is also analogous to the traditional punishment for heretics: being burned alive at the stake. Among them is Farinata degli Uberti, whose family owned property where the Palazzo Vecchio now stands. Dante recalls his place in Florentine history (and that of the preceding generation) in order to leave a record for all time of the internecine conflicts that divided Florence during the middle of the thirteenth century. Farinata (who used this nickname) was born Manente degli Uberti, and was a Florentine nobleman who rose to be the head of the Ghibellines. Under his aegis the Ghibellines banished all the Guelphs from the city in 1248. Two years later the Guelphs managed to return to town, and then sent Farinata into exile in 1258. After the Ghibellines defeated the Guelphs in the Battle of Montaperti in 1260, Farinata was able to return to Florence triumphantly. Peace was made at the Diet of Empoli but Farinata was the only Ghibelline among them who opposed their collective proposal to destroy Florence. He died in 1264 but the Guelphs, having been banished for a second time, were only able to return to Florence in 1267: after the eclipse of Ghibelline power in Italy due to the death of the Holy Roman Emperor Manfred in 1266. Thereafter the Uberti family was permanently exiled from Florence. Their houses and those of other prominent Ghibellines in this neighborhood were torn down and the city began building Palazzo Vecchio in 1299. In the verses above, Farinata stands up proudly in his tomb – as if to recall the great soldier he once was – and asks Dante to stay a while to talk. The eminent Ghibelline recognizes Dante's Florentine accent, and the two fellow citizens recall the events just described above.

82) San Pier Scheraggio   Via della Ninna 7

Turn right from the Lungarno Anna Maria Luisa de' Medici into the central courtyard of the Uffizi museum (Piazzale degli Uffizi). Walk its length and turn right at the next corner, Via della Ninna. You will see the following plaque on your right just around the corner:

Avanzi e vestigia della chiesa di San	Traces and remains of the church of Saint
Pier Scheraggio che dava nome ad uno	Peter Scheraggio, whose name was given
dei sesti della città e fra le cui mura nei	to a city neighborhood. Within its walls
Consigli del popolo sonò la voce di Dante.	Dante's voice was heard at People's Council
	meetings.

Dante and Boccaccio both came to meetings in this church, that was used not only for worship but for neighborhood council meetings as well.

83) *Inferno* X, 91-93   Palazzo Vecchio Courtyard

Retrace your steps to the Piazzale degli Uffizi and turn right into Piazza della Signoria. The Main façade of the Palazzo Vecchio is on your right. Walk up its steps and enter its main entrance into the courtyard. Cross the courtyard and look for the statue of "Sampson and the Philistine" in a niche opposite the building's entrance you just passed through. To the right of the statue are two plaques. On the one nearest the corner are the words:

fu' io sol colà dove sofferto	But where I was alone was there where all
fu per ciascun di tòrre via Fiorenza	the rest would have annihilated Florence,
colui che la difesi a viso aperto.	had I not interceded forcefully.

As at Site 80, these are words spoken by Farinata degli Uberti, who refers to his role as the defender of Florence when all his fellow Ghibellines proposed to raze it to the ground.

84) *Paradise* XVI, 149-154   Palazzo Vecchio Courtyard

The plaque to the left of the previous one lies to the right of the statue of "Sampson and the Philistine."

vid'io Fiorenza in sì fatto riposo,	the Florence that I saw – in such repose
che non avea cagion onde piangesse;	that there was nothing to have caused her sorrow.
con queste genti vid'io glorioso	These were the families, with them I saw
e giusto il popol suo tanto, che il giglio	her people so acclaimed and just, that on
non era ad asta mai posto a ritroso,	her staff the lily never was reversed,
né per division fatto vermiglio.	nor was it made blood-red by factious hatred.

Cacciaguida remembers Florence during times of peace before it was divided by the political struggles between the Guelphs and the Ghibellines. He recalls that Florence's flag hadn't yet been reversed: a reference not only to its first incarnation in which a white fleur-de-lis appeared on a red field, but to the fact that blood shed in battle hadn't yet soiled it. After the war between Florence and Pistoia in 1251 the colors were reversed and the flag consisted of a red fleur-de-lis on a white field, which became the banner adopted by the Guelphs. The Ghibellines continued to display the previous flag as their own. Cacciaguida also indicates that prior to this time his city's flag had never been dragged on the ground in battle as a sign of defeat.

85) *Paradise* XVI, 109-110   **Palazzo Vecchio Courtyard**

Look to the left of the above-mentioned statue for this plaque:

> *Oh quali io vidi quei che son disfatti*   Oh, how great were those
> *per lor superbia!*   I saw – whom pride laid low!

Cacciaguida refers in these verses to the Uberti family, which he says met its downfall because its members refused to compromise their pride and Ghibelline ideals. Notice the reproduction of the coat of arms of the Uberti family above the plaque (see also Sites 80 and 83).

86) *Paradise* XVI, 127-128; 130-132   **Via dei Cerchi 23**

Exit Palazzo Vecchio and turn left through its internal courtyard. You will find yourself in Piazza della Signoria. Walk past the enormous white statue of Neptune and approach the equestrian monument to the Grand Duke Cosimo I de' Medici. Beyond it on your right is Via delle Farine. Follow it past Via della Condotta to Via dei Cerchi, which you should walk along passing Via dei Cimatori and Canto alla Quarconia on your right. After the next cross street on your left, Via dei Tavolini, you will come across this plaque on the left-hand side of Via dei Cerchi, where the della Bella family once lived:

> *Ciascun che della bella insegna porta*   All those whose arms bear part of the great
> *del gran barone ...*   baron's fair ensign ...
>
> *Da esso ebbe milizia e privilegio;*   received knighthood and privilege from him,
> *avvegna che col popol si rauni*   though he whose coat of arms has fringed that ensign
> *oggi colui che la fascia col fregio.*   has taken sides now with the populace.

To put these verses in context, refer first to the explanation of the plaque at Site 77. Cacciaguida refers here in particular to Giano della Bella, whose family had been knighted and allowed to include the coat of arms of Hugh of Brandenburg in his own family crest. As such Giano belonged to the Ghibelline power structure. Nonetheless, in 1293 he personally oversaw the creation of the "Ordinamenti di giustizia" or Orders of Justice, which established new legal norms banning titled nobles from holding political power. It also required all those holding political office to belong to one of Florence's medieval guilds (see Walking Tour 10, Site 57). This law essentially limited political power for the first time to the nascent bourgeoisie. With this act Giano allied himself with a lower social class but also retained the right to participate in Florentine politics.

87) *Paradise* XVI, 101-102   **Via dei Tavolini 1 (red)**

Return to the corner of Via dei Tavolini and turn right into it. High up on the far side of Via dei Tavolini is the address and quotation indicated above:

> *... ed avea Galigaio*   ... and Galigaio, in his house,
> *dorata in casa sua già l'elsa e 'l pome*   already had the gilded hilt and pommel.

The Galigai family lived at this location during the thirteenth century when Dante's ancestor Cacciaguida was alive. This family name would have been highly significant to readers of the *Divine Comedy* in Dante's time, who would have recognized its lofty traditions dating back a century. Cacciaguida just notes here that its members, as knights, had already obtained the right to carry swords with gilded hilts and handles.

88) *Inferno* XXXII, 79-81; 106-108   **Via dei Tavolini 8**

Walk down Via dei Tavolini to your right and you will arrive at this site on the right-hand side of the street shortly before the next cross-street.

> *Piangendo mi sgridò: "Perché mi peste?*   Weeping, he chided then: "Why trample me?
> *se tu non vieni a crescer la vendetta*   If you've not come to add to the revenge
> *di Montaperti, perché mi moleste?"*   of Montaperti, why do you molest me?"
>
> *... un altro gridò: "Che hai tu, Bocca?*   ... someone else cried out: "What is it, Bocca?
> *non ti basta sonar con le mascelle,*   Isn't the music of your jaws enough
> *se tu non latri? qual diavol ti tocca?"*   for you without your bark? What devil's at you?"

Those who were traitors to their homelands (or own political party) are punished in the Second Ring of Cocytus in the Ninth Circle of Hell (called "Antenora" after Antenor, a Trojan who betrayed his city). Dante considered treachery one of the worst sins of all and reserved a place for them here at the very bottom of Hell. Cocytus is a frozen lake where the damned are immersed in its ice at depths that vary according to the kind of treachery committed. In Antenora (one of four Rings that make up Cocytus) the traitors are frozen in ice up to their noses and gaze upward. As Dante and Virgil make their way across it, Dante stumbles on the head of a damned soul, Bocca degli Abati, who reprimands him. Bocca, a Florentine Guelph, caused the defeat of his fellow combatants at the Battle of Montaperti, the bloodiest in all of Florentine history. He cut off the hand of his army's flag bearer, thereby causing its troops to lose all direction and, consequently, the battle itself. Dante asks Bocca to tell him his name and promises to mention it among the living so that he won't be forgotten. When Bocca refuses to tell him, both Dante and Virgil grab him by the hair and tear some of it out. As Bocca screams with pain, a damned soul nearby asks him why and calls him by name, thereby informing Dante unwittingly of Bocca's identity. The plaque here marks the spot where the Abati family had its dwellings.

89) *Inferno* X, 58-63   Via dei Calzaiuoli 11 (red)

Proceed along Via dei Tavolini in the same direction and turn left at the next corner into Via dei Calzaiuoli. Follow this past Via de' Lamberti on your right and you will find the plaque between two second-story windows here on the right side of the street toward the end of the next block.

... *"Se per questo cieco*	... "If it is your high intellect
carcere vai per altezza d'ingegno,	that lets you journey here, through this blind prison
mio figlio ov'è? e perché non è teco?"	where is my son? Why is he not with you?"
E io a lui: "Da me stesso non vegno:	I answered: "My own powers have not brought me;
colui ch'attende là per qui mi mena	he who awaits me there, leads through here
forse cui Guido vostro ebbe a disdegno."	perhaps to one your Guido did disdain."

The Cavalcanti family formerly owned buildings located at this address. To place the quotation here in context, make sure you also read the entry at Site 81. During Dante's conversation with Farinata degli Uberti another soul occupying the same tomb raises his head and addresses Dante. He is Cavalcante de' Cavalcanti, father of Guido Cavalcanti. Guido was a poet and intimate friend of Dante who had married Farinata degli Uberti's daughter, Beatrice. As a poet Guido is also identified with the "Dolce Stil Novo," the poetic school associated most closely with Dante. The word "one" above refers to Dante's beloved, Beatrice, whom he says Guido may have disdained. In this context, Dante's words to Cavalcante indicate that Guido may have doubted the "Dolce Stil Novo's" poetic conceit according to which an angelic woman becomes the means to reach divine understanding.

90) *Paradise* XVI, 110-111   Via dei Lamberti 20 (red)

Continue along Via dei Calzaiuoli in the same direction. At the next corner turn right into Via Porta Rossa. Pass Via Arte della Lana on your right and turn right again into Via Calimala. Turn left at the next cross-street into Via dei Lamberti. Just past Via dei Cavalieri on your right, you will come across this site on the right-hand side of the street:

...*e le palle dell'oro*	...And the gold balls
fiorian Fiorenza in tutt'i suoi gran fatti.	in all of her great actions, flowered Florence.

This plaque marks the site where the Lamberti family lived and owned property. In recalling the great Florentine families of the thirteenth century, Cacciaguida tells Dante that the Lambertis ennobled the city with their deeds as well as with their beautiful coat of arms, reproduced here, displaying golden balls against a blue field.

91) *Inferno* XVII, 58-60   Via dei Tornabuoni 1 (red)

Walking down Via dei Lamberti in the same direction, turn left into Via Pellicceria and then right into Via Porta Rossa. Proceed forward past three streets

on your right: Piazza de' Davanzati, Via Monalda and Chiasso de' Soldanieri.
When you arrive in Piazza Santa Trinita, cross the square and turn left in front of
the church of Santa Trinita. Continue in this direction along Via Tornabuoni till
you find this plaque on the right side of the street just before Via Tornabuoni
intersects Lungarno Corsini:

…com'io riguardando tra lor vegno,	…Looking about – when I had come among them –
una borsa gialla vidi azzurro	I saw a yellow purse with azure on it
che d'un leone avea faccia e contegno.	that had the face and manner of a lion.

The usurers are punished in the Third Zone of the Third Ring of the Seventh
Circle of Hell. Under the same rain of fire that pelts the sodomites, the usurers sit
in a circle as they try to fend off the offending flames. Each wears a purse that
hangs from his neck, and on every purse Dante is able to identify a family coat of
arms. Among them, Dante picks out the crest of the Gianfigliazzi family, allied
with the Black Guelphs. It depicted a blue lion against a yellow field, which you
can see here above the plaque. This site marks the spot where the Gianfigliazzi
family lived.

92) *Paradise* XVI, 140; 142-144   Borgo SS. Apostoli 3

From Via Tornabuoni turn left at the corner into the Lungarno degli Acciaiuoli
and then left again into the Chiasso degli Altoviti. Turn right at the next corner
into Borgo SS. Apostoli. Pass Piazza del Limbo and Chiasso del Bene on your
right. Just before the next corner on your right you will come across this plaque:

O Buondelmonte…	Oh Buondelmonte…

Molti sarebber lieti che son tristi	Many would now rejoice, who still lament,
se Dio t'avesse conceduto ad Ema	if when you first approached the city, God
la prima volta ch'a città venisti.	had given you unto the river Ema!

This plaque is located where the Buondelmonti family lived after arriving from
Montebuoni in 1135, just southeast of Florence. Buondelmonte de' Buondelmonti,
who was engaged to Reparata Amidei and rejected her to marry another young
woman, was murdered in 1215 to avenge this affront. Dino Compagni and Giovanni
Villani, the medieval chroniclers of Florentine history, interpret this event as the
one that initiated the division between Florentine Guelphs (allies of the
Buondelmonti) and Ghibellines (allies of the Amidei).

93) *Paradise* XVI, 136-139   Via Por Santa Maria 11 (red)

Continue along Borgo SS. Apostoli in the same direction and pass Vicolo dell'Oro.
At the next corner turn right into Via Por Santa Maria. You will find this quotation at the address above on the right-hand side of the street.

La casa di che nacque il vostro fleto   The house of Amidei, with which your sorrows
per lo giusto disdegno che v'ha morti   began – by reason of its just resentment,
e puose fine al vostro viver lieto,   which ruined you and ended years of gladness –
era onorata, essa e suoi consorti: was honored then, as were its close companions.

This tower house has always been known as the Amidei Tower or the "bigoncio-la" (small vat). The events recalled in the previous site refer to this one as well. Cacciaguida here addresses Florence itself with the word "your" and emphasizes that the city's "sorrows" began in earnest after Buondelmonte's murder, even though the Amidei family and its allies were highly respected.

94) *Paradise* XVI, 145-147   Ponte Vecchio

Cross Via Por Santa Maria to the opposite side of the street and proceed toward the Ponte Vecchio in front of you. Cross Piazza del Pesce and walk onto the bridge. The plaque here is attached to the portico on your immediate left.

…conveniasi a quella pietra scema   But Florence, in her final peace, was fated
che guarda il ponte, che Fiorenza fesse   to offer up – unto that mutilated
vittima ne la sua pace postrema.   stone guardian upon her bridge – a victim.

Because of his deeds explained at Site 92, Buondelmonte de' Buondelmonti was murdered here in 1215 near the statue of Mars that tradionally stood at this site. Mars had been the patron of Florence during Roman times. Thus it is perhaps fitting that a statue of the Roman god of war is associated with the end of Florence's final period of peace.

95) *Inferno* XIII, 146   Ponte Vecchio 27-29 (red)

Walk across the Ponte Vecchio to its midpoint, where there are three arches overlooking the river on your left. On the wall to the right of the right-hand arch (and underneath the overhanging structure above) is this plaque:

…in sul passo d'Arno   – along the crossing of the Arno –

These words, which at first glance seem to allude to the landscape around Florence's river, are instead a reference to the thirteenth canto of the Inferno, where the suicides and the squanderers are punished. Having thought so little of their own bodies that they did away with them, the former are punished after death by being deprived of human form. They are transformed into trees in which Harpies make their nests. Broken off, the twigs and branches bleed with human blood, and as long as it flows the condemned soul trapped within can speak. One of them, who identifies himself as Florentine, reminds Dante that the ancient Roman city was sacred to Mars (the god of war) and that after the advent of Christianity Saint John the Baptist became the city's patron saint. Indeed, he suggests that it is as if Mars took offense at this and punished the city with its long history of internecine warfare. Yet according to popular Florentine belief, the statue of Mars (described at Site 94 and kept as a talisman on the Ponte Vecchio) protected the city from further destruction and allowed the Florentines to rebuild it in 542 after it was devastated by the Goth Totila. The words in the quotation above refer to this vestige of Mars on the bridge "crossing the Arno."

Bibliography

Addington, Symonds John. *The Life of Michelangelo Buonarroti*. Philadelphia: U. of Pennsylvania P, 2002.

Alfieri, Vittorio. *Vita*. Ed. Gianpaolo Dossena. Turin: Einaudi, 1967.

Alighieri, Dante. *Divine Comedy*. Trans. Allen Mandelbaum. Book-of-the-Month Club, 1980-1986.

Allodoli, Ettore. *Giovanni Milton e l'Italia*. Prato: C. & G. Spighi, 1907.

Artusi, Pellegrino. *La scienza in cucina e l'arte di mangiar bene*. Ed. Piero Camporesi. Turin: Einaudi, 1970.

Astaldi, Maria Luisa. *Tommaseo come era*. Firenze: Sansoni, 1967.

Baccolo, Luigi. *Il signor conte non riceve*. Cuneo: L'arciere, 1978.

Barricelli, Jean-Pierre. *Fireplaces of Civilization*. Riverside: Xenos, 1993.

Bertacchini, Renato. *Il padre di Pinocchio: vita e opere del Collodi*. Milano: Camunia, 1993.

Brown, Allison. *Bartolomeo Scala 1430-1497. Chancellor of Florence: the Humanist as Bureaucrat*. Princeton: Princeton UP, 1979.

Browning, Elizabeth Barrett. *The Poetical Work of Elizabeth Barrett Browning*. Boston: Houghton Mifflin, 1974.

Buonarroti, Michelangelo. *Complete Poems and Selected Letters of Michelangelo*. Trans. Creighton Gilbert. New York: Modern Library, 1965.

Byse, Fanny. *Milton on the Continent: A Key to L'Allegro and il Penseroso*. London: Roussy's English Library, 1903.

The Cambridge History of Italian Literature. Ed. P. Brand and L. Pertile. Cambridge: Cambridge UP, 1996.

Cellini, Benvenuto. *The Autobiography of B. Cellini*. Trans. George Bull. London: Penguin, 1998.

– . *My Life*. Trans. Julia Conaway Bondanella and Peter Bondanella. New York: Oxford UP, 2002.

Clough, Arthur Hugh. *Amours de Voyage*. Ed. Patrick Scott. St. Lucia: U of Queensland P, 1974.

– . *The Correspondence of Arthur Hugh Clough*. Ed. Frederick L. Mulhauser. Oxford: Clarendon, 1957.

– . *Poems and Prose Remains of Arthur Hugh Clough*. London: MacMillan, 1869.

– . *Selected Poems*. Ed. Shirley Chue. Manchester: Carcanet, 1987.

Colvin, Sidney. *Landor*. London: MacMillan, 1909.

Cooper, James Fenimore. *Gleanings in Europe: Italy*. Albany: State U of New York P, 1981.

Dentler, Clara Louise. *Famous Americans in Florence*. Florence: Giunti Marzocco, 1976.

Draper, Ronald P. *D. H. Lawrence*. New York: Twayne, 1964.

Edel, Leon. *Henry James: A Life*. New York: Harper, 1977.

Elliot, George. *Romola*. New York: Thomas Y. Crowell, 1900.

"Fiorentino, Salomone." *Enciclopedia della letteratura*. Milan: Garzanti, 1997 ed.

Fortescue, William. *Alphonse De Lamartine: A Poetical Biography.* New York: St. Martin's, 1983.

Foscolo, Ugo. *On Sepulchres.* Trans. Thomas G. Bergin. Bethany: Bethany, 1971.

Friedrich, Hugo. *Montaigne.* Berkeley: U of California P, 1991.

Gide, André. *The Journals.* Trans. Justin O'Brien. Vol. I. New York: Knopf, 1955.

Grafton, Anthony. *Leon Battista Alberti: Master Builder of the Italian Renaissance.* New York: Hill and Wang, 2000.

Graham, Kenneth. *Henry James: A Literary Life.* New York: St. Martin's, 1995.

Heineman, Helen. *Frances Trollope.* Boston: Twayne, 1984.

Hibbard, Howard. *Michelangelo.* Cambridge: Harper & Row, 1985.

Hughes, Kathryn. *George Eliot: The Last Victorian.* New York: Farrar, 1998.

James, Henry. *Autobiography.* Ed. Frederick Dupu. New York: Criterion, 1956.

– . *Italian Hours.* New York: Grove, 1959.

Johnson, Edgar. *Sir Walter Scott: The Great Unknown.* Toronto: MacMillan, 1970.

Kennedy, William Sloane. *Henry W. Longfellow.* New York: Haskell, 1973.

King, Francis. *Florence: A Literary Companion.* London: John Murray, 1991.

Lamartine, Alphonse de. *Graziella. Raphaël.* Paris: Garnier, 1960.

– . *Poetical Meditations: Méditations Poétiques.* Trans. Gervase Hittle. Lewiston: Mellen, 1993.

Lawrence, D. H. *Aaron's Rod.* New York: Thomas Seltzer, 1922.

– . *D. H. Lawrence and Italy: Twilight in Italy; Sea and Sardinia; Etruscan Places.* New York: Viking, 1972.

Lawrence, Frieda. *Not I, But the Wind.* New York: Viking, 1934.

Lee, Vernon. *The Countess of Albany.* London: John Lane, 1910.

Leopardi, Giacomo. *Leopardi's Canti.* Trans. John Humphreys Whitfield. Napoli: Scalabrini, 1962.

– . *Opere.* Vol. 2. Milan: Ricciardi, 1953.

Lombard, M. Charles. *Lamartine.* New York: Twayne, 1973.

Longfellow, Henry Wadsworth. *The letters of Henry Wadsworth Longfellow.* Ed. Andrew Hilen. 2 vols. Cambridge: Belknap-Harvard UP, 1966.

Lounsbury, Thomas R. *James Fenimore Cooper.* New York: Chelsea, 1981.

Lowell, James Russell. *Literary Essays: Leaves from my Journal in Italy and Elsewhere.* Boston: Houghton Mifflin, 1913.

Lupton, Mary Jane. *Elizabeth Barrett Browning.* Baltimore: Feminist, 1971.

Lyndall, Gordon. *A Private Life of Henry James: Two Women and His Art.* New York: Norton, 1998.

MacCarthy, Fiona. *Byron: Life and Legend.* New York: Farrar, 2002.

MacDonald, Bonney. *Henry James's Italian Hours.* London: U-M-I Research P, 1990.

Marchegiani Jones, Irene and Thomas Haeussler ed. *The Poetics of Place: Florence Imagined.* Florence: Olschki, 2001.

Massie, Allan. *Byron's Travels.* London: Sidgwick & Jackson, 1988.

Micheletti, Emma. *Chiese di Firenze.* Novara: De Agostini, 1959.

Milton John, *Milton on Himself.* Ed. John S. Diekhoff. New York: Humanities, 1965.

– . *The Poems of John Milton.* Vol. 2. Ed. John Carey and Alastair Fowler. London: Longmans, 1968.

Montaigne, Michel de, *The Complete Works of Montaigne: Essays; Travel Journal; Letters.* Trans. Donald M. Frome. Stanford: Stanford UP, 1957.

Neville-Sington, Pamela. *Fanny Trollope: The Life and Adventures of a Clever Woman.* New York: Viking, 1997.

Niccolai Foresto. *Firenze: Le lapidi dei luoghi danteschi.* Firenze: Tipografia Coppini, 1996.

– . *Le lapidi in Firenze.* Firenze: Tipografia Coppini, 1995.

– . *L'urne de' forti.* Firenze: Tipografia Coppini, 1997.

Origo Iris. *Leopardi: A Study in Solitude.* London: Hamish Hamilton, 1953.

Paolucci, Antonio. *Le chiese di Firenze.* Firenze: Bicocci, 1975.

Parker, William Riley. *Milton: A Biography.* 2 vols. Oxford: Clarendon, 1968.

Petrocchi, Giorgio. *Vita di Dante.* Bari: Laterza, 1990.

Piergili, Giuseppe. *Vita di Giacomo Leopardi scritta da lui medesimo.* Centro Nazionale di Studi Leopardiani. Ancona: Transeuropa, 1992.

Pirazzini, Agide. *The Influence of Italy on the Literary Career of Alphonse de Lamartine.* New York: Columbia UP, 1917.

Pirodda, Giovanni. *Mazzini e gli scrittori democratici.* Letteratura italiana Laterza. 45. Bari: Laterza, 1990.

Railton, Stephen. *Fenimore Cooper: A Study of His Life and Imagination.* Princeton: Princeton UP, 1978.

Ransom, Teresa. *Fanny Trollope: A Remarkable Life.* New York: St. Martin's, 1995.

Rodini, Robert J. *Autore Francesco Grazzini: Poet, Dramatist, and Novelliere.* Madison: Wisconsin UP, 1970.

Robertson, Eric S. *Life of Henry Wadsworth Longfellow.* Port Washington: Kennikat, 1972.

Scala, Bartolomeo. *Bartolomeo Scala: Humanistic and Political Writings.* Ed. Alison Prown. Tempe: Medieval & Renaissance Texts & Studies, 1997.

Shelley, Percy Bysshe. *Letters.* Ed. Roger Ingpen. 2 vols. London: G. Bell, 1914.

"Shelley, Percy Bysshe." *The Norton Anthology of English Literature.* Vol. 2. New York: Norton, 1962.

Sheridan, Alan. *André Gide: A Life in the Present.* Cambridge: Harvard UP, 1999.

Smith, Denis Mack. *Mazzini.* New Haven: Yale UP, 1994.

Starr, William Thomas. *Romain Rolland: One Against All, a Biography.* The Hague: Mouton, 1971.

Taplin, Gardner B. *The Life of Elizabeth Barrett Browning.* New Haven: Yale UP, 1952.

Thompson, Andrew. *George Eliot and Italy: Literary, Cultural and Political Influences from Dante to the Risorgimento.* London: MacMillan, 1998.

Tuttleton, James and Agostino Lombardo. *The Sweetest Impression of Life: The James Family and Italy.* New York: New York UP, 1990.

Wagenknecht, Edward. *Longfellow: A Full-Length Portrait.* New York: Longmans, 1955.

Whitehouse, Remsen H. *The Life of Lamartine.* Vol. 2. Boston: Houghton Mifflin, 1918.

Wollstonecraft, Mary. *A Vindication of the Rights of Woman with Strictures on Political and Moral Subjects by Mary Wollstonecraft.* Ed. Ulrich H. Hardt. Troy: Whitston, 1982.

Museums, Churches and Other Buildings Open to the Public

Florence Cathedral (Duomo - Santa Maria del Fiore)

Open: Monday-Friday 10:00 A.M.-5:00 P.M.; Thursdays 10:00 A.M.-5:30 P.M.; First Saturdays 10:00 A.M.-3:30 P.M.; other Saturdays 10:00 A.M.-4:30 P.M.; Holidays 1:30 P.M.-4:45 P.M.

Church of Santa Maria Novella

Open: Weekdays 9:30 A.M.-5:00 P.M.; Fridays 1:00 P.M.-5:00 P.M.; Holidays 1:00 P.M.-5:00 P.M.

Church of San Marco

Open: Every day 6:30 A.M.-12:00 P.M.; 3:00 P.M.-8:00 P.M.

Protestant Cemetery

Open: Mondays 9:00 A.M.-12:00 P.M.; Tuesdays 3:00 P.M.-6:00 P.M.; Fridays; Closed: Saturdays, Sundays & Holidays

Museum of Casa Buonarroti

Open: 9:00 A.M.-2:00 P.M.; Closed: Tuesdays

Medici Chapels

Open: Weekdays 8:15 A.M.-4:50 P.M.; Sundays 8:15 A.M.-4:50 P.M.; Closed: 1st, 3rd, and 5th Mondays of every month

Palazzo Vecchio

Open: Daily 9:00 A.M.-7:00 P.M.; Thursdays & mid-week Holidays 9:00 A.M.-2:00 P.M. (January 6, Easter Monday, April 25, June 2, June 24, November 1, December 8, December 26); Closed: January 1, Easter Sunday, May 1, August 15, December 25

Church of Santa Margherita de' Cerchi (Dante's church)

Open: Weekdays: 10:00 A.M.-12:00 P.M.-3:00 P.M.-6:30 P.M.; Holidays 10:00 A.M.-12:00 P.M.

Badia fiorentina

Open for tourist visits: Mondays 3:00 P.M.-6:00 P.M.; Open to the faithful: Tuesdays 7:00 A.M.-6:00 P.M.; Fridays, Saturdays 8:00 A.M.-6:00 P.M.; Sundays 8:00 A.M.-12:00 P.M.

Index